Leavenworth Papers Number 17

The Petsamo-Kirkenes Operation: Soviet Breakthrough and Pursuit in the Arctic, October 1944

Major James F. Gebhardt

Combat Studies Institute
U.S. Army Command and General Staff College
Fort Leavenworth, Kansas 66027-6900

Library of Congress Cataloging-in-Publication Data

Gebhardt, James F., 1948-
  The Petsamo-Kirkenes Operation : Soviet breakthrough and pursuit in the Arctic, October 1944 / James F. Gebhardt.
    p. cm. — (Leavenworth papers ; no. 17)
  Includes bibliographical references.
  1. World War, 1939-1945—Campaigns—Norway—Kirkenes Region. 2. World War, 1939-1945—Naval operations, Russian. 3. Soviet Union—Armed Forces—History—World War, 1939-1945. 4. Germany—Armed Forces—History—World War, 1939-1945. 5. World War, 1939-1945—Campaigns—Arctic Regions. 6. Kirkenes Region (Norway)—History. I. Title. II. Series.
  D763.N62K554   1990   89-18109
  940.54'21845—dc20   CIP

For sale by the Superintendent of Documents, U.S. Government Printing Office, Washington, D.C. 20402

Contents

Illustrations v
Tables vii
Preface ix
Acknowledgments xi
Introduction xiii

Chapter
1. Strategic and Operational Setting 1
     Strategic Situation 1
     Weather and Terrain 4
     German Defensive Dispositions 6
     Soviet Planning and Preparation 11
2. The Battle, Phase One, 7—15 October 1944 31
3. The Battle, Phase Two, 18—22 October 1944 47
4. The Battle, Phase Three, 23 October—1 November 1944 65
     Attack on Kirkenes 65
     Southward Pursuit 75
5. Northern Fleet Support of Ground Operations 85
     Command Relationship 86
     Preparation 88
     Amphibious Landings 89
     Naval Air Operations 95
     Naval Support of Army Logistic Operations 96
6. Soviet Special Operations 99
     Karelian Front Special-Purpose Forces 99
     Naval Special Operations 107
7. Conclusions 115
     Strategic and Operational Planning 115
     Soviet Command and Control 117
     Combat Forces 119
     Combat Support Operations 122
     Conclusion 125

Epilogue 127
Appendix
   A. 131
   B. 135
   C. 139
   D. 143
   E. 145
   F. 147
   G. 149
Notes 151
Bibliography 171

Illustrations

Maps
1. German withdrawal from Finland 3
2. Petsamo-Kirkenes area of operations 5
3. Deployment of Soviet and German forces 7
4. Disposition of 2d Mountain Division units and Soviet units on the main axis 9
5. Karelian Front offensive plan 16
6. Phase one of the Soviet offensive 34
7. Phase two of the Soviet offensive 48
8. Movement of the 127th Light Rifle Corps, 21–22 October 1944 61
9. 14th Army plan, phase three 66
10. 14th Army northern flank, 22–30 October 1944 67
11. 14th Army southern flank, 23 October–2 November 1944 77
12. Northern Fleet amphibious landings 91
13. 14th Army special-purpose actions 101
14. Krestovyi raid, 11–12 October 1944 108

Figures
1. Organization of the German XIX Mountain Corps, October 1944 6
2. Strongpoint Zuckerhutl 10
3. Organization of the Soviet 14th Army, October 1944 13
4. *STAVKA*-Karelian Front-Northern Fleet command relationship ... 27
5. Karelian Front command and control relationships 28

v

Tables

1. Status of German units on 1 September 1944 8
2. Engineer plan, 99th Rifle Corps 23
3. Soviet planning estimate of force ratios 29
4. Actual Soviet-German force ratios 30
5. Artillery ammunition on hand, 367th Rifle Division, 18 October 1944 50
6. Supply status of rifle divisions of the 31st Rifle Corps 78
7. Amphibious landings 90
8. Northern Fleet support for 14th Army logistic operations 96

Preface

Leavenworth Paper No. 17, *The Petsamo-Kirkenes Operation: Soviet Breakthrough and Pursuit in the Arctic, October 1944*, represents a seminal contribution to a field of historical research that has not been thoroughly explored by our Army's doctrinal community. This campaign and others, such as the defense of the Murmansk axis in 1941, are virtually unknown in the West in spite of their profound impact on the strategic outcome of the Soviet-German war on the Eastern Front. This oversight is not surprising when one considers that our Army's sole combat experience in arctic-type terrain over the last fifty years was the Aleutian campaign of 1942.

The Arctic region increases in strategic value annually. The abundance of oil, minerals, and other natural resources in this region and its proximity to Europe and Asia make conflict in these areas of the world a possibility that military professionals must consider. The Petsamo-Kirkenes Operation is staple fare in Soviet military education. The Soviets' interest stems from a need for firsthand knowledge of the rigors imposed on men and machines during combat operations in the Arctic. Major Gebhardt's work should inspire other historical research in this area that will provide warfighting data to further refine our arctic doctrine.

Contrary to the vast majority of the U.S. peacetime exercise experience in northern regions, the Petsamo-Kirkenes campaign was not fought in the bitter cold and darkness of the arctic winter. Nevertheless, geoclimatic conditions still adversely affected the two opposing armies, even in the arctic autumn. Hypothermia, extended and austere lines of communication, and marginal trafficability are endemic to northern operations and must be considered by commanders, regardless of the season. While lightweight tracked vehicles and helicopters have provided considerable improvements to tactical mobility and unit-level logistic support, the present-day foot soldier is still confronted with the requirement to carry backbreaking loads across the tundra. The ninety-pound rucksack carried by Soviet light infantrymen in 1944 was duplicated by British paratroopers in the Falkland Islands and is similarly shouldered by U.S. Army arctic light infantrymen today. Centers of gravity and culminating points will continue to be profoundly affected by weather and terrain. Therefore, commanders at all levels must continually consider the calculus of exposure and exhaustion on unit combat effectiveness.

This Leavenworth Paper emphasizes another maxim of arctic operations: the necessity for effective joint operations and proper synchronization of the various battlefield operating systems. Soviet use of artillery was hindered in its range by limited ground mobility. While our light artillery today is less road bound, it still may find itself unable to support maneuver forces effectively because of terrain obstacles or the unavailability of helicopter lifts during adverse weather. Since heavy artillery will probably continue to be road bound, close air support and joint air attack team operations are increasingly significant as distances are extended. Air defense artillery systems may be the only protection against hostile air if local weather conditions close friendly airfields.

The combat engineer, always a vital player on the modern battlefield, is a central figure in the Arctic. Combat engineers establish and maintain the roads and airfields that are essential for effective lines of communication to prosecute a campaign. Without a herculean engineering effort, the logistician cannot support any operational plan—no matter how simple its concept. With effective engineering support, the logistician can cope with the substantial demands of the combat arms, albeit with great frustration and difficulty.

This Leavenworth Paper illustrates the demanding requirements imposed by arctic operations and also demonstrates that insightful commanders can achieve significant results in decentralized operations when they allow their subordinates sufficient flexibility to seize the initiative.

HAROLD T. FIELDS, JR.
Major General, USA
Commanding General
6th Infantry Division (Light)

Acknowledgments

I wish to acknowledge the contribution and support of several people to the completion of this Leavenworth Paper. Colonel Louis D. F. Frasché (U.S. Army, Retired) approved and resourced the research project, while Lieutenant Colonels John Hixson, William Connor, and James Holbrook (all U.S. Army, Retired), through their supervision, permitted research and writing to proceed at a steady pace in the midst of competing requirements. Office mates Lieutenant Colonel Gary Griffin (U.S. Army) and Dr. Jerold Brown of the Combat Studies Institute (CSI) provided unrelenting moral support and encouragement, as did Major William H. Burgess. Dr. Samuel Lewis, CSI, spent many hours translating German documents. Mary Jo Nelson of the Combined Arms Research Library, Fort Leavenworth, obtained countless books and articles through interlibrary loan. My colleagues at the Soviet Army Studies Office provided constructive criticism and encouragement during the rewriting of the manuscript. Luella Welch, CSI, typed the manuscript several times; Marilyn Edwards, CSI, edited the final manuscript; Elizabeth Snoke, CSI, edited the notes and bibliography; and Robin Inojos, assisted by John Thomas, of the Fort Leavenworth Media Support Center prepared the cover, maps, and figures. The Sor-Varanger Museum in Strand, Norway, permitted the use of several photographs as did the All-Union Agency for Author's Rights (*VAAP*) of the Union of Soviet Socialist Republics. Photographs of the author's collection were taken during the field research trip in October 1987.

JAMES F. GEBHARDT
Major, Armor
Fort Leavenworth, Kansas

"To the courageous Soviet soldiers in memory of the liberation of the city of Kirkenes, 1944"

Introduction

Where the reindeer has gone—there also will go the Russian soldier, and where the reindeer will not go—just the same the Russian soldier will go.

V. Suvorov[1]

On 7 October 1944, a Soviet combined arms force of 97,000 men of the Karelian Front launched an offensive against the 56,000-man German XIX Mountain Corps, defending in prepared positions on Soviet territory northwest of Murmansk. Assisted by sea, air, and land forces of the Northern Fleet, the Soviet 14th Army defeated the German forces in a three-phased, 24-day operation. Soviet troops captured the Finnish town of Petsamo on 15 October and occupied the Norwegian port of Kirkenes on 25 October. The Petsamo-Kirkenes Operation, as the Soviets have named it, is important in Soviet military history. It was the "tenth crushing blow of 1944," the last in a series of strategic offensive operations conducted by Soviet armed forces that year.[2]

Because this battle is the largest in modern military history fought north of the Arctic Circle, its study is more than a historical exercise. For Soviet military professionals, the Petsamo-Kirkenes Operation provides a model for the study of warfare on arctic terrain. It is the empirical base for their arctic warfare doctrine. Soviet military texts cite historical examples from this operation in support of discussions concerning combat activities in the northern regions.[3]

No equivalent operation exists in the American military experience. In the summer of 1943, in the Aleutians campaign, for example, approximately 16,000 American soldiers of the 7th Infantry Division fought against approximately 9,000 Japanese soldiers on the islands of Attu and Kiska, which lie several hundred miles south of the Arctic Circle.[4] The ground combat actions of this campaign, though violent, were brief, and tactical rather than operational in scope.

The closest American soldiers have ever come to warfare on arctic terrain was in September 1918 when some 5,000 men were sent to Archangel, Russia, as part of the Allied intervention in the Russian Civil War.[5] Archangel lies

135 miles below the Arctic Circle, and the combat zone extended another 200 miles southward in forested terrain. These American troops fought in what is now labeled a "low-intensity conflict," characterized by infantry actions at the small-unit level.[6] Analysis of this combat tends to emphasize its cold-weather aspects.[7]

U.S. Army doctrinal publications reflect this lack of experience in large-scale operations on arctic terrain. The most recent version of Field Manual (FM) 100—5, *Operations*, treats operations on arctic terrain as a subset of winter warfare.[8] The same is true of the preliminary draft of FM 90—11, *Cold Weather Operations*.[9] Both manuals tend to dwell on the impact of cold, ice, and snow on military operations, largely ignoring the fact that arctic regions are not always cold. Neither manual, for example, addresses the difficulties of conducting operations on arctic terrain in the summer, when topography, soil type, and light conditions, not low temperatures and snow, affect the employment of military forces.

This oversight is important for significant reasons. First, in the absence of doctrine, armchair tacticians and strategists tend to invent it. For example, a scenario in a recently published article suggests that the Soviet Union could land several conventional motorized rifle and tank divisions on Alaska's northern coast and drive them southward across several hundred miles of arctic terrain into the Canadian heartland.[10] The authors of this scenario offer no evidence that a movement of this magnitude across Alaskan terrain is possible, while the experience of the Red Army with only a hundred or so armored vehicles in the Petsamo-Kirkenes Operation clearly suggests that it is not.

More important, however, is that U.S. Army units have contingency or mobilization missions to fight on arctic terrain. The commanders and staffs of these units need guidance on how to plan, organize, and conduct military operations on arctic terrain, whether in the dark cold of winter or in the warm light of a long summer night. If such guidance now exists, it is in the institutional memories of units and commanders and is based on exercise experience rather than on combat experience. This guidance certainly is not in the doctrinal publications where it is needed.

In his essay "On Historical Examples," Carl von Clausewitz wrote:

> Historical examples clarify everything and also provide the best kind of proof in the empirical sciences. This is particularly true of the art of war. ... The detailed presentation of a historical event, and the combination of several events, make it possible to deduce a doctrine: the proof is in the evidence itself.[11]

The purpose of this Leavenworth Paper, then, is to provide the evidence by way of a comprehensive analysis of a large-scale military operation conducted on arctic terrain. It does not suggest that a doctrine can be deduced from this single experience but, rather, that a historical example is an excellent place to begin in order to arrive at an empirically based doctrine.

Little has been written about the Petsamo-Kirkenes Operation in English. Typical of what is available is the six-page description, drawn entirely from the German perspective, contained in Department of the Army Pamphlet No. 20—271, *The German Northern Theater of Operations, 1940—1945*, by Earl F. Ziemke, published in 1959.[12] Dr. Ziemke summarized this account in a subsequent work, *Stalingrad to Berlin: The German Defeat in the East*, published in 1968.[13] Other American military historians have, for the most part, ignored the history of this operation.

The opposite is true in the Soviet Union. Two rifle corps commanders collaborated to write a single-volume detailed analysis of the Petsamo-Kirkenes Operation, which was first published in 1959.[14] It was followed in 1963 by a monograph on the war in the Murmansk sector, which added considerably more information to the public record.[15] Since 1963, the Soviet military press has published scores of articles and books pertaining to this operation so that it is now a widely known and discussed campaign in Soviet military historiography. Although the Soviets have published the texts of only a few documents relating to this offensive, many participants have written memoirs, including the commanders of both the Karelian Front and the Northern Fleet, Marshal K. A. Meretskov and Admiral A. G. Golovko, respectively. Lieutenant General Kh. A. Khudalov, the commander of a rifle division on the main axis of the 14th Army, also wrote a detailed memoir in 1974 that provides many insights into the battle at his level. These and many other eyewitness reports, when combined with secondary accounts, many of which are based on archival sources, provide a detailed and fairly objective historical record.

German military records, contained in microfilm collections of the National Archives and Records Administration, provide the other perspective of this operation. Microfilm copies of records and after-action reports exist for the 2d Mountain Division, the unit that received the Soviet main attack, and the Twentieth Army. The only records that survived for the XIX Mountain Corps, the 6th Mountain Division, and other major commands are those in the folders of the Twentieth Army. The German documents were used to establish the strength, location, and mission of the German major units and, after that, to act as a "quality check" on Soviet claims and assertions.

The reasons for relying primarily on Russian-language Soviet accounts are both practical and philosophical. The author of this Leavenworth Paper can read Russian fluently and, therefore, was able to fully exploit every available Russian-language source. On the other hand, all German-language materials had to be translated by another scholar, who did so willingly as a professional courtesy. More important, however, this operation was a Soviet offensive, and its planning and conduct is the focal point of the study.

This work focuses on the operational level of war, with infrequent excursions up to the strategic level and down to the tactical level. It does not discuss the care, feeding, and leading of individual soldiers or small units in a cold-weather environment. It does discuss the employment of infantry, light infantry, tanks and self-propelled guns, towed artillery, engineers, air power, ground and naval special-purpose forces, naval infantry (Soviet marines), and logistic support elements in an operational-level setting.

This Leavenworth Paper begins with a description of the strategic and geographical environment, outlines the deployment of both sides' forces on the terrain, and then gives an account of the three phases of the offensive (chapters 1, 2, 3, and 4). Chapter 5 explains the important contribution of the Northern Fleet to the success of the ground offensive. In chapter 6, a detailed and documented account of Soviet special operations is addressed. The concluding chapter is an analysis that draws on Soviet accounts as well as the author's introspection.

The lessons of the Petsamo-Kirkenes Operation are widely applicable. The very ground over which the battle was fought in 1944 is still strategically important to both NATO and Soviet military planners. Northern Norway guards NATO's left flank, as well as the approaches to the Greenland-Iceland-United Kingdom Gap, through which the Soviet Northern Fleet must pass to enter the North Atlantic Ocean.[16] From the Soviet point of view, the Petsamo-Kirkenes terrain guards the approaches to the headquarters of the Northern Fleet at Poliarnyi, the large port and industrial center of Murmansk, and the strategically vital Kola Peninsula.

However, this study has other applications. The U.S. Army sees light infantry as the "weapon of choice" for arctic warfare. The Red Army employed light infantry in this operation, with mixed results. The joint operations aspects of this battle merit study in their own right, as does the employment of special operations forces. Finally, the operational-level principles that governed the conduct of the Petsamo-Kirkenes Operation are equally relevant to the employment of non-Soviet military forces on arctic terrain in this or other parts of the world, now and in the future.

Strategic and Operational Setting

Strategic Situation

The year 1944 was decisive on the Soviet-German front. In mid-January, the Red Army launched a major offensive south of Leningrad that, by early March, had driven German Army Group North westward to the area of the prewar borders of Estonia and Latvia. From late January to late March, four Soviet Fronts (each Front was roughly equal to a U.S. or British army group) attacked west and south of Kiev, clearing vast areas of the Ukraine of German, Rumanian, and Hungarian forces. In April and May, Soviet forces advanced into the Crimean Peninsula and along the Black Sea coast west of Odessa.

On 1 May 1944, Joseph Stalin stated the immediate military-political goals of the Soviet Union. They included clearing all Soviet territory of German occupation and reestablishing the Soviet Union's national borders along the entire line from the Barents Sea to the Black Sea; pursuing and destroying the wounded German Army; and liberating the Poles, Czechs, and other European peoples from German bondage.[1] These strategic goals determined the conduct of Soviet military operations for the remainder of the year.

In June and July, the Red Army destroyed Army Group Center in Belorussia with an offensive conducted by four Fronts. In a series of encirclements and pursuits, the Soviets reached the Vistula River in Poland by the end of August. Soviet troops attacked German forces in the three Baltic states from late June to the end of October, defeating all but a remnant of Army Group North in Kurland. On 31 August, a week after the Allies' liberation of Paris, Red Army soldiers marched through Bucharest, the capital of Rumania. Bulgaria surrendered a week later without a fight.

Significant events also occurred on the northern flank of the Soviet-German front that were a direct result of the changing political-military relationships in that region. In mid-February 1944, the Finnish and Soviet governments began discussing the terms for Finland's withdrawal from the war. These talks led to further bilateral negotiations in Moscow in March and the Finnish rejection of Soviet demands in mid-April. The Soviet General Staff then recommended that the Leningrad and Karelian Fronts launch an offensive against Finnish forces in the sector from Leningrad to Petrozavodsk.[2] The strategic objective of the offensive was to defeat the Finnish Army and force Finland from the war.

On 10 June 1944, the Red Army began the offensive against Finnish forces north of Leningrad and quickly captured Vyborg, thereby threatening the capital, Helsinki (see map 1). As soon as the Finnish military command transferred forces from southern Karelia to meet this threat, Soviet forces of the Karelian Front, under Army General K. A. Meretskov, attacked northward and westward out of Soviet Karelia and quickly advanced through the area between Lakes Ladoga and Onega. This offensive, known as the Svir-Petrozavodsk Operation, continued until 9 August and was strategically significant in that it led to the reopening of bilateral negotiations between Finland and the U.S.S.R. on 25 August. On 4 September, the two sides signed an armistice that required Finland to expel or disarm all German troops still on its soil by 15 September.[3]

Finland's withdrawal from the war left the German Army units deployed there in a precarious position. These forces belonged to the Twentieth Mountain Army, commanded by Colonel General Lothar Rendulic, and were located both north and south of the Arctic Circle (see map 1). The German military presence in northern Finland began in June 1941, when German units, as part of Operation Barbarossa, attacked from Norway on 29 June into Soviet territory along the Murmansk axis. Their mission was to capture the port of Murmansk and interdict the Murmansk-Leningrad railroad, which connected the ice-free port with the Soviet interior.[4] Stiff Soviet resistance halted this drive in September—October 1941 at the Litsa River, fifty kilometers northwest of Murmansk, where the Germans then dug in and built defensive positions.

From these defensive positions, during the period of October 1941 to October 1944, the German Army in the Murmansk sector accomplished two basic missions. Organization Todt workers extracted nickel ore from mines located southwest of Petsamo and iron ore from a Norwegian mine near Kirkenes. Additionally, the units of the German Twentieth Mountain Army protected the air and naval bases along Norway's arctic coastline from ground attack. From these bases, German air and naval forces mounted attacks against Allied shipping in the Norwegian and Barents Seas. During the three-year stalemate, both sides engaged in local and long-range reconnaissance activities and small-unit actions to achieve local objectives.[5]

When Finland began negotiations with the Soviet Union in late August 1944, Colonel General Rendulic began to withdraw his two southernmost corps northward to form a new defensive line across northern Finland from Lyngen through Ivalo to Petsamo. Operation Birke, as this plan was called, commenced on 6 September 1944, and by mid-September, both the XVIII and XXXVI Mountain Corps had moved back into Finnish territory on their respective axes (see map 1).[6]

During the second half of September, the XVIII and XXXVI Mountain Corps withdrew westward toward Rovaniemi and to the routes of their Birke

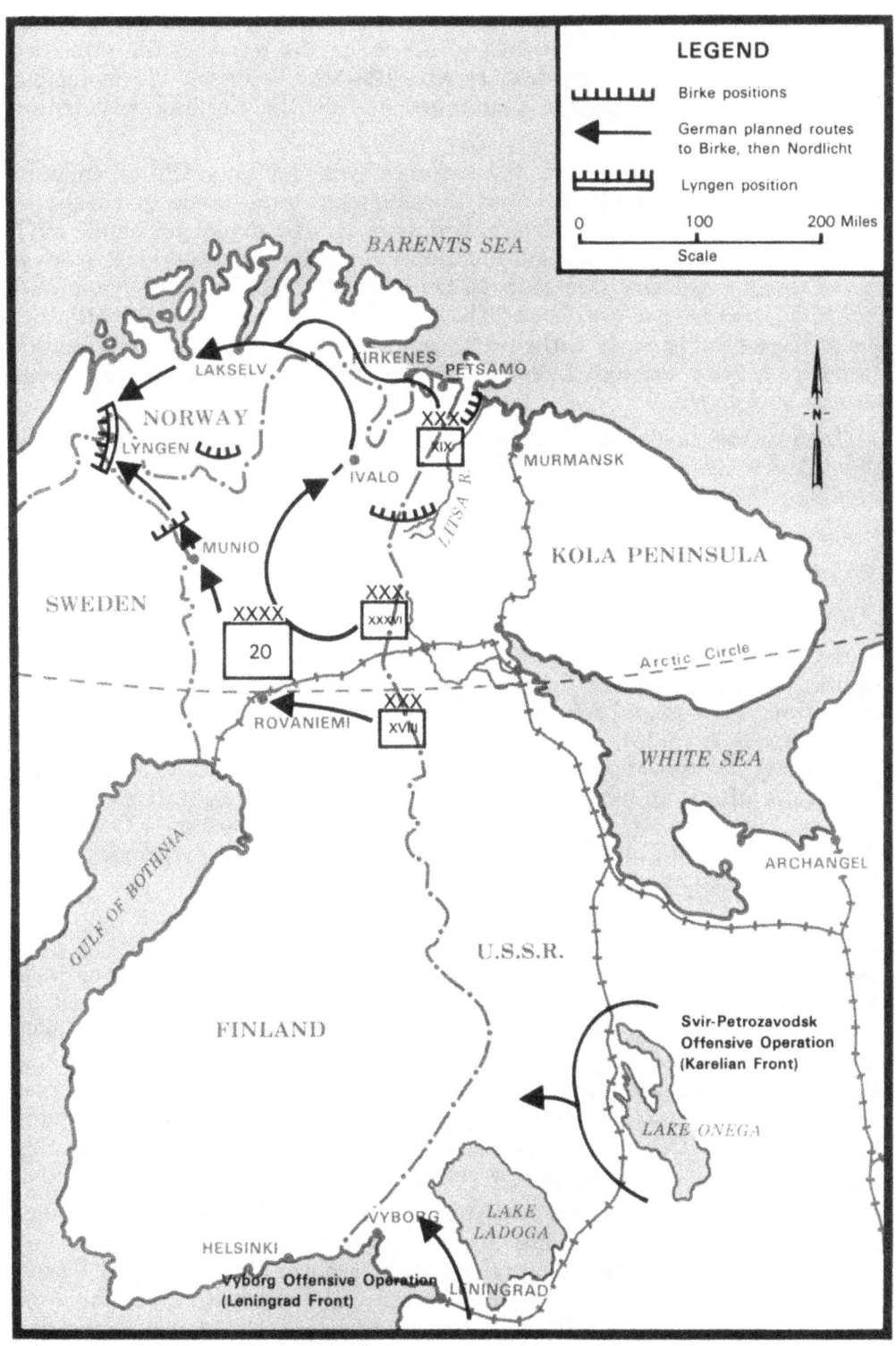

Map 1. German withdrawal from Finland

positions. Not satisfied with the slow German withdrawal and under strong political pressure from the Soviets to adhere to the terms of the armistice, Finnish forces engaged the withdrawing German units on 28 September. After some relatively minor exchanges of fire, the German withdrawal continued.

At the end of September, the German Armed Forces High Command (*OKW*) Operations Staff reviewed the strategic importance of occupying northern Scandinavia and determined that it was no longer vital. *OKW* recommended that the Twentieth Mountain Army be withdrawn into Norway to the Lyngen position (see map 1). On 3 October, Adolph Hitler approved this plan, code-named Nordlicht.[7] The XIX Mountain Corps would withdraw along Highway 50 from Kirkenes through Lakselv, the XXXVI Mountain Corps from Ivalo through Lakselv, and the XVIII Mountain Corps through Muonio to Lyngen.

During the preparation phase of Operation Nordlicht, Soviet forces of Meretskov's Karelian Front launched the Petsamo-Kirkenes offensive by attacking the XIX Mountain Corps on 7 October 1944.

Weather and Terrain

The area of operations of the Petsamo-Kirkenes offensive lies between 69 and 70 degrees north latitude, between Murmansk, U.S.S.R., and Kirkenes, Norway, about 200 miles north of the Arctic Circle (see map 2). Strong moist winds blow inland from the cold but unfrozen Barents Sea. In October, temperatures normally range from -5° to +5° Centigrade (23° to 41° Fahrenheit). Precipitation in the form of snow or a mixture of rain and snow falls often, and heavy fog frequently forms when gulf stream air meets colder arctic air. Daylight decreases from 13.5 hours on 1 October to 10 hours on 30 October. At this time of the year, the sun traverses a low arc across the southern sky.

Along the coast, the terrain is primarily tundra interspersed with hills of barren rock covered by moss and lichen.[8] Farther inland, steep rock-strewn hills rise to elevations of up to 1,900 feet above sea level. Hundreds of streams flow into scores of swamps and lakes that are drained by northeastward-flowing rivers. Vegetation consists of scrub trees and heavy low bushes, permitting clear fields of view from surrounding elevations. Numerous ravines and gullies cut between elevations, allowing unobserved dismounted movement only during periods of limited visibility. The ground is not frozen in October and is water-logged and broken. Therefore, only the roads can support any kind of vehicular traffic.

The existing road network was thus of great significance to the Germans and the Soviets for conducting and supporting military operations. Two main supply routes (MSRs) serviced the German XIX Mountain Corps. Highway 50, an all-weather road, followed the Norwegian coastline from the south all the way north and east to Kirkenes, the major Norwegian city and port facility in the area. A secondary road continued east as far

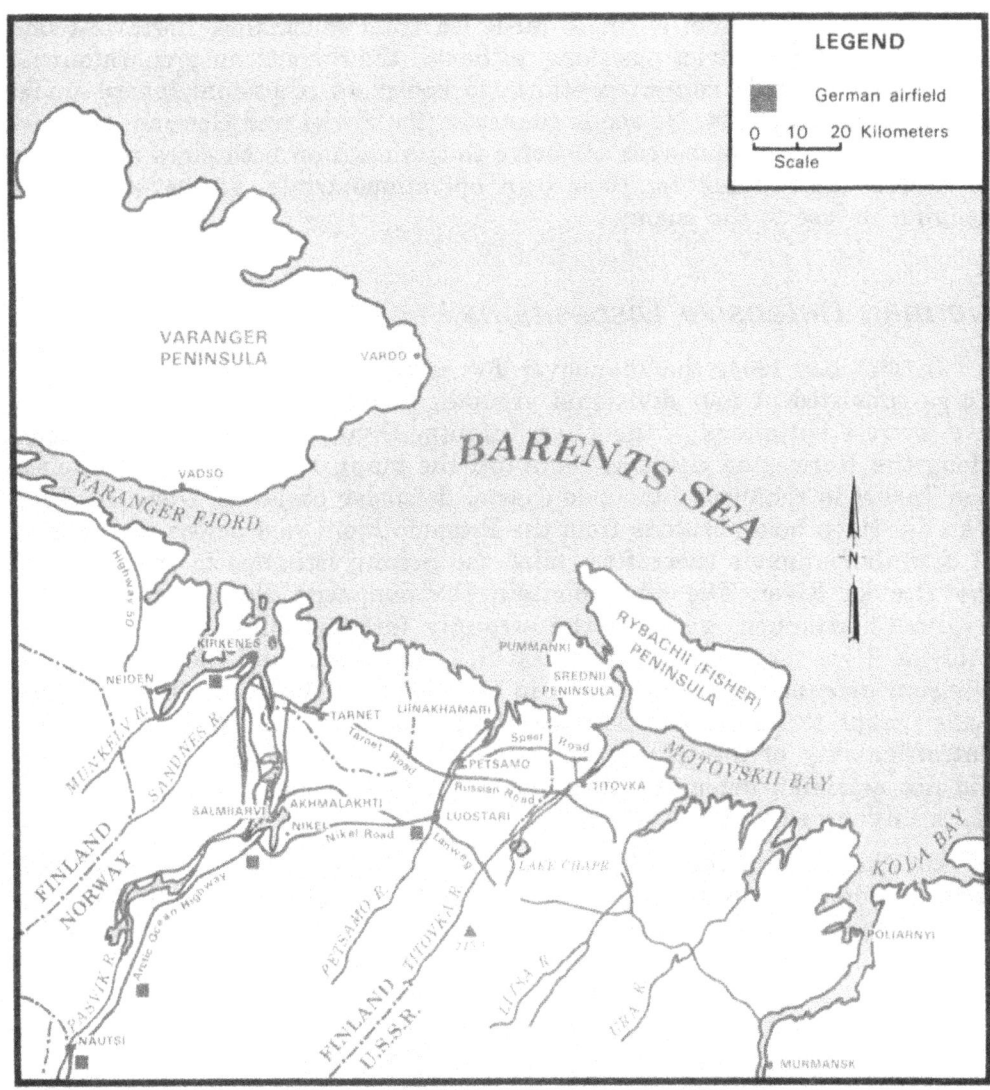

Map 2. Petsamo-Kirkenes area of operations

as Tarnet, and in 1943—44, using prisoner-of-war labor, the Germans extended this road to Petsamo. The other German MSR, Arctic Ocean Highway, originated in Rovaniemi, Finland, and led northward to Ivalo, then northeastward to Nautsi, Salmiiarvi, Akhmalakhti, Luostari, Petsamo, and Liinakhamari. Lateral routes connected this MSR with Kirkenes along both sides of the Pasvik River. A road also joined Salmiiarvi, Nikel, and Luostari. East of Petsamo and Luostari were three trunk roads that supported the three division-size groupings of the XIX Mountain Corps. Speer Road connected Petsamo and the village of Titovka, Russian Road linked Petsamo with the 6th Mountain Division units in their Litsa front positions, and Lanweg joined Arctic Ocean Highway at Luostari with the 2d Mountain Division positions along the Titovka River.

On the Soviet side, a single MSR led from Murmansk northwestward to the rear of the Soviet positions, although the Soviets, in preparation for the offensive, made concerted efforts to construct additional lateral routes in the summer of 1944. No roads connected the Soviet and German defensive sectors. The entire three-week offensive thus hinged on both sides attempting to exploit the roadnet for their own operations while, at the same time, denying its use to the enemy.

German Defensive Dispositions

In October 1944, the maneuver forces of the German XIX Mountain Corps consisted of four divisional groupings (see figure 1 and map 3). The five fortress battalions of the 210th Infantry Division were widely scattered along the Norwegian coast at Tana (off the map), Vardo, Vadso, Kirkenes, and Tarnet in relatively immobile coastal defensive positions. Division Group Van der Hoop held positions from the Petsamo Fjord east across the isthmus of Srednii Peninsula (hereafter called the Srednii isthmus) to the mouth of the Titovka River. The 6th Mountain Division, with the 388th Grenadier Regiment attached, guarded the strongly fortified Litsa front from the Titovka River mouth south and west to Lake Chapr, and the 2d Mountain Division defended in strongpoints in front of the Titovka River south from Lake Chapr to Hill 237.1. Because of the unavailability of forces and the untrafficability of the terrain, the commander of the XIX Mountain Corps did not establish defensive positions south of Hill 237.1, leaving his right flank unguarded.[9]

On the surface, the XIX Mountain Corps appeared to be a formidable fighting force. Its units were at or near full strength in regular personnel but lacked the usual complement of auxiliaries.[10] On 1 September 1944, the maneuver divisions of the corps were at an average of 90.2 percent of their

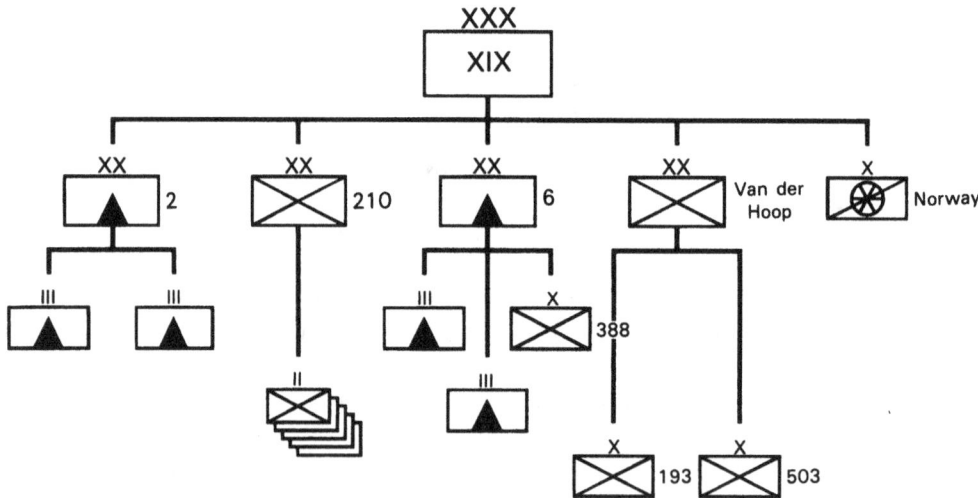

Figure 1. Organization of the German XIX Mountain Corps, October 1944

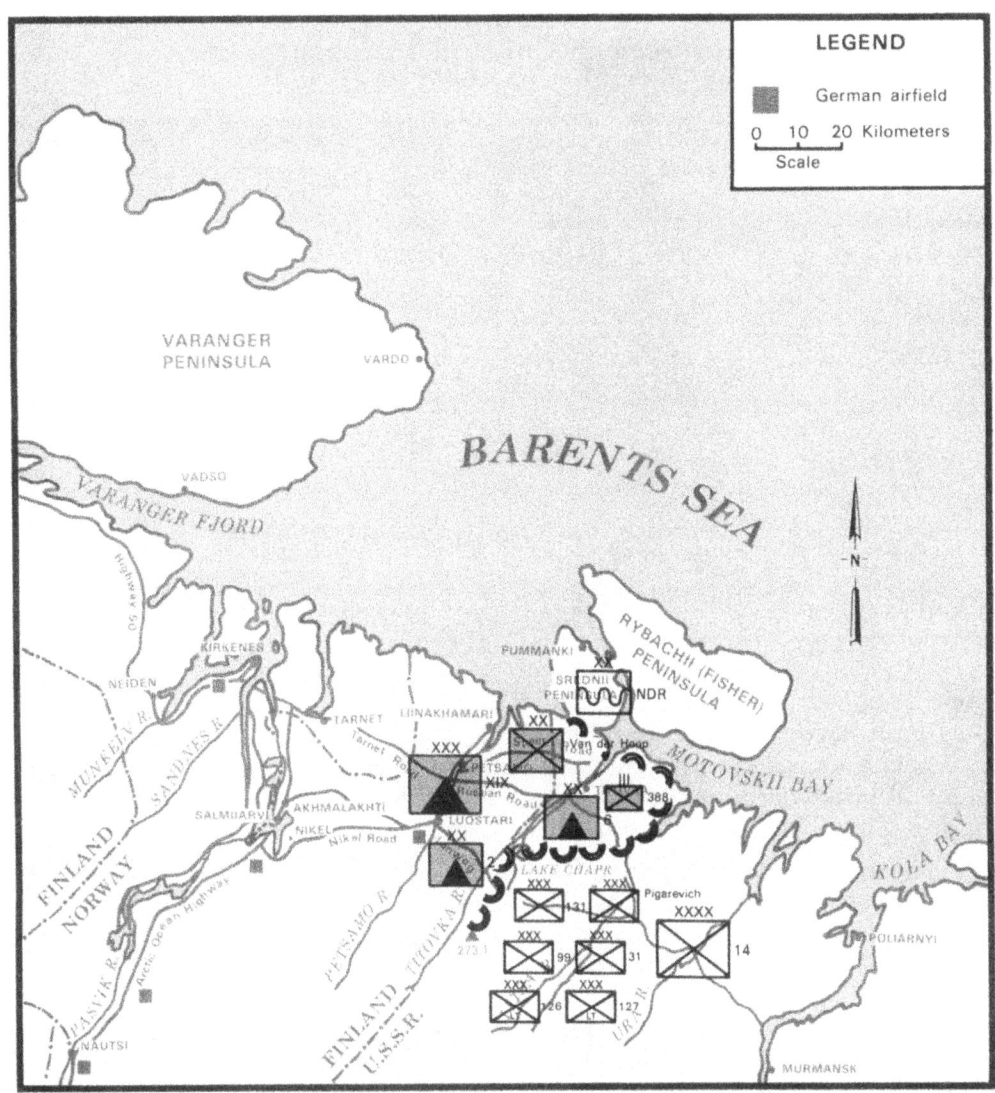

Map 3. Deployment of Soviet and German forces

authorized strength and were well stocked with ammunition and provisions (see table 1).[11] But they were generally deficient in transport and thus could not move all their required tonnage with organic means. Additionally, having been stationed in the Arctic for three years, with relatively little large-scale or intense combat activity, corps units were inexperienced.

The XIX Mountain Corps' mission was to defend its position while thousands of tons of stockpiled supplies were evacuated through the ports at Petsamo and Kirkenes.[12] To conduct a defense, the corps relied on the strongpoint system (*stutzpunktlinie*), constructed during their three-year occupation of the Litsa front. The first belt of the system was occupied, and the second and third belts were prepared for use as needed. Within

TABLE 1
Status of German Units on 1 September 1944

	XIX Mountain Corps, All Units	2d Mountain Division	6th Mountain Division[2]	Division Group Van der Hoop	210th Infantry Division	Bicycle Brigade Norway[3]
Assigned strength	56,000[1]	16,026 92.8%	18,020 90.6%	3,992 90.0%	5,914 82.7%	2,130
Rifles and submachine guns	51,888	13,873	12,621	NA	5,700	
Machine guns	1,979	514	774	331	391	
Tanks	0	—	—	—	—	
Field guns	135	45	36	0	77	
Antitank guns[4]	261	6	9	0	20	
Mortars[5] (8.0 cm)	245	NA	NA	NA	NA	
Horses	—	3,672 69%	5,074 80%	657 64.5%	305 92%	

1. Corps strength figure is as of 1 July 1944; all subunit strength figures are as of 1 September 1944.
2. This figure includes the attached 388th Grenadier Brigade.
3. Authorized strength of this unit is shown; no data is available on the actual personnel or materiel status.
4. Corps total includes 120 3.7-cm Paks and 109 8.8-cm rockets. Subunit figures are only for 7.5-cm Pak 40s.
5. Figures do not include six 21.0-cm mortars. German records show no 120-mm mortars.

Source: This data was compiled from several German documents. See note 11.

their assigned sectors, German units selected dominating hilltops on which they built covered concrete and steel-reinforced bunkers, firing points, trench systems, ammunition and supply caches, and command posts. Each strongpoint allowed for all-around observation and fire and was surrounded by barbed-wire obstacles and minefields, as needed.

The size of each strongpoint varied in relation to the terrain and troops available (see map 4). In the 2d Mountain Division sector, for example, Strongpoint Zuckerhutl was manned by a company of mountain infantry, a reinforced engineer platoon, and an artillery observation section. This force was armed with thirteen light machine guns (145,000 rounds), four heavy machine guns, two 80-mm mortars (2,100 rounds), two light infantry guns (1,600 rounds), and two 37-mm antitank guns (770 rounds) (see figure 2).[13] In the entire division sector, there were ten reinforced company-size strongpoints and several smaller positions occupied by a platoon or less. The commander of the 137th Mountain Infantry Regiment and three battalion headquarters controlled these strongpoints. The 111th Mountain Artillery Regiment provided indirect-fire support with a battalion in direct support of each infantry battalion and an additional artillery battalion designated for crisis situations.

Direct and indirect fires, engineer obstacles, minefields, and patrols covered the low ground between strongpoints, which varied in width to as much as two to four kilometers. Realizing that these gaps constituted a major weakness in the defensive system, the 2d Mountain Division units constructed or improved additional intermediate positions in the week before the Soviet offensive began.

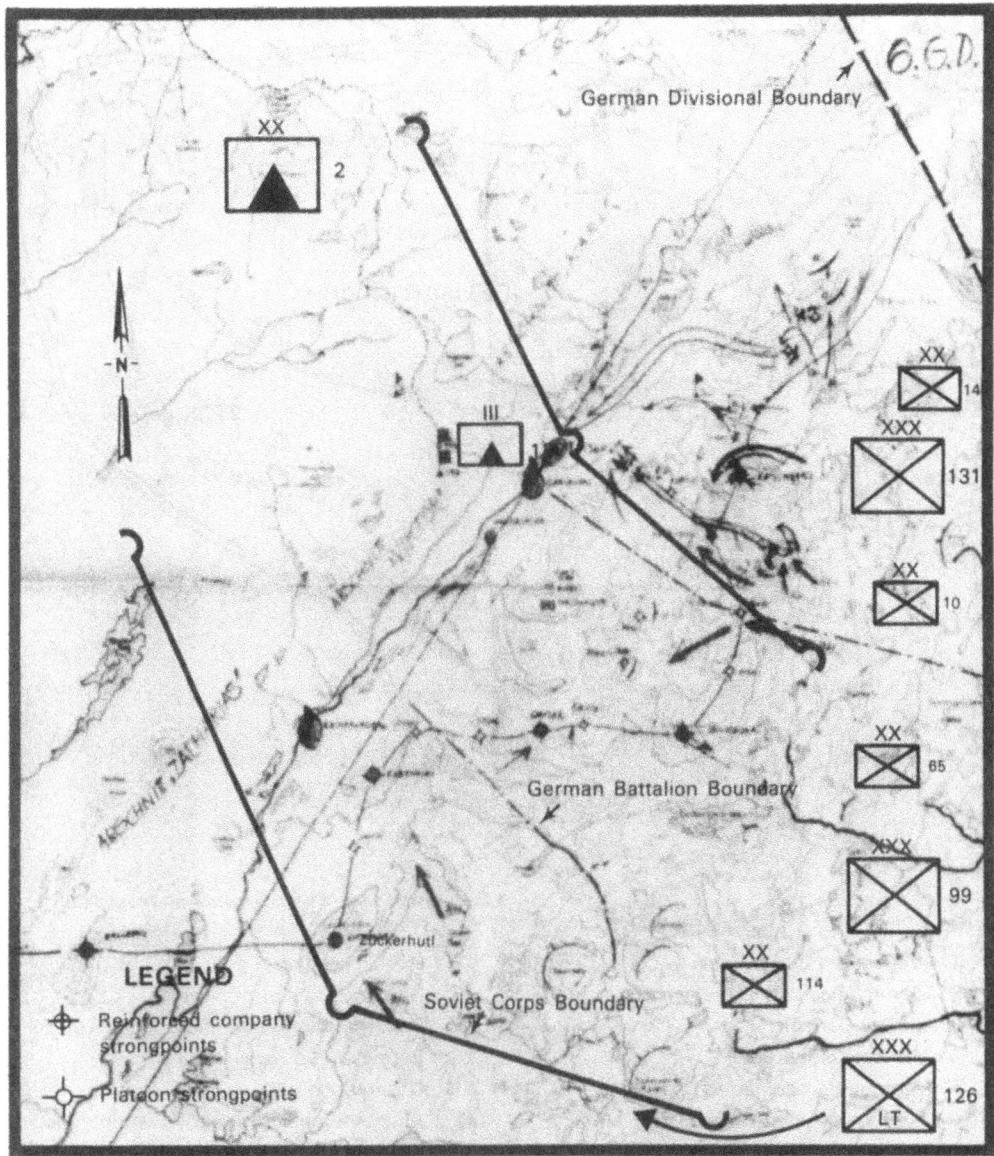

Map 4. Disposition of 2d Mountain Division units and Soviet units on the main axis

The second defensive belt ran along the west bank of the Titovka River, ten to twelve kilometers behind the first belt. It consisted of individual strongpoints covering approaches to the river, primarily where there were roads or paths. The rear defensive belt lay twenty to twenty-five kilometers farther west, behind the Petsamo River. Its strongest positions guarded the approaches to Petsamo and Luostari. Additional defensive positions protected the mines at Nikel, the port at Liinakhamari north of Petsamo, and Kirkenes with its airfield and port.[14]

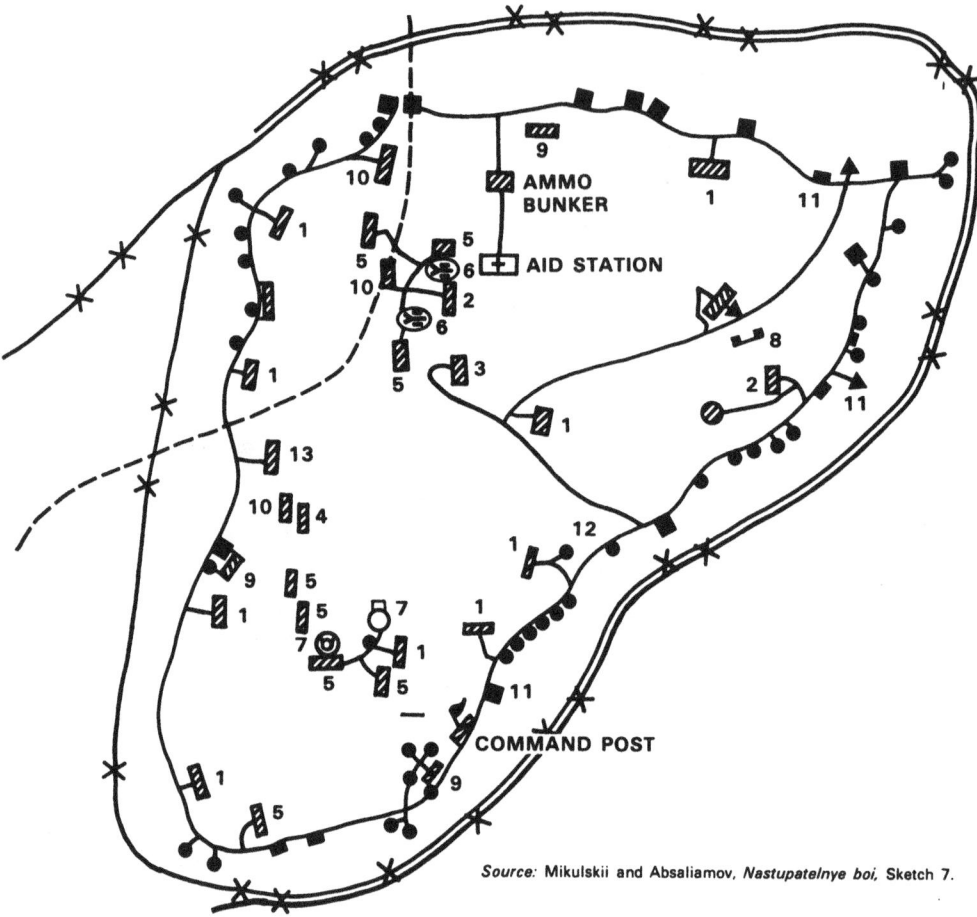

1. Dugout for two squads
2. Communications center and generator
3. Officer barracks
4. Administration point
5. Ammunition dump
6. Artillery position number 2
7. Mortar position
8. Artillery position number 1
9. Underground ammunition dump
10. Barracks and repair shop
11. Observation post
12. Air observation and early warning post
13. Kitchen

Figure 2. Strongpoint Zuckerhutl

The German XIX Mountain Corps units were aware of the Soviet buildup and knew that a major offensive was imminent. Lieutenant General Hans Degen, commander of the 2d Mountain Division, told his soldiers as much in a proclamation issued on 12 September (see appendix D).[15] A ten-page divisional order issued on 28 September contained more detailed information concerning the impending Soviet offensive.[16] This order correctly identified Lanweg as the main axis of the Soviet attack and prescribed a number of measures to be taken by divisional units to strengthen their strongpoints. However, there was nothing in the order that suggested a German plan to

Marshal K. A. Meretskov, commander, Karelian Front, who was promoted to that rank after the successful conclusion of the Petsamo-Kirkenes Operation

withdraw from their long-held defensive positions; rather, it presumed that the strongpoint line would hold. Hitler had not yet agreed to Operation Nordlicht, which required the corps to withdraw into Norway.

Soviet Planning and Preparation

Soviet planning for an operation to clear the Germans from the Murmansk sector began in February 1944, when Meretskov replaced Colonel General V. A. Frolov as Karelian Front commander.[17]

At the age of forty-seven, Meretskov was an experienced Soviet commander. He joined the Red Army in 1918, was a veteran of the Russian Civil War, and during the interwar period had served in progressively higher command and staff positions. In 1936, Meretskov was an adviser in Spain; in 1937, he became deputy chief of the Soviet General Staff; and in 1938, he took command of the Leningrad Military District. Meretskov commanded Soviet forces in the initial, less successful phase of the 1939—40 war with Finland, then briefly served as chief of staff of the Red Army. In 1941 and from 1942 to 1944, he commanded the Volkhov Front, which was adjacent to the Leningrad Front on its southern flank. Meretskov was chosen for this new position in part because he was available. His Volkhov Front forces had been absorbed into other commands when the lines were shortened.

Lieutenant General V. I. Shcherbakov, commander, 14th Army

But more important, he was familiar with the terrain of Soviet Karelia, having fought there in 1939—40. Stalin reminded him of this when the two met in Moscow on 13 February:

> You know the Northern Direction well. You have acquired the experience of the conduct of offensive operations in the difficult conditions of forested and swampy terrain. You have the maps, and more importantly, you commanded the army on the Vyborg Direction in 1939—40, during the Soviet-Finnish War, and broke through the Mannerheim Line. To name another person, who knows nothing at all about the peculiarities of this theater of military operations, and who does not have experience in the conduct of battles in the conditions of Karelia and the polar region, to the Karelian Front at this time would be inexpedient. This would prolong the organization of the defeat of the enemy. Any other commander would have to be retrained, which would take much time. And this is something we do not have.[18]

In April and May 1944, with guidance from Stalin and the Headquarters of the Supreme High Command (*STAVKA*) in hand, Meretskov and his subordinate army commanders conducted operational-tactical war games that were oriented on subsequent offensive operations. Similar exercises occurred at divisional and regimental headquarters.[19]

The 14th Army, which had defended the approaches to Murmansk since the beginning of the war, was commanded by Lieutenant General V. I. Shcherbakov, a 43-year-old civil war veteran who had commanded a division in Meretskov's 7th Army during the Soviet-Finnish War in 1939—40. Shcherbakov took command of the 14th Army in March 1942 and was promoted to lieutenant general in 1943. As an old acquaintance of Meretskov from his service in the Leningrad Military District, he enjoyed the new Front commander's confidence.[20] During June and July of 1944, while the Karelian Front's major effort focused on the Svir-Petrozavodsk Operation in southern Karelia, Shcherbakov used his limited forces of two rifle divisions and two light rifle brigades to close the gap between his army and the XIX Mountain Corps units, pushing the Soviet positions forward another ten to twelve kilometers. In the 14th Army rear, Soviet infantry and engineer units improved the approaches to the battlefield by building and improving roads and bridges.[21]

In August, Soviet reinforcements necessary for the planned offensive began arriving on the Murmansk-Leningrad railroad from the recently completed operations in the Svir-Petrozavodsk area of southern Karelia and from the Kandalaksha area just north of the Arctic Circle. Between 9 August and 7 October, six rifle divisions, two rifle corps headquarters, and a light rifle corps headquarters with three brigades detrained at Kola Station south of Murmansk and moved forward along dirt roads to new staging areas. Tank and heavy artillery units detrained farther north and crossed the bay on barges before driving to the staging areas. By early October, regrouping was completed, and Meretskov's force was assembled (see figure 3).[22]

On the eve of the offensive, the 14th Army infantry units were of various origins and levels and types of combat experience. The 126th and 127th Light Rifle Corps (LRCs) were composite units formed in March 1944 from naval rifle brigades and separate army ski units under a ground force corps headquarters. The 126th LRC was commanded by Colonel V. N. Solovev,

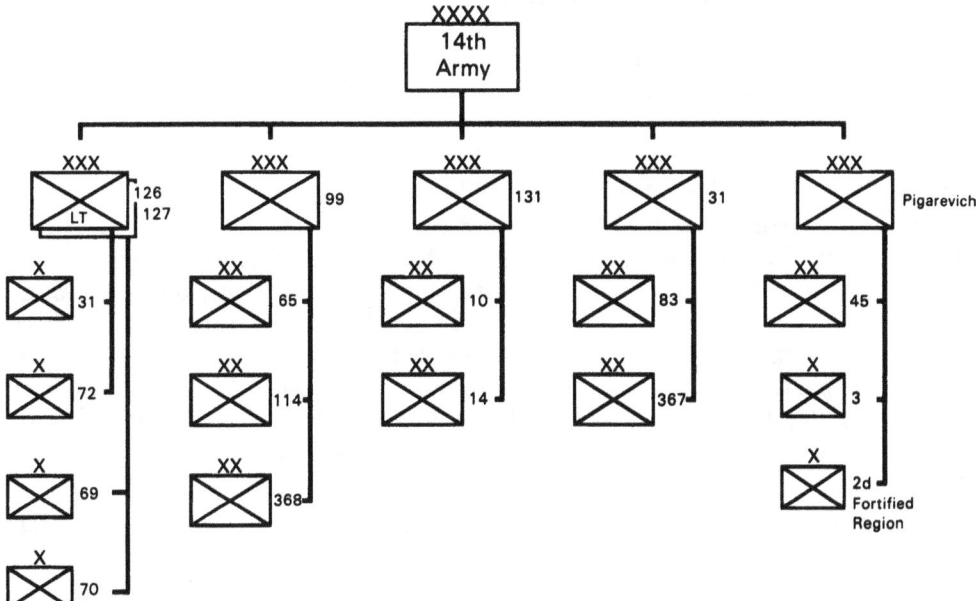

Figure 3. Organization of the Soviet 14th Army, October 1944

who was intimately familiar with the terrain, having previously commanded a regiment in the 10th Guards Rifle Division.[23] The 126th consisted of the 31st Light Rifle Brigade, probably an army unit, and the 72d Naval Rifle Brigade.[24] Major General G. A. Zhukov, who had previous experience as a rifle division commander in the Karelian Front,[25] commanded the 127th LRC, which also was composed of two brigades, the 69th and 70th Naval Rifle Brigades.[26]

All four brigades in these two corps were structured similarly. They had three rifle battalions with 715 men each, an artillery battalion with eight 76-mm guns, an antitank artillery battalion with twelve guns, a mortar battalion with a mix of sixteen 82-mm and eight 120-mm mortars, a company of submachine gunners, a reconnaissance company, a company of antitank rifles, an antiaircraft platoon, a signal battalion, an engineer company, a transportation company, and a medical company. The authorized strength of a brigade was 4,334 people, 178 vehicles, and 818 horses.[27] In personnel, a full-strength, two-brigade light rifle corps was thus slightly smaller than a full-strength, standard Soviet rifle division.

As is often the case, however, neither corps was configured exactly according to the standard tables of organization and equipment at the time of this offensive. Since none of the brigades had vehicles or even carts, they used pack animals to transport all their heavy infantry weapons, artillery, mortars, communications equipment, and ammunition.[28] According to one Soviet source, the 126th LRC had five batteries of 76-mm pack howitzers and three batteries of heavy mortars.[29] Another source indicates that each light rifle corps contained an artillery battalion of twelve 76-mm mountain guns and a mortar battalion of twelve 120-mm mortars.[30] Pack horses transported the guns, reindeer the ammunition. Of the two corps, the 127th had the most combat experience, having just participated in the Svir-Petrozavodsk offensive in southern Karelia. However, this experience apparently came at the cost of casualties and may explain the 14th Army commander's decision to place the 127th LRC in the army second echelon.[31] Each corps probably had about the same personnel strength as the average rifle division in the 99th and 31st Rifle Corps.[32]

The 14th Army also had three standard rifle corps—the 99th, the 131st, and the 31st. Lieutenant General S. P. Mikulskii, who had earlier commanded a rifle corps under Meretskov in the Volkhov Front, took command of the 99th Rifle Corps in June 1944 and led it through the Svir-Petrozavodsk Operation. Two of his three rifle divisions (the 114th and the 368th) also participated in that operation; the 65th Rifle Division had been part of Mikulskii's corps in the Volkhov Front. When the offensive began, the 99th was at about 65 percent of its authorized strength (see appendix E).

The 131st Rifle Corps headquarters was created in late August 1944 and, in early October, was commanded by Major General Z. N. Alekseev, who had commanded the 127th LRC in combat during the Svir-Petrozavodsk Operation.[33] His two rifle divisions, the 10th Guards and the 14th, had spent the entire war in the Murmansk sector and were experienced in arctic warfare. The actual strength figures of the 131st are not available. Major General M. A. Absaliamov, who earlier had commanded a rifle division in Meretskov's Volkhov Front and then in the Svir-Petrozavodsk Operation, commanded the 31st Rifle Corps.[34] Absaliamov's 83d and 367th Rifle Divisions were veteran units of the Karelian Front but had limited combat experience. When the 31st was committed to battle, the corps was at about 60 percent of its authorized strength (see appendix F).

The remaining infantry formation of the 14th Army was Group Pigarevich, a composite corps-size unit named after its commander, Lieutenant General B. A. Pigarevich. A World War I veteran of the Imperial Army who joined the Red Army in 1918, commanded a battalion in the civil war, and served mostly in staff positions during the interwar period, Pigarevich had been chief of staff of the 14th Army during the Soviet-Finnish War of 1939—40. After two years of staff service in the West Front, he returned to the Karelian Front as its chief of staff in 1943.[35] In August 1944, Meretskov replaced Pigarevich with a younger, more energetic and experienced officer after the Svir-Petrozavodsk Operation.[36] Group Pigarevich comprised the 45th Rifle Division, from the Karelian Front's 26th Army; the 3d Naval Rifle Brigade, recently in combat in southern Karelia; and the 2d Fortified Region, which had come from Meretskov's Volkhov Front.[37]

On 8 September, General Meretskov discussed his plan for the offensive with the commander of the Northern Fleet, Admiral A. G. Golovko, whose air, sea, and land forces would support the coastal flank of the 14th Army.[38] In late September, Meretskov sent his draft plan to Moscow for *STAVKA*'s approval. *STAVKA* accepted the draft with minor adjustments, and on 29 September, Meretskov published the order to his subordinate units (see appendix A).[39]

The plan was straightforward and uncomplicated (see map 5). The 14th Army was to attack with the main effort on the left, in the sector from Lake Chapr south to Hill 237.1, to defeat the 2d Mountain Division and seize the Petsamo-Luostari area by frontal attack. On its left, the 126th and 127th Light Rifle Corps, deployed in two echelons, would envelop the German right flank to block the Arctic Ocean Highway west of Luostari and the Tarnet Road west of Petsamo to prevent German retreat and reinforcement. On the 14th Army right flank, from Lake Chapr to the east and north, Soviet forces would conduct an economy-of-force operation against the German 6th Mountain Division. On the far right flank, naval infantry forces would attack across the Srednii isthmus and along the coastline west of it, against Division Group Van der Hoop, to cut that unit's path of retreat and reinforcement.

On the main axis, Meretskov formed the first echelon with the 99th and 131st Rifle Corps (five divisions), the 126th LRC (two brigades); and tank and artillery units. His second echelon consisted of the 31st Rifle Corps (two rifle divisions) and the 127th LRC (two brigades). Group Pigarevich would execute the economy-of-force mission on the Soviet right flank.

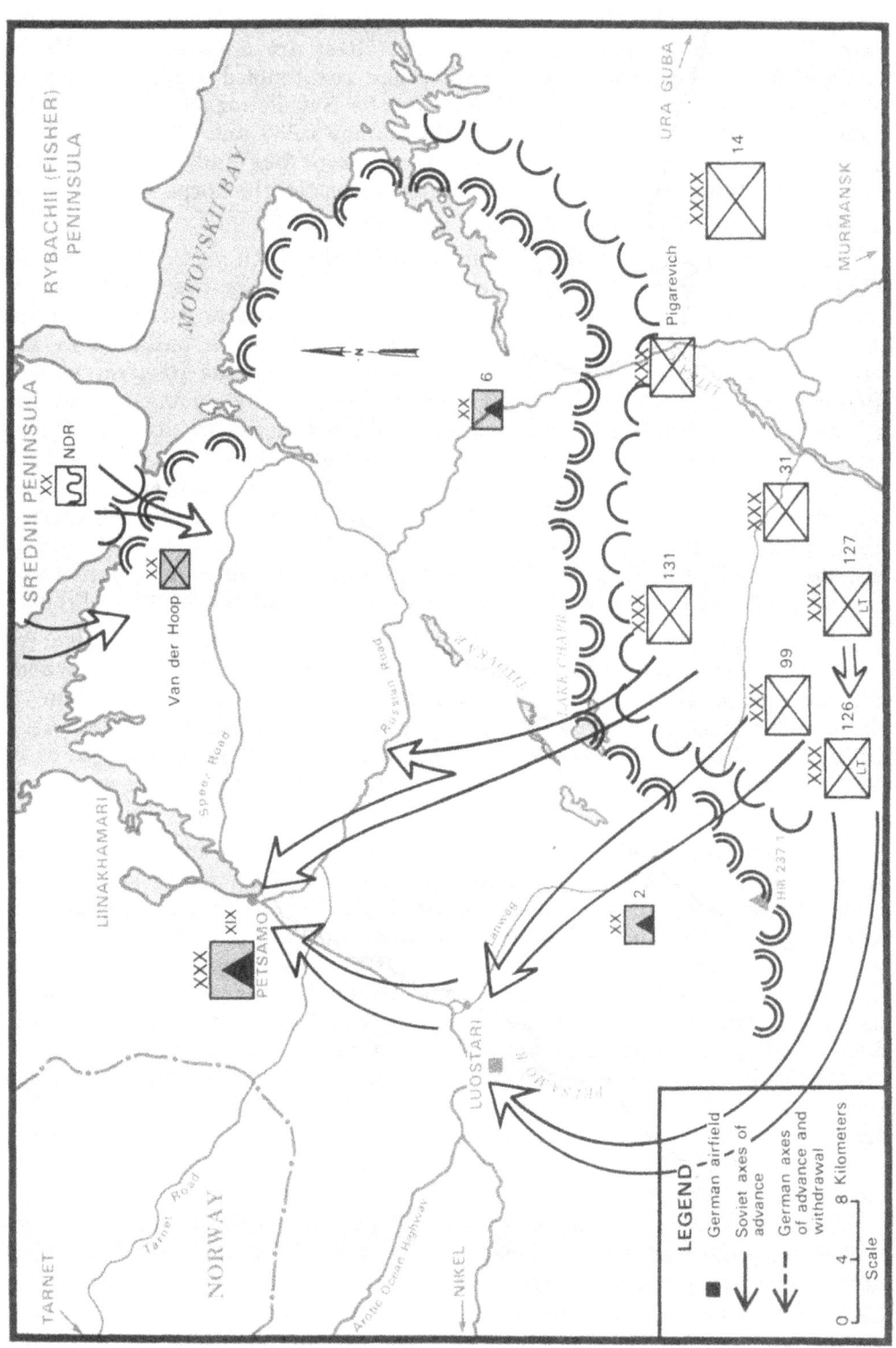

Map 5. Karelian Front offensive plan

Admiral Golovko would employ the Northern Defensive Region (NDR) with one naval infantry brigade attacking across the Srednii isthmus and another naval infantry brigade landing in an amphibious assault to the west of the isthmus.

To support the operation, Meretskov ordered his chief of artillery to plan a two-hour and thirty-five minute artillery preparation, fired by mortars and artillery numbering more than 150 tubes per kilometer of front on the main axis. Their primary mission was to knock out the enemy's artillery and then to support the breakthrough, the crossing of the Titovka River, and the infantry's attack into the intermediate German positions. Lieutenant General Mikulskii, the 99th Rifle Corps commander, ordered his artillery to silence enemy indirect-fire assets, suppress or destroy enemy troops and weapons systems, create openings in enemy obstacles large enough for two to three companies to attack through, support the crossing of the Titovka River, and deny the enemy the opportunity to counterattack or withdraw.[40]

The artillery forces amassed to support this operation were formidable. Each rifle regiment had from twelve to eighteen 82-mm and four to six 120-mm mortars and three to four 76-mm guns. Each rifle division had an artillery regiment equipped with a mix of twenty-eight to thirty-two 76-mm and 122-mm howitzers. The total organic indirect-fire assets varied slightly from division to division but averaged fifty 82-mm mortars, sixteen 120-mm mortars, thirty 76-mm guns, and twelve 122-mm howitzers.[41]

To reinforce the 14th Army, at least seven mortar and seventeen artillery regiments were brought in from the 7th and 32d Armies and other units in the Karelian Front.[42] These included regiments of 120-mm mortars, 76-mm guns, and 122-mm howitzers; one regiment of captured German 150-mm guns; and regiments of 152-mm towed guns. In addition, Meretskov gave Shcherbakov three regiments and two brigades of multiple rocket launchers (MRLs). The total artillery and mortar tube count was 2,100, to which can be added 120 MRL systems.[43] Two Soviet sources report a density of 156 and 168 tubes per kilometer of front in the main attack sector of two divisions. But one of these divisions belonged to the 99th Rifle Corps, and its commander, Lieutenant General Mikulskii, plainly states that, in that division sector, the density was ninety-five guns and mortars and twenty-three MRL systems per kilometer of front.[44] One indisputable fact emerges from all the accounts: over half of the tube density on the main axis came from mortar systems. The number of 76-mm and 122-mm artillery pieces employed in a direct-fire mode to supplement the 45-mm antitank guns was relatively small. In the 65th Rifle Division, for example, twenty-one 76-mm guns and six 122-mm howitzers were set aside for direct fire.[45]

In accordance with standard Soviet practice, indirect-fire support systems were organized into army, corps, divisional, and regimental groups. An army artillery group was made up of long-range artillery and MRLs. The long-range artillery was to suppress enemy artillery, his reserves, and his command and control nodes. MRLs were targeted on the two German strongpoints believed to be the strongest—a 24-system regiment on each.

American lend-lease trucks mounted with Katyusha multiple rocket launchers

The corps artillery group consisted of up to two regiments of long-range artillery (150-mm or 152-mm) and a regiment of MRLs (twenty-four systems). This group was to execute counterbattery fire in the breakthrough sector.

The division artillery group varied in size depending on the division's mission. The 65th Rifle Division's artillery group in the main attack was a regiment of twenty-four 122-mm howitzers. Regimental artillery groups also varied in size and were a combination of mortar and field artillery units. The regimental artillery group of the 65th Rifle Division had two battalions of 120-mm mortars and five battalions of field artillery. In contrast, the 114th Rifle Division's regimental artillery group consisted of one mortar battalion and two field artillery battalions. As a result of these groupings, in the 99th Rifle Corps first-echelon regiments, each rifle battalion was supported by one or two artillery battalions and one or two mortar batteries. On the main axis, the support ratio was even greater: one mortar and two artillery battalions per rifle battalion. This resulted in each attacking rifle company enjoying the support of two or three artillery and mortar batteries.[46]

Counterbattery fires were planned on the basis of "instrumental reconnaissance" conducted during the preparatory period.[47] Forty-three Soviet batteries were targeted on the twenty-one German batteries that were plotted in this manner, a ratio of 2 to 1. A counterbattery mission would be 3 to 5 minutes of fire, achieving a density of 25 to 30 rounds per hectare (an area 100 meters square) or 2,500 to 3,000 rounds per square kilometer. Counter-battery fires—a combination of mortar and artillery units firing 200 rounds per German battery—were to suppress German mortar batteries in the zone of the main attack.[48]

To mask their location from German observation, the mortar and artillery batteries of all Soviet units, including those of the second-echelon corps, were brought into firing positions at night. Most of the artillery units were positioned by 24 September, and late-arriving units sent quartering parties ahead to select and prepare firing postions.[49]

The Front order specified the details of the artillery preparation as follows (see appendix A):

- 5 minutes—Barrage by all indirect-fire weapons, except MRLs, on strongpoints and centers of communication and command and control.
- 30 minutes—Registration.
- 60 minutes—Destruction of known targets; creation of passage lanes in barbed-wire obstacles.
- 30 minutes—Aerial bombing while artillery continues to suppress important targets.
- 20 minutes—Artillery plus two brigades of MRLs suppress newly acquired targets.
- 10 minutes—Maximum density of fire by all systems directed at initial defensive positions, immediate depth, and enemy artillery and mortar batteries.

Just for the preparation, the Soviets allocated a total of 140,000 rounds—84,000 mortar and 56,000 artillery. They also planned to fire 8,200 to 8,500 rounds of MRL projectiles per square kilometer on selected strongpoints, a total of 97 tons of MRL ordnance.

When the infantry attacked following the artillery preparation, the artillery was to use the standard "successive concentration of fire" to a depth of 2.5 kilometers.[50] Under this system, the direct support indirect-fire assets were to concentrate their fires on successive lines immediately in front of the attacking troops, shifting their fires forward as the attack advanced. The 82-mm and 120-mm mortars were to fire successive volleys, each 150 meters beyond the previous volley. This method of employment, by exploiting the high angle-of-fire capability of mortars, aided in reaching targets on reverse slopes, which artillery fires often missed, and also reflected the relatively greater amount of mortar tubes and ammunition on hand.

After the infantry broke through the enemy's initial positions, mortar and artillery units would continue to support the attacking troops. MRL support would be available only on those axes of advance that were capable of supporting wheeled-vehicle traffic. Tank units would control their supporting artillery fire through a forward observer riding in a radio-equipped combat vehicle.[51]

The 14th Army did not have an organic tank or self-propelled artillery unit.[52] All armored forces belonged to the Karelian Front, and for the Petsamo-Kirkenes Operation, Meretskov brought in three tank and two self-propelled artillery units. Four of these formations that had recently participated in the Svir-Petrozavodsk Operation in southern Karelia were the 7th Guards Tank Brigade (7th GTB) with thirty-seven T-34 tanks, the 89th Separate Tank Regiment (89th STR) with eighteen T-34s, the 339th Guards Heavy Self-Propelled Artillery Regiment (339th GHSPAR) with seventeen JSU-152s, and the 378th Guards Heavy Self-Propelled Artillery Regiment (378th GHSPAR) with seventeen JSU-152s.

General Meretskov personally asked *STAVKA* for the fifth armored unit. Having considered the nature of the German antitank defenses and their lack of tanks, Meretskov believed that his forces should include a regiment of the heavy KV tanks. After some deliberation, *STAVKA* approved Meretskov's request, and he obtained the 73d Separate Guards Heavy Tank Regiment (73d SGHTR) with twenty-one KV tanks.[53]

From 1 to 5 October, all the armored units arrived by rail at Murmansk, were transported by barge across the bay, and then were driven on dirt roads to their unit assembly areas eight to twelve kilometers from the Germans' initial positions. From these units' time of arrival in the assembly area until 7 October, they performed maintenance duties, trained drivers, and coordinated with supported units.[54]

The 73d SGHTR was paired with the 378th GHSPAR and attached to the 131st Rifle Corps. From the beginning of the operation, Major General Alekseev had planned to use his tanks and guns for direct support of infantry and, therefore, attached them to his left-flank 10th Guards Rifle

KV-85 heavy tank, specifically requested by Meretskov for this operation

Division. The 7th GTB was paired with the 339th GHSPAR and attached to the 99th Rifle Corps. Lieutenant General Mikulskii, influenced probably by his recent combat experience in southern Karelia, formed a mobile group by combining his armor, an engineer battalion, and infantry from his second-echelon rifle division. After the breakthrough, it was to develop the offensive in depth. Since the 89th STR did not arrive in the area until after 7 October, it was placed in army reserve.[55] General Shcherbakov's 14th Army had a total of 110 tanks and self-propelled artillery pieces. As far as can be determined, the Germans had none.

Soviet planning for engineer support of the offensive was comprehensive, taking into account the underdeveloped road network; the geological composition of the terrain, that is, its swamps and bogs, solid rock, boulders, and mixtures thereof; and the extensive hardening of the German defensive positions. In his Front order, Meretskov directed the engineer troops to prepare assembly areas for the army, support the rapid forcing of water obstacles on the main axis of attack, and support the maneuver of the attacking forces after the breakthrough. In addition, they were expected to support the surprise breakthrough of the enemy's forward defensive positions in the initial attack.[56]

To accomplish these missions, the Soviets employed approximately thirty engineer battalions. Each of the eight rifle divisions had its own divisional engineer battalion. The 20th Svirsk Motorized Assault Combat Engineer Brigade and the 13th Assault Combat Engineer Brigade had six battalions each. The 1st Motorized Engineer Brigade had three battalions. Five separate engineer battalions included two pontoon bridge units, a road exploitation battalion, a road construction battalion, and a battalion of demolition specialists.[57]

Although not engineer units in name, the 275th and 284th Separate Special-Purpose Motorized Battalions were certainly engineer equipped. Each had ninety-four American-made amphibians.[58] The 284th Battalion was attached to the 99th Rifle Corps before 7 October and remained with it for the duration of the operation.[59] The other battalion supported the 131st Rifle Corps.

The Soviets' river-crossing equipment included both heavy and light pontoon sets, a captured German bridge set, 50 meters of class 60 bridging, 300 assault boats, and 1,200 sets of waders. The 14th Army commander controlled the heavy pontoon and bridge units, while the light pontoon and all the remaining crossing materials were distributed among the first-echelon divisions.[60]

Another element of the operations plan was the building of roads and bridges. Special road-bridge detachments at division and corps level were to build roads on the axes of advance for each of the four rifle divisions in the first echelon. A division detachment consisted of engineer troops of company to battalion size, plus a battalion of infantry. A corps detachment was two to three combat engineer and road construction battalions combined with an infantry regiment. These specially created organizations were also

A Ford ¼-ton amphibian, given to the U.S.S.R. in lend-lease and employed by the 14th Army to cross water obstacles

to rebuild fallen or destroyed bridges while moving behind the combat formations of the first echelon.[61] To help tank units maintain mobility during the offensive, each platoon had a squad of engineer troops equipped with explosives to remove concrete or rock obstacles and with logs to negotiate swampy terrain.[62]

During the initial assault on German defensive positions, engineer troops were organized to conduct reconnaissance, remove German obstacles, and destroy reinforced positions. Divisional and army engineer units conducted reconnaissance during the concentration and deployment phases by determining the nature of German positions, approach routes, suitable terrain for the future construction of cross-country vehicular roads and footpaths, and possible crossing sites on the Titovka River.

To remove German obstacles and destroy reinforced positions, the Soviets created assault groups and obstacle detachments within first-echelon infantry units. An assault group usually consisted of a specially trained rifle platoon reinforced with a heavy machine gun or 45-mm antitank gun, one or two flamethrower teams, and one or two engineer squads. A rifle battalion would have one such composite platoon. Engineer troops for these composite detachments came from regimental or divisional engineer units.[63] Table 2 shows Lieutenant General Mikulskii's allocation of engineer units and how he planned to use them.

Soviet Army air forces had a significant role in supporting the offensive.[64] Meretskov's 29 September Front order specified the standard missions of close air support (CAS), interdiction, and air superiority. CAS tasks included assisting Soviet artillery during the preparatory fires to break through the German defenses, disrupting enemy command and control, suppressing artillery and mortar batteries, and accompanying tanks and infantry during the battle to support their attacks. Interdiction tasks were to locate and engage enemy operational and tactical reserves and to prevent their commitment, destroy river-crossing sites to deny the enemy the ability to withdraw, destroy enemy command posts and communications centers, and strike at his means of mobility. The Soviets were to maintain air superiority in two ways. Bombers targeted German airfields at Luostari, Salmiiarvi, and Kirkenes for strikes, and fighter planes covered the battle area, protecting both air and ground forces. Although the Front order did not specify a reconnaissance mission, the various air units had this capability and continuously exercised it.

General Meretskov's air forces came from various commands. His own 7th Air Army provided four mixed air divisions, an interceptor division, and the command and control apparatus. From the national air defense forces, he acquired an additional interceptor division that, throughout the operation, defended Murmansk and the Murmansk-Leningrad railroad. Finally, *STAVKA* reserve provided a bomber division. Soviet aircraft types included the Il-2 ground attack aircraft; Pe-2 dive-bomber; Il-4 medium bomber; Lag-5, Yak-3, and Yak-9 fighters; and Po-2 utility aircraft. In addition, the 7th Air Army had a number of American lend-lease P-40s, P-39s, and P-63s.

TABLE 2
Engineer Plan, 99th Rifle Corps

Engineer Units	Number of Battalions	Number of Companies	Engineer Equipment (Special)	Missions or Attachments
Engr bns of the 65th, 114th, and 368th Rifle Divs	3	6	—	Per decision of division commander
20th Motorized Cbt Engr Bde (2d, 109th, 135th, 222d, and 447th Cbt Engr Bns, 28th Flamethrower Bn)	6	18	Light crossing park with 50% transport	2d Cbt Engr Bn attached to the 7th Gds Tk Bde 109th and 135th Cbt Engr Bn with pontoon assets attached to the 65th Rifle Div for Titovka crossings and participation in assault groups 222d Cbt Engr Bn attached to the 114th Rifle Div for participation in assault groups 447th Cbt Engr Bn for rebuilding class 60 wood bridge across Titovka 28th Flamethrower Bn for participation in assault groups along corps front
50th Sep Rd Exploitation Bn	1	2	—	Build road in zone of the 65th Rifle Div
218th Sep Rd Const Bn	1	2	—	Build road in zone of the 114th Rifle Div
168th Brg Const Bn	1	2	—	Erect class 60 bridge across Titovka
Total	12	30		

Source: Mikulskii and Absaliamov, *Nastupatel'nye boi*, 34—35.

A Bell P-39 Aircobra, given to the U.S.S.R. in lend-lease and flown by naval and army air forces. Note that the 37-mm nose cannon has been replaced with a machine gun.

The total air strength in the Karelian Front was 132 bombers; 52 Po-2 utility aircraft; 189 ground attack aircraft; 308 fighter-interceptors; and 66 assorted reconnaissance, forward observer, and liaison aircraft—a total of 747 aircraft.[65] Although the air arm of the Northern Fleet contained an additional 275 aircraft, they were not used to support army ground forces. (Naval air operations are discussed in detail in chapter 5.)

By 6 October, the commander of the 7th Air Army, Lieutenant General of Aviation I. M. Sokolov, assumed operational command of all army air units.[66] He, in turn, allocated a mixed air division each to the 99th and 131st Rifle Corps, which were attacking on the main axis. The commanders of these two air units were located at their supported rifle corps command posts. A liaison officer with communications equipment was attached to the command post of each rifle division in the main attack to aid in directing CAS strikes. Also, an additional liaison officer was attached to the tank forces of each corps.[67] Lieutenant General Sokolov controlled the remaining two mixed air divisions, the fighter divisions, and the bomber division from his command post collocated with Lieutenant General Shcherbakov's 14th Army command post.

Two plans were developed for air operations, one for good flying weather and the other for bad. In the event of good weather, all assets were to be used. During bad weather, bombers would not fly, but fighters and CAS aircraft would. Specific air operations were planned only for the breakthrough phase of the offensive, but this still amounted to over 4,000 sorties.[68]

The Soviets estimated German air strength in the immediate area to be 160 aircraft, half of which were fighters.[69] The most common German aircraft were the Arado 66 night bombers, Ju-87 Stukas, Bf-109 fighters, and FW-190 fighter-bombers. The Soviets thus enjoyed a 6-to-1 superiority in air strength.

Logistic support, essential to all military operations, was especially significant in the far north. Soviet logistic planners for the Petsamo-Kirkenes Operation were given several imperatives.[70] Logistic units were to stockpile the necessary supplies prior to the operation, provide medical evacuation and treatment to the wounded and sick, accomplish timely repair of combat equipment, build and maintain the lines of communication, provide the troops with everything they needed for combat and survival, and provide rear area protection against enemy attacks.[71]

The hub of logistic support of the operation was Murmansk, the northern terminus of the rail link to Leningrad, and its outlying rail and water transport facilities. Materiel delivered by rail was either stored on the ground in the Murmansk area or shipped forward by truck or barge to supply bases in the 14th Army rear. At the beginning of the operation, these bases were forty to fifty road kilometers northwest of Murmansk.

From the rear supply bases, cargo was pushed forward on dirt roads, most of which were either built or improved by engineers in support of the operation. By the first week in October, each corps of the first echelon had at least one road and one cross-country track in its sector for logistic support.[72]

The first priority of supply was ammunition, and in early September, artillery units began to stockpile ammunition in all calibers. By the time the operation began, artillery ammunition supplies averaged nearly 2.2 units of fire,[73] and the total accumulation of all types of ammunition came to 17,000 metric tons. Petroleum, oils, and lubricants (POL) were also stockpiled at the user level, at refueling points on roads, and at army dumps—a total of slightly over 3,000 metric tons.[74]

Food for troops and draft animals was critical. By the beginning of the operation, units had a six-day supply of food and forage, of which two days' worth was in the hands of the troops. At army level was another seven days' supply of food and fourteen days' supply of forage, with an additional ten days' supply of food and more forage stored in the Murmansk area. The ration supply plan called for the preparation of 50,000 dry rations, many of which were later air-dropped to units.

In view of the weather conditions in the area of operations, clothing issue was critical to the forces' survivability. In addition to sheepskin coats, caps, underwear, mittens, blankets, and sleeping bags, thousands of white camouflage smocks were issued. Medical kits were restocked, thousands of tack items were repaired or replaced for pack animals, and boots and shoes were repaired. Direct-exchange stockage was established in units. To provide heating fuel for medical treatment and maintenance facilities, the army stockpiled 64,500 cubic meters of firewood. Additional firewood was to be gathered by the troops when and where needed.[75]

Daily, approximately 800 metric tons of supplies were required to keep the army fed, fueled, and firing. Various types of naval vessels and army trucks moved the supplies forward from Murmansk. While discrepancies exist between Soviet sources as to the exact number, the 14th Army and Karelian Front together had seven truck battalions capable of moving 1,761 metric tons in one lift. In early September, however, the Front withdrew three of the truck battalions from the 14th Army and placed them under Front control. To keep the truck fleet moving, the 14th Fixed Automotive Repair Shop provided a depot-level repair capability in Murmansk, while the 224th Separate Repair-Renewal Battalion operated a shop in Murmansk and a forward collection and repair point in the army rear. Three army repair shops, aided by Front assets, took care of the problems with artillery and infantry weapons.

In the absence of suitable roads, especially in the battalion and regimental areas, most of the supplies were moved by pack animals. The 14th Army had an animal-drawn transport company of 141 horses and 2 army reindeer companies totaling over 500 reindeer (a horse could carry 250 pounds, a reindeer 75 to 80 pounds).[76] In the case of the 10th Guards Rifle Division, 99th Rifle Corps, five rifle battalions employed teams of soldiers to carry ammunition and supplies into their positions on fourteen consecutive nights in late September.[77] Since the animals were so important for tactical and logistic transport operations, Soviet planners established rear area and forward veterinary services for the hundreds of horses, reindeer, and dogs in the force.[78]

Medical support was handled by several hospitals in the Murmansk area. Surgical field hospitals and a medical transport unit were deployed to the rear of the combat zone and handled up to 6,000 to 7,500 patients. As the area of operations shifted westward, so too were the field hospitals.

A Soviet supply column of horses transporting boxed ammunition

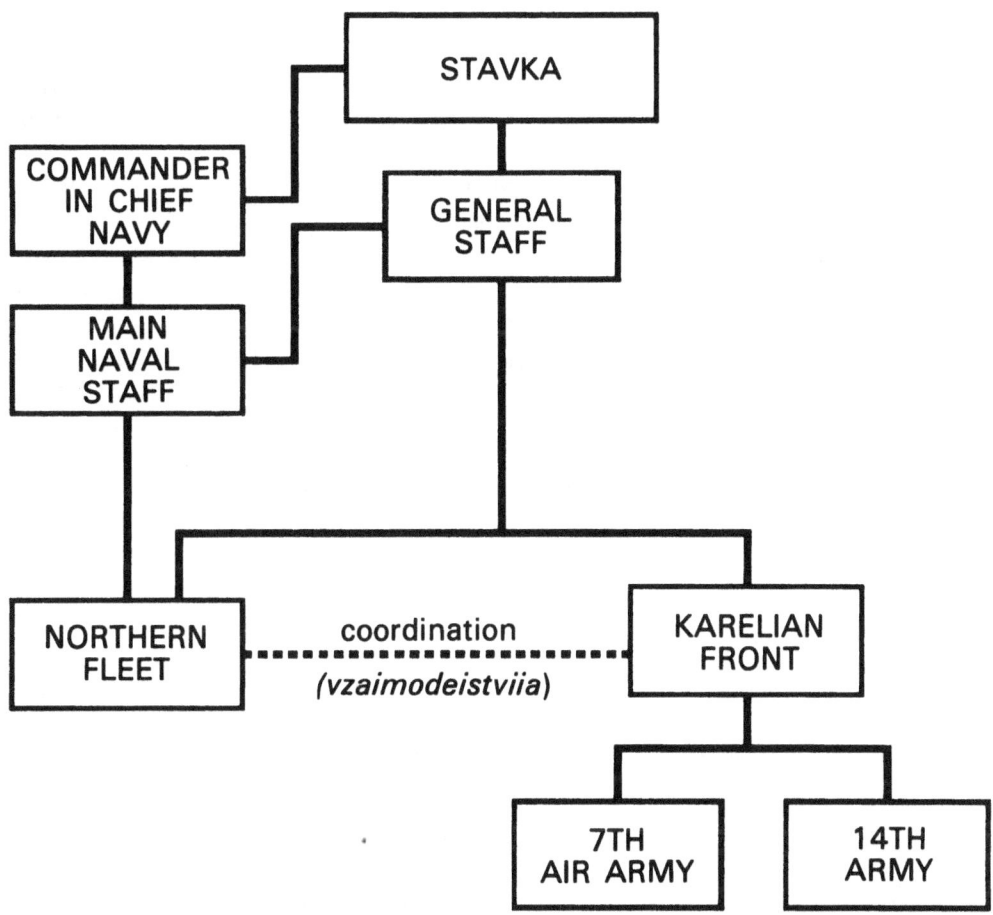

Figure 4. *STAVKA*-Karelian Front-Northern Fleet command relationship

Dogs would detect wounded soldiers left on the battlefield. These casualties would then be removed on sleds, on litters, in flat-bottomed boats, or by horses or reindeer. Once treated at the field station, casualties were to be evacuated to the rear either in ambulances or in cargo trucks returning to the supply base area. A limited number of patients would be transported by air.[79]

The chiefs of rear service at the Front and army levels, both general officer positions, supervised logistic support operations. The Front and army military councils paid close attention to logistic planning and, at army level, conducted at least two formal inspections of logistic units during the operation's preparatory phase.[80]

Command and control of the Petsamo-Kirkenes Operation was exercised through a system that had evolved through three years of combat experience. At the top of the command hierarchy was *STAVKA* (see figure 4). Through its action agency, the General Staff, *STAVKA* exercised national command authority over all Front and fleet commanders concerning the planning and conduct of military operations. General Meretskov reported to and received orders from *STAVKA* through the General Staff. As a former chief of the General Staff, however, Meretskov enjoyed a special relationship with *STAVKA*. He personally talked with Stalin in February, when he took command of the Karelian Front, and again in May concerning the preparations for the June offensive.[81] This personal relationship with Stalin and also with several officers of the General Staff gave Meretskov ready access to *STAVKA*.

At the Karelian Front level, Meretskov exercised command and control of his ground and air forces through the Front staff and commanders of branches and chiefs of service (see figure 5).[82] Operational command and control was accomplished by direct personal contact between commanders. Directorates of branches and services at the Front level coordinated with and supervised analogous sections at the army level, and staffs coordinated with staffs. Above it all at the Front level sat the Front Military Council, made up of the commander, the deputy commander for political affairs, and the chief of staff. An analogous triumvirate existed at all levels down to division. The 7th Air Army was also subordinate to the the Main Staff of Air Forces in Moscow for administrative, supply, basing, and other nonoperational issues.

Meretskov had a long-standing professional relationship with at least two important members of his Front staff. His chief of engineer troops, Lieutenant General A. F. Khrenov, had served in the same capacity with Meretskov in the Leningrad Military District in 1938—40 and then followed

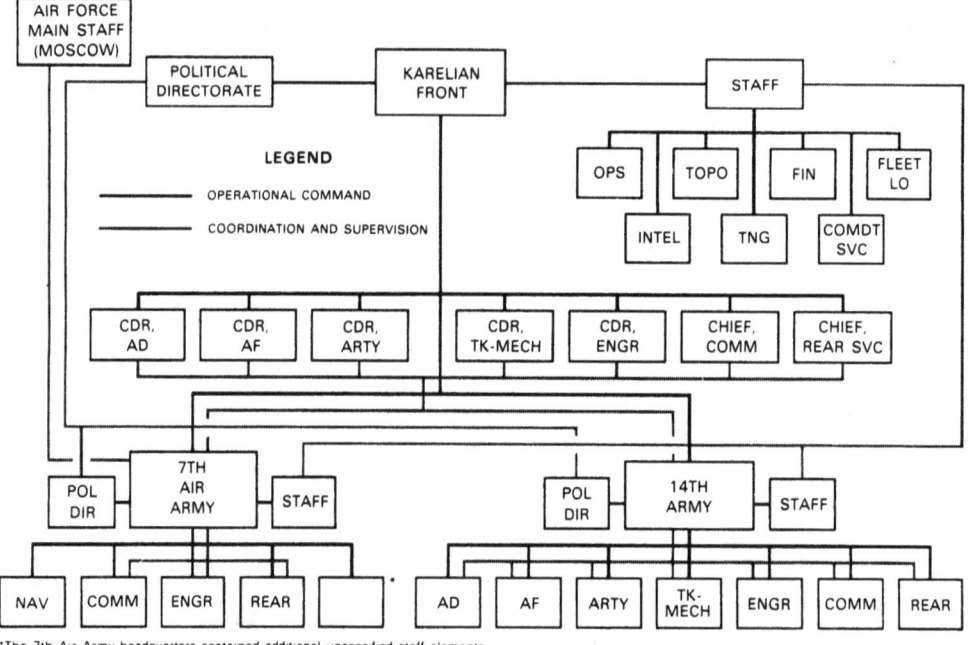

*The 7th Air Army headquarters contained additional unspecified staff elements

Figure 5. Karelian Front command and control relationships

TABLE 3
Soviet Planning Estimate of Force Ratios

	A On the Entire Front- age of 14th Army			B On the Axis of the Main Attack of 14th Army			C On the Sector of the NDR of Northern Fleet		
	Soviet Forces	German Forces	Ratio	Soviet Forces	German Forces	Ratio	Soviet Forces	German Forces	Ratio
Men	96,806	45,529	2.1:1	69,652	21,655	3.2:1	11,390	5,100	2.2:1
Rifles and Sub-machine guns	76,911	37,264	2.0:1	54,837	18,394	3.0:1	5,028	4,106	1.2:1
Machine guns	3,319	1,513	2.2:1	2,446	735	3.3:1	439	233	1.8:1
Tanks	98	27	3.6:1	90	0	—	11	0	—
Guns (field and antitank)	1,032	371	2.7:1	792	226	3.5:1	167	62	2.7:1
Mortars of all calibers	1,090	383	2.8:1	882	205	4.3:1	182	72	2.5:1

Source: Rumiantsev, *Razgrom vraga*, 172. The data in this table is from the Archives of the Soviet Ministry of Defense.

Meretskov to the General Staff. The two went separate ways in March 1941 but met again in June 1942, when Khrenov became chief of engineer troops in Meretskov's Volkhov Front.[83] Lieutenant General T. F. Shtykov, Meretskov's deputy commander for political affairs, had served on the military council of Meretskov's 7th Army in the Leningrad Front in 1939—40 and in the same capacity in the Volkhov Front since April 1943.[84] Both Khrenov and Shtykov joined the Karelian Front with Meretskov in February 1944. On 1 September 1944, General Meretskov selected Lieutenant General A. N. Krutikov as his new Front chief of staff. Krutikov had commanded the 7th Army since April 1943 and had apparently impressed Meretskov during the Svir-Petrozavodsk Operation.[85] These few documented examples illustrate another aspect of the Soviet command and control system: the infusion of personal relationships into the chain of command. By surrounding himself with trusted, hand-picked subordinates, in both staff and command positions, Meretskov overlaid a system of personal fealty on the already rigidly hierarchical chain of command, thus strengthening his role as commander.

When all the preparations for the operations were completed, Soviet planners calculated a relative Soviet strength advantage of just over 2 to 1 on the 14th Army front (see table 3, column A) and even higher in the main attack sector opposite the German 2d Mountain Division (see table 3, column B). Actually, the Soviet planners had underestimated the size of the XIX Mountain Corps by approximately 10,000 men (45,529 versus 56,000), while overestimating the strength of the 2d Mountain Division (21,655 versus 16,026). Thus, Soviet superiority in the sector of the main attack was significantly more favorable than the Soviets had expected (see table 4, column B).

TABLE 4
Actual Soviet-German Force Ratios

	A On the Entire Frontage of 14th Army			B On the Axis of the Main Attack of 14th Army			C On the Sector of the NDR of Northern Fleet		
	Soviet Forces	German Forces	Ratio	Soviet Forces	German Forces	Ratio	Soviet Forces	German Forces	Ratio
Men	96,806	56,000	1.7:1	69,652	16,026	4.3:1	11,390	3,992	2.8:1
Rifles and Submachine guns	76,911	51,888	1.5:1	54,837	13,873	4.0:1	5,028	NA	—
Machine guns	3,319	20,953	1.6:1	2,446	514	4.8:1	439	331	1.3:1
Tanks	98	0	—	98	0	—	11	0	—
Guns (field and antitank)	1,032	396	2.6:1	792	NA	—	167	NA	—
Mortars of all calibers	1,090	245	4.4:1	882	NA	—	182	NA	—

Source: The author compiled this table from data in tables 1 and 3.

On 2 October, Lieutenant General Shcherbakov, the 14th Army commander, spent four hours discussing the operation with Major General Mikulskii, the commander of 99th Rifle Corps. That same day, Mikulskii reconnoitered the terrain with his three division commanders for six hours. On the morning of 3 October, the division commanders walked the terrain with their regimental commanders and, in the afternoon, regimental commanders with battalion commanders. On 4 October, the battalion commanders spent the entire day in reconnaissance with staff and company commanders.[86] On 6 October 1944, the 14th Army commander ordered the artillery preparation to begin at 0800 on 7 October, and the attack two and one-half hours later.[87]

The Battle, Phase One, 7—15 October 1944

Soldiers of the 2d Mountain Division!
... We will permit the enemy to hurl himself against our diligently and solidly built strongpoints, and then destroy him through a counterattack. ... We must here show the Russians that there is still one front on which their hunger for territory will not be satisfied. ... I put my trust in you! We will master every situation, no matter how and when it may develop.

/s/ Degen
Generalleutnant,*
Commander[1]

On the day of the offensive, the weather conditions generally favored the attacking Soviet infantry. Wind from the north was bringing fog to all the low areas and occasional mist to the high ground. Visibility, however, was a problem because of low cloud cover and falling snow. The artillery preparation began as scheduled at 0800, and in two and one-half hours, the Soviets fired more than 100,000 rounds.[2]

The same low visibility that favored the attacking infantry, however, prevented Soviet aviation from providing full air support. Since artillery planners had not prepared for this, the volume of fire was weak for the thirty-minute period beginning at 0935. Poor visibility likewise complicated the artillerymen's tasks of observing and adjusting fires. As a result, particularly in the 99th Rifle Corps sector, German positions were not suppressed or destroyed, and the Soviet attack did not achieve the expected success. Lieutenant General Mikulskii, the 99th's commander, acknowledged that the German defenders in his sector (the 2d Mountain Division) were able to maneuver by fire effectively from strongpoints after the preparation was completed.[3]

At 1035, when the Soviets shifted their artillery fires, both first-echelon rifle corps attacked. Their first day's objective was to break through the initial German strongpoints and seize bridgeheads on the west bank of the Titovka River, a distance of nine to ten kilometers.[4] The 131st Rifle Corps

---

*Lieutenant General Degen's rank is equivalent to a major general's in the U.S. Army.

on the right quickly moved through or past the German defenders in its sector and, by the end of the day, had secured a bridgehead on the west bank. This corps' success was due entirely to infantry attacks supported by artillery and limited ground attack aircraft sorties. The tanks and self-propelled guns attached to the corps could not move from their initial positions because of the absence of roads and untrafficable terrain.[5]

On the left flank of the main axis, however, the 99th Rifle Corps met heavy German resistance at several strongpoints on the eastern approaches to the river. After a day of hard fighting, at 1830, Mikulskii ordered his division commanders to halt the attack for five hours so their units could rest and reorganize. At midnight, both first-echelon divisions were to attack again, with no artillery preparation, and to seize river crossings by dawn on 8 October.[6]

During the night, the 99th Rifle Corps assault groups re-formed and continued to press their attacks against individual German strongpoints. From the evening of 7 October to midday on 8 October, groups of up to twenty-five German close air support aircraft attacked advancing Soviet troops and rear areas of the 99th Rifle Corps.[7] One by one, however, the 2d Mountain Division positions began to give way. Soviet units defeated several local counterattacks and, by the evening of 8 October, had reached the east bank of the Titovka River.

The Soviet offensive was developing rapidly to the north of the 99th Rifle Corps. On 7 October, both the 10th Guards and 14th Rifle Divisions reached the Titovka River, first with small groups of infantrymen and later with entire units. During the night, eleven soldiers of the 24th Rifle Regiment, 10th Guards Rifle Division, swam the icy river in their underwear, pushing their uniforms, weapons, and equipment wrapped in ponchos in front of them. On the far shore, they dressed hurriedly and went about their mission of attracting the German defenders' attention so that the main body of the battalion could capture the existing bridge.[8] In the ensuing

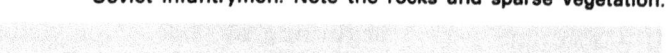

Soviet infantrymen. Note the rocks and sparse vegetation.

battle, despite the courageous efforts of these men, the German defenders demolished the bridge before withdrawing. Inside a damaged and abandoned Opel staff car, Soviet troops found maps and documents, including Lieutenant General Degen's 12 September proclamation. The maps accurately showed the Soviet attack positions and axes of advance, indicating clearly that the Germans expected a Soviet offensive.[9]

On the morning of 8 October, engineers put a light pontoon bridge across the river at the destroyed bridge site. Using this footbridge, fords, and makeshift rafts, the 131st Rifle Corps units expanded their bridgehead westward toward Lanweg to cut the road and isolate the German units still on the east bank and advanced northward toward the boundary between the German 2d and 6th Mountain Divisions (see map 6).

On this, the second day of the offensive, infantry troops moved out of the range of their supporting artillery, which could not move forward due to the untrafficability of the terrain. Therefore, as Soviet units moved away from their artillery support, close air support became critical, especially in the 131st Rifle Corps sector. To speed up the process of building roads leading westward, all troops of the 14th Army second echelon were committed to engineer work.[10] This included both divisions of the 31st Rifle Corps, as well as artillery and other special units that were otherwise uncommitted.

On the far left, the 126th Light Rifle Corps had moved up to the Titovka River on 7 October, crossed it on 8 October, and pushed northwestward toward its objective unopposed. The extremely rough terrain, laced with bogs, streams, boulder fields, and two significant rivers, was opposition enough. The men carried enough food for eight days, personal weapons and ammunition, and additional ammunition for crew-served weapons—up to ninety pounds. Horses hauled the 76-mm pack guns and 120-mm mortars, reindeer the ammunition for both. The reindeer moved easily through their natural habitat, while the horses frequently lost their footing and had to be unloaded, put aright, and reloaded. To preserve the security of the column, fires were prohibited; thus, the soldiers ate cold rations. Smoking was permitted, but at night only under a poncho. Corps units crossed all water obstacles at fords, because constructing foot bridges would expose their route to German air reconnaissance.[11]

Although the German Twentieth Mountain Army may have been aware of the 126th LRC's movement, the Twentieth did not discern the 126th's objective. On the morning of 8 October, for example, the Twentieth Army chief of staff warned the XIX Mountain Corps chief of staff of the possibility of a breakthrough toward Nikel. Additionally, in his report to *OKW* that evening, Colonel General Rendulic, the Twentieth Mountain Army commander, expressed concern about a deep envelopment of the southern flank.[12] Despite these concerns, he did not send out a force to fix or engage the 126th.

The 127th Light Rifle Corps in the second echelon followed the 126th LRC's general route but started from a point farther in the rear. The men of the 70th Naval Rifle Brigade were weighted down with 15 boxes of

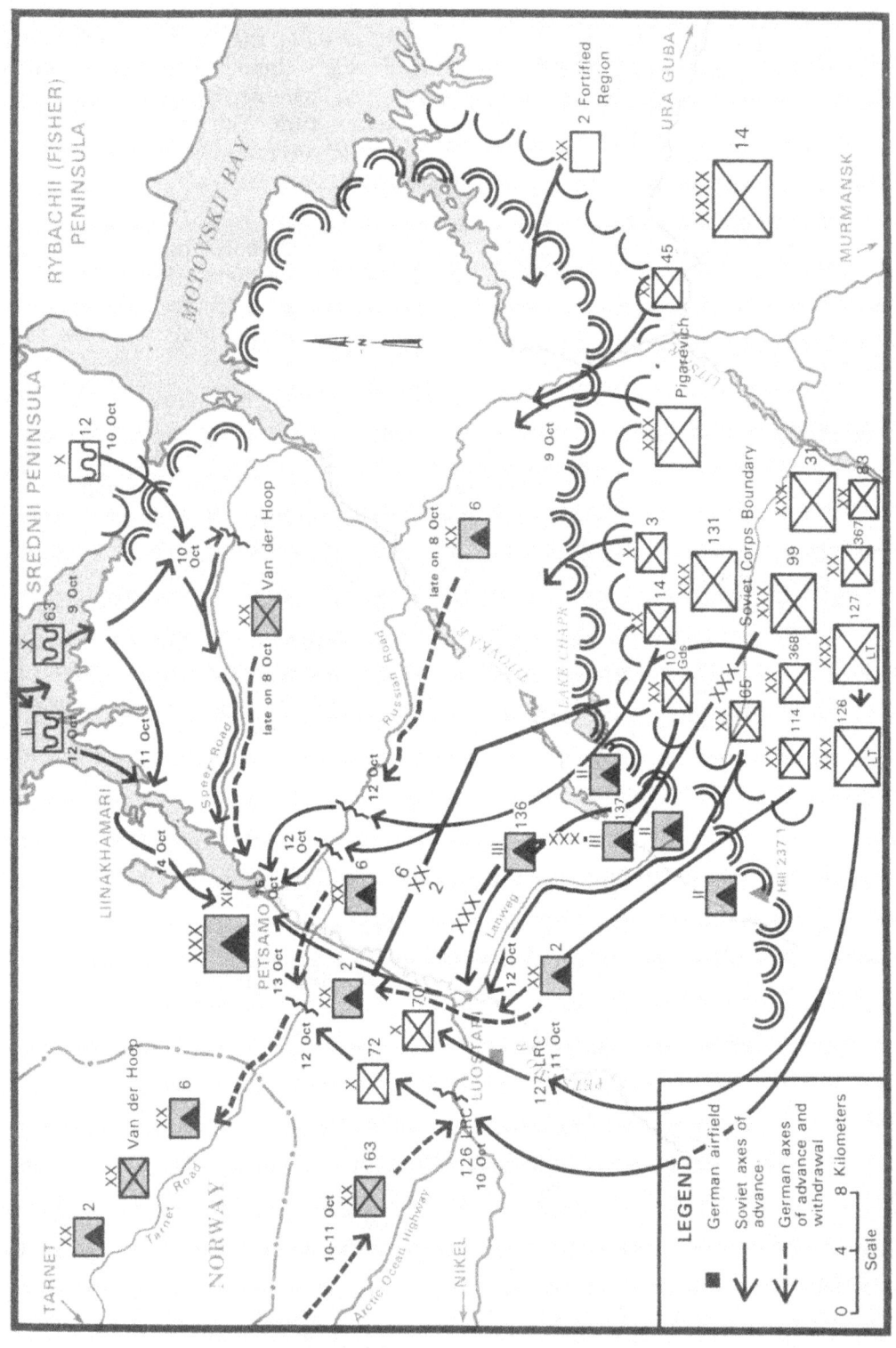

Map 6. Phase one of the Soviet offensive

American rations (food for 5 days), a rifle or submachine gun with 1,500 rounds of ammunition, and 6 hand grenades. The communications platoon carried 25 kilometers of wire, and pack animals carried 6 mountain guns with 200 rounds, 24 mortars with 420 rounds, and other provisions and equipment.[13] This brigade began moving on 6 October and did not cross the Titovka River until 9 October. The men and animals endured drenching rain, numbing cold, and terrain that alternated between frozen moss-covered tundra; solid or broken rock; and deep, soft bogs.

In the breakthrough sector, after two days of fighting, the German XIX Mountain Corps position was deteriorating rapidly. The 2d Mountain Division had sustained heavy casualties and was in danger of partial encirclement. This division's defeat would threaten the 6th Mountain Division and other units positioned along the Litsa front.[14] Late in the afternoon of 8 October, Colonel General Rendulic authorized General Jodl, commander of the XIX Mountain Corps, to begin withdrawing the 6th Mountain Division to positions along the Titovka River.[15] The written order, which was published about six hours later, instructed the 6th Mountain Division units to deceive the enemy as long as possible; maintain strict communications security; and move quickly, but only at night. Also, the 2d Mountain Division was to withdraw to positions east of Luostari. Rendulic expected the XIX Mountain Corps to hold these new positions for fourteen days so that supplies could be evacuated.[16] In a report transmitted to *OKW* late than evening, he reiterated these points.[17]

Meanwhile, on the Soviet side, General Meretskov, the Karelian Front commander, clearly understood the precarious situation the German 6th Mountain Division now faced. At 2300 on 8 October, in an attempt to cut off any withdrawal of the 6th from its positions along the Litsa River, Meretskov ordered the 14th Army to interdict Russian Road and to capture Luostari by nightfall on 9 October. To reinforce the 131st Rifle Corps, the Front commander transferred the uncommitted second-echelon 368th Rifle Division of the 99th Rifle Corps to the 131st Rifle Corps in exchange for the heavily committed 10th Guards Rifle Division on the left flank of the first echelon of the 131st.[18] This enabled the 131st Rifle Corps to sustain its forward movement.

Early on the morning of 9 October, while it was still dark, units of the 99th Rifle Corps began crossing the Titovka River on log rafts and at fording sites along a broad front. However, encircled German strongpoints on the east bank continued to resist, thus delaying road construction. The second-echelon 65th Rifle Division of the 99th Rifle Corps was ordered to eliminate these pockets while the first echelon expanded the bridgehead.

The absence of roads was seriously affecting the battle: combat units could not replace their quickly depleting ammunition stocks, bridging assets could not be brought up to the river, and artillery units could not reposition.

The night before, Soviet forward observers had crossed the river with the infantry to help improve fire support, but that did not compensate for range inadequacies. By noon on 9 October, artillery troops in old positions had been detailed to road-building tasks. In fact, in the entire 99th Rifle Corps sector, only sixty-four long-range guns, firing at maximum range, were able to provide indirect-fire support.[19] This lack of artillery support slowed the offensive and enabled German units to withdraw safely to subsequent battle positions.

To solve this problem, on 9 October, General Mikulskii, the 99th Rifle Corps commander, pulled all but one battalion of engineer assets back from divisions and assigned them road- and bridge-building tasks. He named the commander of the 20th Assault Combat Engineer Brigade as commander of the Titovka River crossing site and gave him the troops of various corps and division logistic units and one regiment from the second-echelon 65th Rifle Division.[20] Shcherbakov, the 14th Army commander, also abandoned the plan for building a road in each division sector and went to constructing a single road for the entire corps.[21] This road was the ten- to twelve-kilometer stretch connecting the existing Soviet and German roads through the breakthrough area in the 99th Rifle Corps sector.

Good weather enabled both sides to commit their air forces on 9 October. Soviet air units flew over 1,000 sorties of close air support and interdiction, with good results. On 9 October, General Jodl, commander of the German XIX Mountain Corps, remarked that "Army headquarters must consider that command and control of units is very difficult because air attacks have almost uniformly destroyed our wire communications."[22] The rocky soil had precluded the Germans from burying their communications wire; instead, they strung it alongside roads, making it easy prey for flying bomb shrapnel. Close air support was particularly important on 9 October because the infantry units of both the 99th and 131st Rifle Corps had advanced beyond the range of their artillery support.[23] According to Soviet sources, the Ger-

A reindeer sled delivering ordnance to a Pe-2 dive bomber

Soviet infantrymen clear a German trench

mans flew over 200 sorties on 9 October against Soviet ground forces, with unspecified results.[24]

At midday, Colonel General Rendulic expressed concern over the Soviets' continued forward progress. He urged the XIX Mountain Corps to exert strong leadership over the 2d Mountain Division, which in his view had been overwhelmed by events. He also encouraged General Jodl to regain control of the battle by launching a strong counterattack. General Jodl responded to this message at 1600, indicating that he planned to counterattack with corps assets at 1000 on 10 October.[25]

Meanwhile, the Soviet offensive continued unabated, with the 99th Rifle Corps driving toward Luostari and the 131st Rifle Corps toward Petsamo. Soviet air reconnaissance on 9 October detected signs of the withdrawal of the 6th Mountain Division. In accordance with his Front plan, which called for the launching of attacks against the German left flank as soon as the breakthrough was achieved on the main axis, General Meretskov, late on 9 October, ordered Group Pigarevich on the right flank to attack. He also requested Admiral Golovko, commander of the Northern Fleet, to begin his ground and amphibious attacks.

Subunits of the 63d Naval Infantry Brigade had been alerted on the morning of 9 October and, by 2100, were loaded onto their vessels in three detachments, a landing force of approximately 2,800 men.[26] The main amphibious force was to land to the west (left) of the German positions opposite Srednii isthmus and, in a night attack, strike the German positions on the left flank. These forces, opposed only by German shore battery fire, landed between 2330, 9 October, and 0150, 10 October (see map 6).[27] With the aid of a smoke screen and counterbattery fire from Srednii Peninsula, the landing force quickly moved inland toward its objectives, incurring minor casualties. A special 195-man raiding party landed at the same time and was to move 30 kilometers to the southwest and seize a German shore battery guarding the approaches to the port of Liinakhamari (this raid is described in detail in chapter 6).

As the amphibious landing was being reported to the Twentieth Mountain Army, the XIX Mountain Corps chief of staff requested that the corps counterattack be postponed from 10 October to 11 October because of the difficulty in assembling scattered units. About an hour later, Rendulic granted the request.[28] The situation was indeed bleak: the XIX Mountain Corps was now faced with an envelopment of its right flank by the 126th Light Rifle Corps, a breakthrough toward Luostari and Petsamo, and an envelopment on its left flank by naval infantry.

As the Soviet naval infantry brigade fought its way inland, at 0330 on 10 October, artillery units of the Northern Defensive Region began firing a 47,000-round, 90-minute artillery preparation against the German positions along the Srednii isthmus. At 0500, Soviet troops of the 12th Naval Infantry Brigade launched their attack across minefields covered by ten inches of fresh snow.[29] By midday on 10 October, the attacking ground forces had broken through the German positions and were linking up with troops of the amphibious force. By evening, German forces were retreating westward along Speer Road as the Soviet naval infantry forces attempted to cut them off.[30]

Farther south, on the axis of the main attack, the Soviet units were making critical gains. By 0800 on 10 October, the 126th LRC had lodged itself on the road junction west of Luostari, having marched over forty kilometers in the seventy-two hours since the offensive had begun. At the objective, the 31st Rifle Brigade dug in facing west to prevent passage of German reinforcements, and the 72d Naval Rifle Brigade dug in facing east to block the road to retreating German units. The corps, supported by its organic mortars and artillery and air assets, defeated several local counterattacks on 10 October. According to one veteran of the 126th LRC, his unit also fired 600 captured German mortar rounds during this battle.[31]

In the trackless terrain to the south, the 127th LRC units crossed the Petsamo River on the morning of 10 October. Now in their fifth day of movement, both animals and men were exhausted. Many horses had lost their protective horseshoes, had broken hooves, and refused to go in the water. To enable the horses to go on, the artillerymen wrapped the horses' hooves in protective canvas wrappings made from tentage. Without forage, the horses were weakening rapidly. Their American rations eaten, the men began tightening their belts. Knowing that no supplies would be delivered to his corps, Major General Zhukov ordered both brigades to continue to move. They had to attack the enemy and eat his food and forage.[32]

Soviet naval infantrymen move a 45-mm antitank gun into position

A Soviet 82-mm mortar crew in action, often along with the 120-mm, the only fire support for Soviet infantry units

On the Luostari axis, the 99th Rifle Corps units continued to attack without artillery support against prepared German positions on dominating terrain. Progress was slow. By 1000 on 10 October, the second-echelon troops had completed the road connecting Soviet and German roads, and the engineers had put in two bridges and two fording sites. Before any tanks or artillery could cross the river, however, the road destroyed by the retreating Germans had to be repaired.[33] The road problem, which had adversely affected the movement of combat equipment since the first day of the battle, now began to manifest itself in the logistic support of the battle. A regiment of the 10th Guards Rifle Division, which had captured an important piece of high ground along the road to Luostari, ran out of ammunition and had to surrender its hard-won position.[34] The ammunition was available in the supply system but could not be pushed forward until the road in the territory formerly occupied by the Germans was repaired.

The heaviest fighting on 10 October occurred in the 131st Rifle Corps sector, where a Soviet force cut Russian Road at noon. The Twentieth Mountain Army headquarters, reacting strongly to this development, ordered the 6th Mountain Division units to attack and reopen the road.[35] As these German units counterattacked, the Soviet 131st Rifle Corps commander hurriedly deployed his 368th Rifle Division into the action, but it arrived too late. On the morning of 11 October, lacking artillery, close air support, and ammunition, the Soviet rifle regiment astride the road fell back, and German units continued their westward flight. Soviet reinforcements arrived late in the day on 11 October.[36] An all-night battle ensued, during which the Soviets cut the road for the last time. On 12 October, several German attempts to break through were defeated, resulting in heavy casualties on both sides and the dispersal of the remaining German units across the tundra. The 131st Rifle Corps then turned west and attacked units of the 6th Mountain Division in their prepared positions along the east bank of the Petsamo River, defeating several German counterattacks. By late in the day on 14 October, the 131st was positioned to attack Petsamo from the southeast.

Meanwhile, on 10 October, the Twentieth Mountain Army headquarters initiated two actions that demonstrated its concern over the ominous developments in the XIX Mountain Corps sector. At 1345, the army chief of staff ordered that the nickel mine and processing facilities at Nikel be destroyed. At 1600, the XXXVI Corps chief of staff was told to dispatch an artillery battalion immediately and to prepare to commit his 163d Infantry Division to the XIX Mountain Corps sector.[37] However, on 10 October, this 12,000-man division was south of the XIX Mountain Corps area of operations, near Rovaniemi on the Arctic Circle. The 163d quickly loaded onto trucks and began its 400-kilometer journey northward.

In the 99th Rifle Corps sector, on the night of 10—11 October, all thirteen regiments of supporting heavy mortars and artillery moved forward across the Titovka River and deployed along Lanweg, the single road. However, because of the inability to deploy this fire support across the corps front and the range limitations of many of the weapons systems, only half of it could fire on German positions.[38] With the transfer of the 10th Guards Rifle Division to his corps, Lieutenant General Mikulskii now had two sizable

Soviet 152-mm towed artillery in column

armored forces: twenty-one KV tanks and seventeen 152-mm self-propelled guns in the armor package with the 10th Guards Rifle Division and thirty-seven T-34 tanks and seventeen 152-mm self-propelled guns in the corps second echelon. These units also crossed the Titovka River during the night of 10—11 October. In the reorganization of the corps for combat on 11 October, all ninety-plus tanks and self-propelled guns were attached to the 65th Rifle Division attacking along the road.[39] The crossing of all these tank, artillery, and mortar units, coupled with the impossibility of deploying any of them off the road due to terrain restrictions, resulted in massive congestion on the west side of the Titovka River on 11 October.

At 1830 on 10 October, General Meretskov, commander of the Karelian Front, while at the 99th Rifle Corps command post five kilometers east of the river, approved Mikulskii's plan for the next day. Two hours later, Mikulskii personally telephoned his orders to his division commanders.[40] On the morning of 11 October, the 99th Rifle Corps attacked toward Luostari with three rifle divisions abreast. The 114th Rifle Division, which moved cross-country south of the road, was the most successful. It linked up with the 69th Naval Rifle Brigade of the 127th Light Rifle Corps south of Luostari by nightfall on 11 October. The other two divisions, attacking along and north of Lanweg, were repeatedly halted by the 2d Mountain Division units fighting from prepared positions on high ground.

Soviet tanks and self-propelled artillery on Lanweg were unable to deploy and could not move without infantry and engineer support. Soviet infantry attacked and neutralized each German antitank position, while engineer troops cleared the road of mines and filled in craters. By the end of the day, the 99th Rifle Corps units had stalled just east of Luostari. Attacks during the night of 11—12 October failed to dislodge the German defenders east of the settlement.

On 11 October, on the German left flank, the Soviet naval infantry forces continued to fight their way south to Speer Road, which they interdicted by the end of the day. But their advance was slow, and Soviet artillery units fell behind, allowing withdrawing German units to escape. Approximately five hours elapsed between the time the Germans broke contact during the night of 11—12 October and the naval infantry began pursuit on the morning of 12 October. The Germans' success in breaking contact is attributed to the naval infantry's inexperience and lack of training in night operations.[41]

While Soviet ground forces were steadily grinding forward on all axes, Soviet air forces were striking at the German airfield south of Nikel. In an 11 October raid, the Soviets used eighteen ground attack aircraft and thirty-six fighters in the first flight and fifty-five fighters with externally carried bombs in the second. The Soviets claimed to have destroyed thirty-three of sixty German aircraft on the ground and five more in the air.[42]

Numerous air battles were also waged during the first week of the offensive, by which the Soviet air forces established almost total control of the airspace over the battle area. (This conclusion is corroborated both by

Soviet sources and an analysis of descriptions of ground operations. Reports of interference by German air forces in Soviet maneuver or logistic operations are extremely rare.)

The German situation grew more critical by the hour. On the Germans' far right, local counterattacks against units of the 126th LRC had failed to dislodge them from their blocking positions, and the 163d Infantry Division's forward units were still on the road. On the morning of 11 October, the 70th Naval Rifle Brigade of the 127th LRC crossed Arctic Ocean Highway west of Luostari en route to a blocking position on Tarnet Road.[43] In the center, Luostari was in danger of falling to the 99th Rifle Corps, while the 131st Rifle Corps was fighting toward Petsamo. Naval infantrymen were turning westward on Speer Road, trying to regain contact with retreating German units.

During the night of 11—12 October, the Twentieth Mountain Army chief of staff implored his counterpart at XIX Mountain Corps to hold the Luostari road junction and prevent the forces of the Soviet main attack from linking up with the 126th LRC.[44] But that is exactly what happened the next day. On the morning of 12 October, Soviet units attacked Luostari from the south, east, and northeast and took this important road junction by noon. While Soviet units consolidated and reorganized to hold Luostari and, at the same time, continued the attack northward toward Petsamo, the German 163d Infantry Division arrived on the battlefield. In the words of the division operations officer:

> After a motorized march of more than 400 kilometers, the 307th Regiment literally detrucked on the battlefield. Soldiers almost frozen stiff had to be committed in battle immediately after leaving their vehicles because the enemy had already penetrated westward beyond the road fork.... The bulk of the 307th Regiment arrived by the afternoon of 12 October and received orders to attack in the evening, to drive back the enemy, and to occupy the road fork as its first objective.[45]

But while the 163d Infantry Division units were being committed to piecemeal counterattacks, the Soviet 14th Army continued to develop the offensive. On the night of 11—12 October, by order of General Meretskov, several tons of ammunition and provisions were air-dropped to the 126th Light Rifle Corps.[46] On 12 October, elements of the 114th Rifle Division from Lieutenant General Mikulskii's 99th Rifle Corps arrived from the Luostari area and relieved the 72d Naval Rifle Brigade in place. The 114th continued to fight off determined counterattacks by the German 163d Infantry Division, which had just arrived in trucks from the south. Heavy combat for control of the road west of Luostari continued until 14 October, when the German units withdrew to their local starting positions.

The decision on 12 October to relieve one brigade of the 126th Light Rifle Corps was probably wise, because the brigade, by this time, was no doubt weak from physical exhaustion and personnel losses from both movement and combat. But rather than allow the unit to stand down and rest and recover, Lieutenant General Shcherbakov, the 14th Army commander, ordered it to move northward cross-country fifteen kilometers to Tarnet Road to help the 127th LRC block the Germans' last remaining escape route. The 70th Naval Rifle Brigade had reached Tarnet Road on the morning of 11 October but without its mortars and artillery, which had fallen behind on the rocky ground. Without fire support, the infantry had fought all day in a futile effort to defeat the German position guarding the road.[47] Around midday, German dive-bombers bombarded the 70th, but it suffered no personnel casualties. The Soviet cooks prepared a hot meal from the pack horses killed in the air attacks.

On the night of 12—13 October, the 72d Naval Rifle Brigade of the 126th LRC cut Tarnet Road just east of the Norwegian border, thus blocking the Germans' path of retreat to the west. The 70th Naval Rifle Brigade of the 127th LRC continued fighting for high ground on the south side of the road farther to the east.

Late in the evening of 12 October, General Meretskov was visiting the 99th Rifle Corps command post on the southeast outskirts of Luostari. There, Mikulskii was issuing an order to his 10th Guards Rifle Division commander for the next day's activities.[48] Meretskov expressed concern about the approach of German reinforcements from the south, which were, in fact, already arriving by truck. On the morning of 13 October, the 163d Infantry Division launched counterattacks west and north of Luostari, while the 2d Mountain Division units consolidated in defensive positions between Luostari and Petsamo along Arctic Ocean Highway. These actions delayed the 99th Rifle Corps' northward offensive approximately twenty-four hours, time the German units east of Petsamo needed to withdraw westward.

On 12 October, on the Soviet northern flank, the 12th and 63d Naval Infantry Brigades moved westward along the axis of Speer Road. Early that morning, a naval special operations detachment had attacked and neutralized the German shore batteries opposite Liinakhamari that covered the entrance to Petsamo Bay. This detachment, supported by naval close air support and air-dropped supplies, continued to hold out against several counterattacks. Naval planners hurriedly gathered and organized another amphibious landing force made up of volunteers from the rear areas. This 600-man force landed in the harbor at Liinakhamari at 2250 on 12 October. On the 13th, this force, with the help of naval close air support, defeated the local German garrison. Units of the 12th and 63d Naval Infantry Brigades were closing up from the east and had established contact with the ground forces of the 131st Rifle Corps to the south.

On the morning of 13 October, Soviet units were poised to attack toward Petsamo from the north, east, and south. The night before, elements of the 126th Light Rifle Corps had occupied blocking positions west of Petsamo on Tarnet Road, denying that route to German elements attempting to withdraw westward. German units continued to occupy and fight from good positions north of Luostari and east of Petsamo along the axes of the roads to Petsamo. In light of this new development, the XIX Mountain Corps commander, General Jodl, could no longer expect his two beleaguered divisions to attack eastward. Their single escape route lay westward, along the now-blocked Tarnet Road. At 1500 on 13 October, he communicated his views to the Twentieth Mountain Army commander and requested a directive. After some delay, army headquarters ordered the XIX Mountain Corps to open Tarnet Road and establish new battle positions just inside Norwegian territory.[49]

Meanwhile, the Soviet forces continued to close in on Petsamo. On the night of 13—14 October, Soviet naval infantry of the 12th and 63d Naval Infantry Brigades crossed Petsamo Bay at Liinakhamari and attacked southward along the west side. At the same time, German troops of the 2d Mountain Division, under pressure from the 99th Rifle Corps attacking from Luostari, defeated the Soviet blocking force on Tarnet Road west of Petsamo and broke out. Thus, on 14 October, the remainder of the 2d Mountain Division, 6th Mountain Division, and Division Group Van der Hoop withdrew westward into Norway.[50] By Soviet estimates, 15,000 to 18,000 German troops escaped along this route.[51]

The first Soviet troops entered Petsamo from the east at 2200 on 14 October. While Germans and Soviets fought inside the town, other Soviet units outside the city engaged German units retreating in columns from the Litsa front. By 0500 on 15 October, Petsamo was captured. Those Germans who survived escaped in small groups to the northwest across the tundra, leaving behind many dead, as well as 150,000 shells and mines and several warehouses of equipment that they had not been able to destroy or remove.[52]

In nine days of combat, the Soviet forces had achieved a breakthrough on the main axis, advanced from thirty-five to sixty kilometers across extremely difficult terrain, crossed three rivers, landed two amphibious assault groups, and captured three built-up areas. Estimated German troop losses for this phase of the offensive were approximately 6,000.[53] German equipment losses were also severe; Soviet losses for the same period are not available.

The Soviet attackers were exhausted, however. Many units had wholly used up their supplies of food, fuel, and ammunition. The existing road network was inadequate to maintain the needed logistic support, and even the availability of the Luostari airfield after 12 October for aerial resupply flights did not alleviate the supply problem. To enable the troops to take a much-needed rest and the logistic system to catch up, Lieutenant General Shcherbakov, commander of the 14th Army, ordered a three-day pause in combat. Both sides used this time to reconstitute, reorganize, and resupply. Phase two of the Soviet offensive was to begin on the morning of 19 October.

The Battle, Phase Two, 18—22 October 1944   3

As the Soviet 14th Army paused after the capture of Petsamo, Colonel General Rendulic personally visited the battle area to assess the situation. On 15 October, after consulting with General Jodl, the XIX Mountain Corps commander, and General Ruebel, the 163d Infantry Division commander, at Ruebel's command post, Rendulic ordered the 6th Mountain Division to defend the Kirkenes axis, Battle Group Ruebel to defend the roads east of Akhmalakhti and Nikel, and the 2d Mountain Division to assemble at Salmiiarvi to subsequently support Battle Group Ruebel. Rendulic's intent was to hold Kirkenes as long as possible in order to permit the continued evacuation of supplies. General Rendulic rejected a request from the commander of the XXXVI Mountain Corps for operational control of Battle Group Ruebel, leaving General Jodl in full command of the defensive battle. The XIX Mountain Corps staff correctly discerned that the main Soviet effort would be directed against Battle Group Ruebel and anticipated that the offensive would resume on the morning of 18 October.[1]

Meanwhile, Soviet units were busy resupplying, reorganizing, and repositioning. The air delivery of supplies to the Luostari airfield, which had begun soon after its capture on 12 October, continued unabated until 19 October, with a total of eighty-six tons of various commodities being delivered, much of it for the 126th Light Rifle Corps.[2] Soviet forces continued to push reconnaissance elements forward in their sectors, clearing away German stragglers and determining the locations of German defensive positions. In the area west and northwest of Petsamo, the 131st Rifle Corps pushed forward to the Norwegian border and then halted. In the zone west of Luostari, Soviet troops of the 99th Rifle Corps attacked the German covering forces along Arctic Ocean Highway and drove them back into the German main defensive positions.

Lieutenant General Shcherbakov, the 14th Army commander, moved all five of his rifle corps into a single echelon (see map 7).[3] In the north, the 131st Rifle Corps was deployed along and north of Tarnet Road. This corps now had three rifle divisions, having received the 45th from Group Pigarevich. The 14th Army also gave the 131st Rifle Corps an unspecified quantity of multiple rocket launcher systems[4] and, for armor support, the 7th Guards Tank Brigade.[5] The engineer support to the corps included the

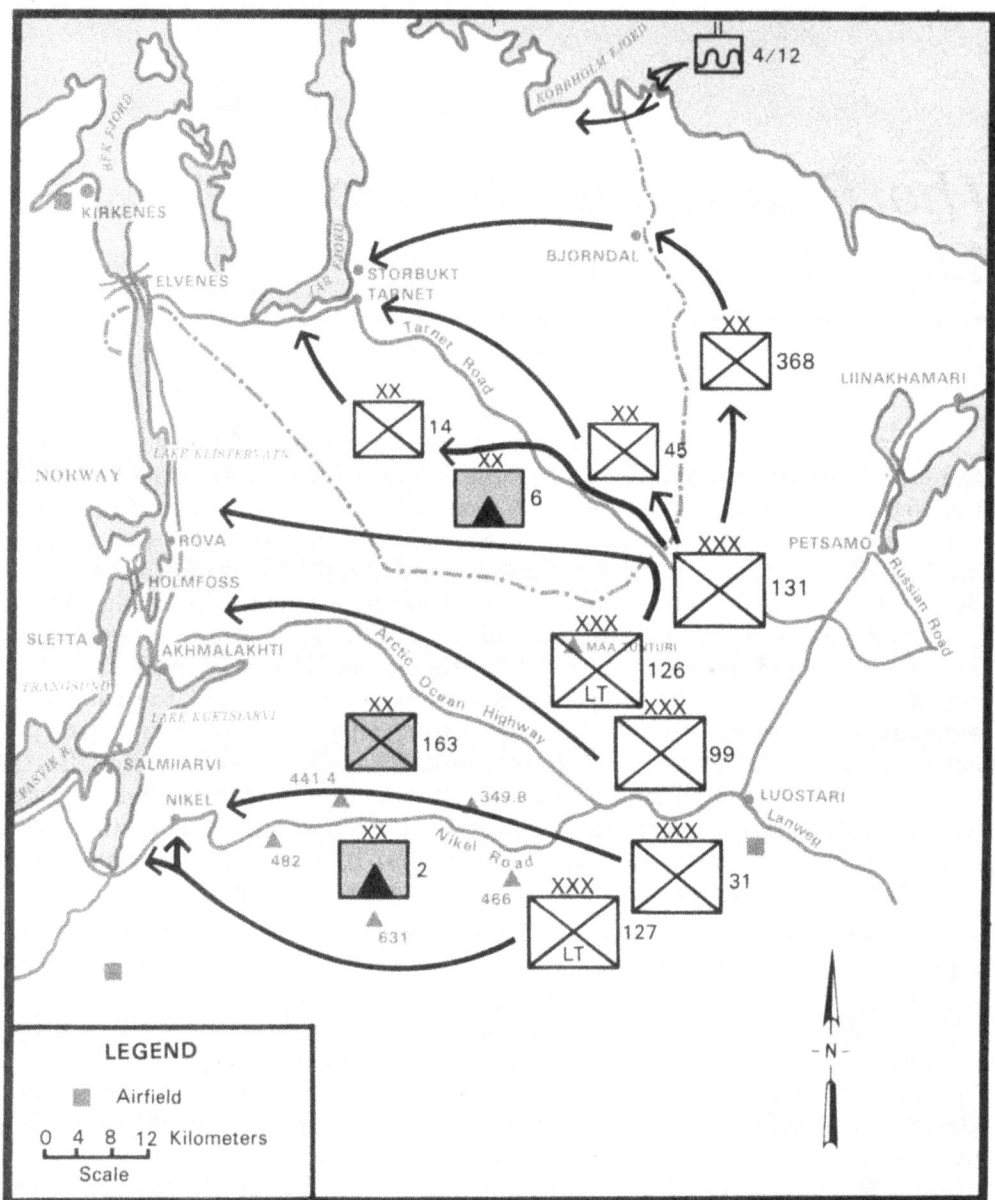

Map 7. Phase two of the Soviet offensive

275th Separate Special-Purpose Motorized Battalion, which was equipped with over ninety American 2½-ton amphibians.

Initially, the 131st's mission was to protect the right flank of the renewed offensive by clearing the zone along the Norwegian border from the Barents Sea coast to the westward turn of the border south of Tarnet Road. In order to pursue the fleeing German units into Norway, General Meretskov, the Karelian Front commander, requested permission from *STAVKA* late on 17 October or early on 18 October to cross the Norwegian border. When *STAVKA* gave this permission on 18 October, the 131st Rifle Corps' mission was changed.[6] Now the 131st was to conduct a supporting attack northwestward along the axis of Tarnet Road and pursue the retreating German units into Norway toward the port of Kirkenes.

The 99th Rifle Corps commander, General Mikulskii, consolidated his three rifle divisions—the 10th Guards from the Petsamo area, the 65th, and the 114th—west of Luostari and prepared them to advance along the axis of Arctic Ocean Highway toward Akhmalakhti and the Norwegian border at the Pasvik River west of there. The 73d Separate Guards Heavy Tank Regiment, equipped with KV tanks, and the 339th Guards Heavy Self-Propelled Artillery Regiment, equipped with JSU-152s, provided armor support. The corps still had a battalion of ¼-ton jeep amphibians, as well as a heavy pontoon bridge battalion. Lieutenant General Shcherbakov ordered the 126th Light Rifle Corps to support the 99th Rifle Corps on the 99th's northern flank.

South of the 99th Rifle Corps, along the Luostari axis, the 31st Rifle Corps was still east of the Titovka River in the 14th Army second echelon on 16 October. The 31st Rifle Corps had been assigned to the 14th Army on 27 September, and its last units closed on the Murmansk area on 7 October, the day the offensive began. One of its rifle divisions, the 45th, was immediately detached and sent to Lieutenant General Pigarevich at the Litsa front, leaving the corps with two rifle divisions, the 83d and the 367th. Each of these divisions consisted of three rifle regiments and an artillery regiment and had approximately 6,000 men. (For a complete table of organization and equipment listing of the 31st Rifle Corps, see appendix F.)

The 31st Rifle Corps had little combat experience, having spent the entire eighteen months of its existence in the relatively quiet Karelian Front. The troops were fully acclimated and trained for operations in the swampy forests of central Karelia but found the mountainous terrain around Murmansk to be much more difficult. During phase one, as part of the 14th Army second echelon, the 31st Rifle Corps units had constructed and repaired roads and, at the same time, became familiar with the unique terrain of the area. According to the corps commander, Major General Absaliamov, his troops were sufficiently prepared to successfully accomplish their combat missions by the time of their commitment in phase two. A severe shortage of serviceable trucks, however, weakened the corps' logistic readiness for combat. Artillery ammunition, hand grenades, provisions and forage, and petroleum products were still in short supply when phase two commenced.[7]

On 16 October, the 83d Rifle Division was still in its assembly area forty kilometers southeast of Luostari. The 367th Rifle Division, which had been repairing and constructing roads in the army rear area, was twenty to thirty kilometers southeast of Luostari. On the night of 16—17 October, under cover of rainy (nonflying) weather, both divisions, with the 367th Rifle Division leading, began moving forward to their attack positions west of Luostari. On 17 October, units of the 367th Rifle Division began replacing the 114th Rifle Division units (99th Rifle Corps) in positions along the

Luostari-Nikel road, a task to be completed by the morning of 18 October. At 0200 on 18 October, Absaliamov received his combat order from Shcherbakov, the 14th Army commander (see appendix B). Stated simply, corps units were to be prepared to attack by 2400 on 18 October in two echelons along the Luostari-Nikel road, with the 367th Rifle Division leading. In cooperation with the 127th Light Rifle Corps, they were to seize Nikel and, subsequently, the road junction three kilometers southeast of Salmiiarvi.

The 14th Army reinforced the 31st Rifle Corps with two mortar and three artillery regiments, two full regiments of multiple rocket launchers, a regiment of T-34 tanks, a depleted regiment of 152-mm self-propelled guns, and a three-battalion brigade of combat engineers.[8] The most serious problem facing corps artillery units on 18 October was a severe ammunition shortage. According to Absaliamov, his divisional and regimental artillery units went into battle with only one-fourth to one-third of a unit of fire (see table 5).[9]

South of the Luostari-Nikel road, the 127th Light Rifle Corps was to attack cross-country in support of the 31st Rifle Corps and to cut the main road southwest of Nikel, thus isolating the German defenders east of Nikel. Lieutenant General Shcherbakov designated the axes of the 31st and 99th Rifle Corps as the main attack.

Although Shcherbakov initially had planned to resume the offensive on the morning of 19 October, his first-echelon divisions actually began moving forward on the morning of 18 October.[10] On the Soviet right flank, in the 131st Rifle Corps sector, the 45th Rifle Division moved forward along the Petsamo-Tarnet road into the vicinity of the Norwegian border on the night of 17—18 October. While this division occupied attack positions, early on the morning of 18 October, Soviet naval infantry, in support of the 131st Rifle Corps, landed in two places along the coast to clear the Germans from the area.[11] Just before dawn on 18 October, the 485-man 4th Battalion, 12th Naval Infantry Brigade, landed at two points four to five kilometers apart. With naval close air support, the naval infantry forces attacked westward through several scattered German positions, including shore batteries, lighthouses, and signal and observation stations. By the end of the day on 19 October, they had reached the Norwegian border.

TABLE 5
Artillery Ammunition on Hand, 367th Rifle Division, 18 October 1944

Caliber	Percentage of Norm
82-mm mortar	20
120-mm mortar	20
45-mm antitank gun	40
76-mm regimental artillery	30
76-mm divisional artillery	25
122-mm howitzer	20

Typical terrain along Tarnet Road: lakes at all elevations, many rocks, and no cover or concealment

Meanwhile, at 1350 on 18 October, the 45th Rifle Division crossed the Norwegian border and, by the end of the day, had pushed forward to a strongly defended German position along a river line five kilometers inside Norway. From 19 to 21 October, this division continued to attack along the axis of Tarnet Road against the 6th Mountain Division's delaying positions adroitly placed on dominating elevations. The terrain along this road from the Soviet-Norwegian border to Tarnet had sparse vegetation, steep and rocky hills, lakes and swamps at all elevations, and large dense masses of boulders. By evening on 21 October, the 45th Rifle Division had advanced over twenty kilometers but was still meeting determined resistance from prepared positions near Tarnet.

That morning, the 14th Rifle Division, which had followed the 45th Rifle Division, joined the attack on the southern (left) flank of the 45th Rifle Division. Despite the untrafficability of the terrain, the Soviets attempted to maneuver a small tank force south and west of Tarnet Road with the 14th Rifle Division. This effort failed when the tanks could not negotiate a swamp just four kilometers off the main road.[12] The armor turned back to Tarnet Road and advanced with and behind the 45th Rifle Division in small packets.

The 368th Rifle Division, in the corps second echelon back at the Norwegian-Soviet border, moved one regiment northward to Bjorndal, where it linked up with naval infantry forces.[13] On 22 October, the naval infantry along the coast and soldiers of the 1226th Rifle Regiment crossed the Norwegian border, the naval infantry attacking westward and the 1226th southwestward. By evening, the naval infantry reached the hills overlooking Kobbholm Fjord, and the soldiers drove halfway between Bjorndal and Storbukt along the road.

During the night of 21—22 October, the 45th Rifle Division seized the German positions opposing them, and by evening on 22 October, together with the 14th Rifle Division and the 1226th Rifle Regiment, controlled the east and south shores of Jar Fjord. In five days, the 131st Rifle Corps had advanced twenty-five to thirty kilometers into Norwegian territory against light to moderate resistance, and the naval infantry had cleared the coastline of German positions up to Kobbholm Fjord. As the German 6th Mountain Division units withdrew toward Kirkenes, they fought delaying actions from carefully chosen positions on dominating terrain.

To the south, on the 14th Army's main axis, heavier combat was being waged. On 18 October, the 99th Rifle Corps deployed in two echelons. The 10th Guards Rifle Division, which had spearheaded the corps' attack on Petsamo, now became the second echelon and was not committed again until 23 October. The 65th Rifle Division, poised eighteen kilometers west of Luostari, prepared to attack along the road. The 114th Rifle Division was in contact with German defensive positions at Hill 234.[14] The initial frontal attack on this German position failed, but a subsequent envelopment

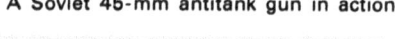

A Soviet 45-mm antitank gun in action

A Soviet 7.62-mm Maxim machine-gun crew moves to a new position

from both flanks, in conjunction with the frontal assaults, drove the German defenders westward during the night of 18—19 October to another prepared defensive position. On 19 October, the 114th Rifle Division units attacked this position all day, gaining success only by nightfall.

On 20 October, the corps second-echelon 65th Rifle Division attacked along the road on the southern flank of the 114th Rifle Division, and together, these two divisions drove forward five to seven kilometers. One regiment of the 65th succeeded in cutting the road west of the withdrawing German units, forcing them to abandon their vehicles and retreat cross-country. Although the 99th Rifle Corps had both tanks and self-propelled guns to support its advance, the armored vehicles quickly fell behind the advancing infantry due to the destruction and heavy concentration of mines in the road. Vehicles moving singly and in pairs on the road were also easy prey for German antitank guns firing from prepared positions. On the afternoon of 20 October, units of the Soviet 7th Air Army flew several close air support missions for the 99th Rifle Corps and destroyed or suppressed several German artillery batteries.[15]

On 21 October, the 14th Army commander ordered the 99th Rifle Corps to destroy the enemy in the Akhmalakhti area and reach the Norwegian border between Rova and Salmiiarvi by the day's end. Subsequently, the corps was to prepare to attack toward Kirkenes from the south. But, due to stronger than anticipated German resistance, this mission was not accomplished in the stated time. The 99th moved forward seven to eight kilometers and, by evening, was still three to seven kilometers short of the Norwegian border. Consequently, corps units continued the attack that night and the next day, reaching the border and the Pasvik River by the evening of 22 October.

Two regiments of the 114th Rifle Division crossed the Pasvik River at Holmfoss and Sletta, using makeshift rafts and the lend-lease American jeep amphibians of the 284th Separate Special-Purpose Motorized Battalion.[16] The forward detachment of the 65th Rifle Division crossed in its sector and seized a small bridgehead at Trangsund. On the night of 22—23 October, with only limited artillery fire from the Germans, the 97th Separate Motorized Pontoon Bridge Battalion put in a 250- to 275-meter-long floating bridge at Holmfoss.[17] The construction of this bridge was critical to the 99th Rifle Corps' northward movement in the last phase of the offensive.

On the northern flank of the 99th Rifle Corps, the 126th Light Rifle Corps was to perform a screening mission. Ultimately, the 126th was to cut the lateral route that connected Akhmalakhti and Kirkenes on the east side of the Pasvik River. Between 14 and 19 October, the 126th LRC received fifty-one tons of supplies.[18] Whether the corps' personnel losses had been made up during this pause in the offensive, as well as the fighting condition of the corps at this time, is unknown. On 18 October, the corps moved cross-country east from the vicinity of Mount Maa Tunturi and then

At this site, Holmfoss, on 22—23 October 1944, the Soviets placed a pontoon bridge. It came into the photograph from the left. This is the exit.

Author's collection

north, crossing the Norwegian border behind the 131st Rifle Corps units on Tarnet Road in the afternoon. Thereafter, the 126th left the road and marched due west, more or less parallel to the border. By the evening of 19 October, the corps had progressed only ten kilometers, against light resistance. On 20 October, the 126th LRC moved westward another thirteen to fifteen kilometers, against little opposition, but over difficult cross-compartmented terrain. On 21 October, the corps recrossed the border onto Finnish territory, approached Lake Klistervatn from the east, and engaged and defeated elements of the German Bicycle Reconnaissance Brigade Norway.[19] By the end of the day, the main body of the corps was two to three kilometers east of the lake, with elements astride the main road leading north from Akhmalakhti to Kirkenes. Logistic constraints, primarily shortages of provisions and ammunition, held the 126th here until 23 October. In four days, the 126th LRC had moved thirty to thirty-five kilometers across trackless terrain and fought a single successful engagement. However, the corps may have had a greater influence on the course of the battle on the main axis had it attacked in concert with the 99th Rifle Corps along the 99th's immediate right flank. Not only could the 126th have added its combat power to the fight on the main axis, but also, it could have been supported logistically.

The heaviest fighting during the second phase of the offensive occurred on the Soviet left flank along the road from Luostari to Nikel. The German forces facing the 31st Rifle Corps and the 127th Light Rifle Corps consisted of elements of the 163d Infantry Division (Battle Group Ruebel), bolstered by additional combat elements from the XXXVI Mountain Corps. Soviet planners estimated the German strength at approximately 15,000 men, about equal to the combined strength of the two Soviet corps.[20] In order to delay the Soviet offensive long enough to continue the evacuation of supplies stored in Kirkenes, the Germans were planning a stubborn defense. The Soviets, however, had a 2-to-1 advantage in mortars and artillery, enjoyed the support of tanks and self-propelled guns, and still had overwhelming air superiority.

Bald, rocky hills, interspersed with ravines and swampy depressions, marked the terrain between Luostari and Nikel. The highest elevation, Hill 631, was 1,900 feet above sea level, and several other hills along the axis of attack were over 1,000 feet. Numerous lakes at various elevations dotted the area. The high ground was totally devoid of vegetation and, therefore, in good weather, open to air observation.

Due to the terrain, all vehicular movement was absolutely road bound. The only forces that could maneuver cross-country were light units equipped with machine guns and 82-mm mortars. Marshy approaches or sheer, rocky banks turned even small streams into difficult obstacles. The German troops skillfully incorporated the single road, which passed like a bridge over and between countless swamps, lakes, streams, or ravines, into their defensive plan. They employed mines, craters, and barricades and, wherever the terrain permitted, overwatched it from defensive positions, some of which were used in the 1939—40 Soviet-Finnish War.[21]

The 31st Rifle Corps' first contact with the enemy came on the morning of 18 October, when a regiment of the 367th Rifle Division, performing reconnaissance, engaged a German screening force along the road. Heavy Soviet supporting fire and the threat of envelopment on their northern flank forced the Germans to pull back while giving little resistance. The Soviet

Soviet soldiers moving a 7.62-mm Maxim machine gun

regiment continued to push forward until strong German fire from Hill 466, overlooking the road, halted it some six to seven kilometers from the starting point. The 367th's remaining two regiments, instead of engaging the enemy, became stacked up on the road behind the lead regiment. The tanks and self-propelled artillery supporting the lead regiment were unable to deploy on either side of the road and were forced to fire from selected positions, thus assuming the role of infantry support.[22]

The rapid fallback of the German screen and the lack of additional reconnaissance reports led the 14th Army commander to conclude that the Germans would continue retreating. So, during the afternoon of 18 October, Lieutenant General Shcherbakov changed his previous order and directed that Nikel be captured on 19 October instead of 21 October. Major General Absaliamov, the 31st Rifle Corps commander, altered his plan and issued his own order (see appendix C).

In accordance with the Soviet commanders' assumptions and orders, the 367th Rifle Division commander organized his forces for pursuit rather than attack, with two regiments up and one back. Of the 31st's six rifle regiments, only two would thus be in contact; the remainder would follow with be-prepared-type missions.

The events of 19 October proved the inaccuracy of Soviet assumptions and the inadequacy of Soviet reconnaissance. The Germans were in no hurry to leave and continued to defend each carefully sited and prepared position. The 367th Rifle Division attacked at 0900 on 19 October with just one reinforced regiment but did not defeat Hills 466 and 349.8 until noon. Several kilometers down the road, the Germans halted the Soviet attack with another strongpoint around Hill 441.4.[23]

Another regiment of the Soviet 367th Division, advancing cross-country south of the road, met only scattered opposition and moved approximately twenty kilometers by the end of the day on 19 October.

South of the 31st Rifle Corps, the 127th Light Rifle Corps moved into an assembly area.[24] Although the 127th had rested and eaten well during the period of 15—17 October, it had not received any new issue of clothing or footgear. Some of the men repaired their boots with the hides from slaughtered horses. On the evening of 18 October, the corps began another long westward march across the tundra. The 69th Naval Rifle Brigade was to attack Nikel from the southern flank while the 70th Naval Rifle Brigade cut the main road southwest of Nikel by 1700 on 20 October.

The 70th Naval Rifle Brigade moved fifteen kilometers during the night of 18 October. During a breakfast halt on 19 October, German aerial reconnaissance appeared, followed shortly by a flight of dive-bombers. Four times during the short arctic day, the bombers appeared, inflicting casualties—five killed and eight wounded—in the brigade. The wounded were sent to the rear either walking or riding on horseback. The survivors found ground that could be dug by hand, where they buried the dead. In great hardships, the brigade moved on in a column that extended over two kilometers. When it rained, the men became wet and cold, and at times,

A Soviet 7.62-mm Maxim machine-gun crew in combat

the wind blew so hard that a man could not stand erect. In places, the soft soil and low bushes pulled at their feet and clothes. When the sky cleared, German reconnaissance aircraft searched for them.

Not satisfied with his formations' 19 October accomplishments, Shcherbakov, the 14th Army commander, issued another combat order at 2400, reiterating his imperative to capture Nikel. Again, Major General Absaliamov, the 31st Rifle Corps commander, assigned this mission to the 367th Rifle Division. As before, he ordered the 83d Rifle Division to follow in the second echelon and to be prepared to pursue the withdrawing German units to the south along Arctic Ocean Highway after the capture of the Nikel area. One regiment of the division was to assist the engineers in repairing and improving the road.[25]

On 20 October, the 31st Rifle Corps commander was actually fighting two battles. Immediately in front of the corps was an exceptionally strong German position on Hill 441.4 that blocked the advance of the corps along the road. While part of his corps maneuvered to attack this position, other corps elements pressed forward in the north and south toward Nikel. Strong German fire concentrations drove back the initial assault on Hill 441.4, and attacking Soviet troops could not penetrate the obstacles in front of this strongpoint. Indeed, the engineer troops supporting the corps' advance were busy. The following excerpt from Absaliamov's memoir gives a good picture of the scope of the engineers' problems.

> Thus, for example, in the sector of road from Lake Pilguiarvi to Hill 441.4, a distance of approximately ten kilometers, an engineer platoon that

was supporting the movement of tanks and self-propelled guns removed from the roadbed and some sections of shoulder 230 T-43 antitank mines, 84 assorted high explosives, 42 250-kilogram aviation bombs, and 96 antipersonnel mines.[26]

Due to severe ammunition shortages, Soviet artillery was not particularly effective against Hill 441.4. This ammunition shortage was chronic and resulted directly from the inability of logistic support units to move ammunition forward. Also, the Soviets' overwhelming superiority in armor was of no great value. Armored columns could advance on a front of one vehicle, which too frequently fell prey to a well-sited German antitank gun. Tanks and self-propelled guns were committed in groups no larger than platoon to company in size, with the remaining vehicles waiting in the rear for their turn to fire. The infantry used armor firepower to destroy hardened German positions. Along with the logistic and mobility problems, the Soviet commanders experienced difficulty in conducting coordinated attacks. Units attempting to outflank Hill 441.4 became engaged and could not execute their supporting assaults in a coordinated manner. Because of these difficulties, Hill 441.4 did not fall on 20 October.

Other Soviet units pressing toward Nikel converged from both flanks to within two kilometers of the settlement in the north and four kilometers in the south. Combat on both flanks was intense, with both sides using close air support. Sometime before noon on 20 October, having difficulty communicating with the lead element of his southern regimental-size pincer, the 31st Rifle Corps commander, Major General Absaliamov, gave up control of that element to the 127th Light Rifle Corps, whose command post was

Soviet engineer troops probing for mines. Note the openness of the terrain.

only two kilometers from the unit.[27] Units from the 127th Rifle Corps did not engage any enemy forces early on 20 October and continued to press forward. At 2400, the 127th LRC commander reported that his corps had cut the main supply route southwest of Nikel.[28] Based on this report, the 14th Army commander, Lieutenant General Shcherbakov, believed that the German forces in and around Nikel had been surrounded on three sides, with their backs to the water.[29]

Consequently, Shcherbakov ordered the 31st Rifle Corps to destroy the encircled German forces around Nikel on 21 October with the 367th Rifle Division reinforced with a regiment from the 83d Rifle Division and with assistance from the 127th Light Rifle Corps. He also ordered a second regiment of the 83d Rifle Division to move cross-country and seize the German airfield located ten to fifteen kilometers south and west of Nikel.[30]

The 127th LRC's penetration to the main road southwest of Nikel came as an unpleasant surprise to the Germans. Alerted by aerial reconnaissance, German ground reconnaissance patrols had detected the main body of the 127th as it moved south of German defensive positions (see map 8). But the forward element of the corps, approximately 1,000 men according to German estimates, avoided detection and infiltrated to the road. The Germans' first indication of a problem in their rear was when, at around 1700 on 20 October, they discovered a Soviet force occupying a portion of the main road about 700 meters northeast of the southeast corner of Lake Kuetsiarvi. In fact, the 2d Mountain Division commander, while traveling in his staff car, narrowly escaped death in an ambush by this Soviet force.[31]

On the morning of 21 October, in a coordinated effort led by the commander of the 137th Mountain Rifle Regiment, a composite German force attacked and destroyed the Soviet forward element, thus clearing the road. The Germans claimed to have killed or captured about 850 men, including the Soviet battalion commander and his commissar. Another 150 Soviets escaped to the northeast. The Germans lost approximately 100 men.[32] As a result of this German tactical victory, 1,000 German troops fighting in the Nikel area were able to withdraw later on 21 October.

On 21 October, Soviet units attacked the German strongpoints in front of Nikel again and, before noon, pushed past Hill 441.4, only to be halted at Hill 482. The 367th Rifle Division finally defeated this position by 1900 and continued to attack westward, still two to three kilometers east of Nikel. Meanwhile, the 127th Light Rifle Corps closed in on Nikel from the south. However, even with close air support, the 31st and 127th Light Rifle Corps could not quickly destroy the German defenders in and around the settlement and mine works. There were indications though that a German withdrawal was imminent. Beginning on the afternoon of 21 October, the Soviets heard loud explosions and saw large fires in Salmiiarvi, Akhmalakhti, and Nikel.

General Shcherbakov's order for 22 October called for seizing Nikel by noon and capturing the airfield by the end of the day. Soviet troops continued to attack during the night of 21—22 October, and by 0200 on 22 October, the first elements of the 69th Naval Rifle Brigade, 127th Light

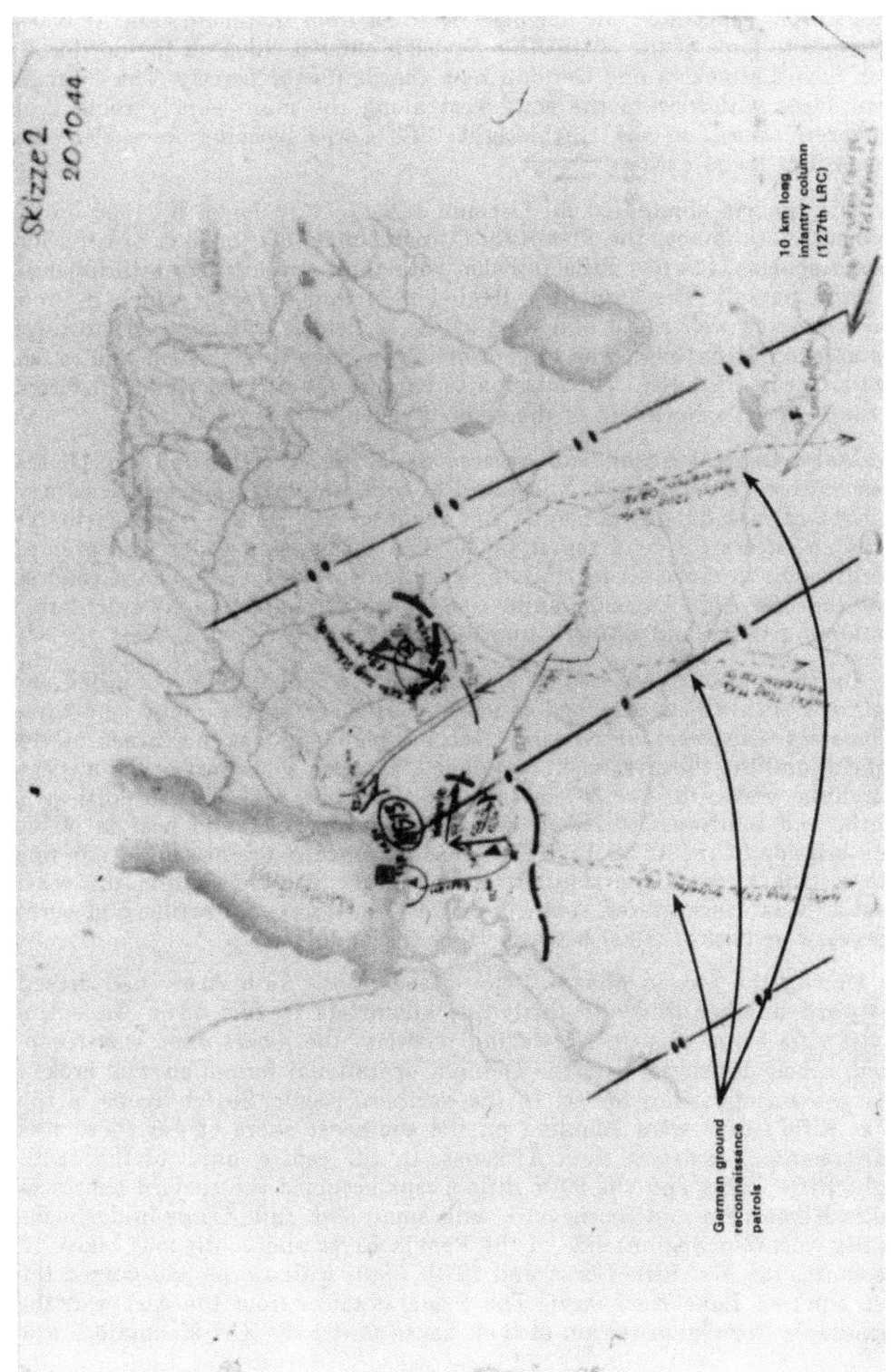

Map 8. Movement of the 127th Light Rifle Corps, 21—22 October 1944

Rifle Corps, penetrated the defenses of Nikel from the southwest. At 0500, a composite force of the 367th Rifle Division entered Nikel on the northeast. Both Soviet attackers and German rear guards fought fiercely. The German main force withdrew to the southwest along the main supply route that had been cleared of the 127th Light Rifle Corps blocking force elements twenty-four hours earlier.

The Soviets eliminated all German resistance in Nikel by 1000 on 22 October. Absaliamov, the 31st Rifle Corps commander, quickly ordered his second echelon, the 83d Rifle Division with tank and artillery attachments, to begin pursuit. The 26th Rifle Regiment of that division, which by now had wandered well south and west of the airfield it was supposed to have captured on 21 October, was to continue its westward movement and to cut Arctic Ocean Highway. The mission to capture the airfield was transferred to the 11th Rifle Regiment of the same division.

Major General Absaliamov ordered the 367th Rifle Division to clear the area around Nikel to Lake Kuetsiarvi of any remaining enemy troops and then to release quickly all units not required for combat missions to the corps engineers for road repair tasks. The corps commander also ordered the division to move all its units and equipment to the side of the road so that the 83d Rifle Division units could pass through, and he transferred reinforcing tanks and artillery from the 367th to the 83d.

By the end of phase two on 22 October, the 83d Rifle Division had one regiment with all its attached tanks and artillery on the main road three kilometers southwest of Nikel. A second regiment was northeast of the airfield, and the third regiment was four kilometers southwest of the airfield, marching westward. The 367th Rifle Division units were located northwest, north, and southwest of Nikel, with the division command post in Nikel. One brigade of the 127th Light Rifle Corps reached the destroyed crossing site on the river at the southern end of Lake Kuetsiarvi, and the other brigade was concentrated south of Nikel. The tanks and artillery of corps reserve were east of Nikel between Hills 482 and 441.4.

During the second phase of the offensive, the 14th Army had driven westward another thirty to thirty-five kilometers in five days. An entire Soviet rifle corps was on Norwegian territory, the nickel mine was recaptured, albeit destroyed, and the German operational formation was broken into two unsupporting forces. In the northern sector, Soviet troops of the 131st Rifle Corps were standing on the southeast shore of Jar Fjord less than twenty kilometers from Kirkenes. In the center, units of the 126th Light Rifle Corps and the 99th Rifle Corps occupied the eastern shores of Lakes Klistervatn and Bjornevatn, with small 99th Rifle Corps bridgeheads on the west (Norwegian) side of the Pasvik River and contiguous lakes. In the south, the 31st Rifle Corps and 127th Light Rifle Corps had gained the east bank of Lake Kuetsiarvi. The Soviet attacks from the east and the impassable Norwegian terrain at their backs forced the XIX Mountain Corps (minus the 2d Mountain Division) to withdraw northward toward Kirkenes and the 163d Infantry and 2d Mountain Divisions to withdraw southwestward toward Nautsi and Ivalo. Having thus split the Germans' combat power into two isolated axes, Soviet commanders prepared their units for the final phase of the operation.

The Battle, Phase Three, 23 October—1 November 1944

4

The German withdrawal on two axes, north to Kirkenes and south toward Ivalo, forced the Soviet Front commander to split his force likewise. General Meretskov ordered pursuit in both directions but left the 14th Army commander, Lieutenant General Shcherbakov, to organize it.[1] He and his staff elected to attack northward with three corps and pursue southward with two (see map 9).

The 14th Army planned a coordinated assault on the 6th Mountain Division that was defending the Kirkenes area. Shcherbakov ordered the 131st Rifle Corps to push toward Kirkenes from the east, force a crossing on Bek Fjord, and, in cooperation with the 99th Rifle Corps to its left (south), seize Kirkenes. He ordered the 99th Rifle Corps to screen its left (west) flank with one division and, with the remainder of its forces, attack and seize Kirkenes from the south. The 126th Light Rifle Corps was to march cross-country west and north to Munkelv and, there, cut Highway 50, which was the German main supply route and the sole land escape route from Kirkenes.

On the northern flank, Admiral Golovko's Northern Fleet would continue to conduct operations at sea to deny the Germans escape or relief from that direction. In addition, the fleet continued to support the land battle with amphibious landings. The first one came ashore in Kobbholm Fjord early on 23 October. A portion of this landing force cleared the coastline to the west; the remainder marched inland and arrived at Jar Fjord on 25 October (see map 10).

Attack on Kirkenes

On 23 October, in the 131st Rifle Corps sector, the 14th Rifle Division defeated several German counterattacks along the road from Tarnet to Kirkenes, which were supported by naval gunfire and shore batteries from Kirkenes. The division moved forward only two kilometers during the day. That night, the 45th Rifle Division crossed Jar Fjord in their American-made amphibious trucks and locally procured fishing boats. On 24 October, this division met little resistance as it advanced cross-country to the area of Jakobselv, across the fjord from Kirkenes. Its tanks and multiple rocket

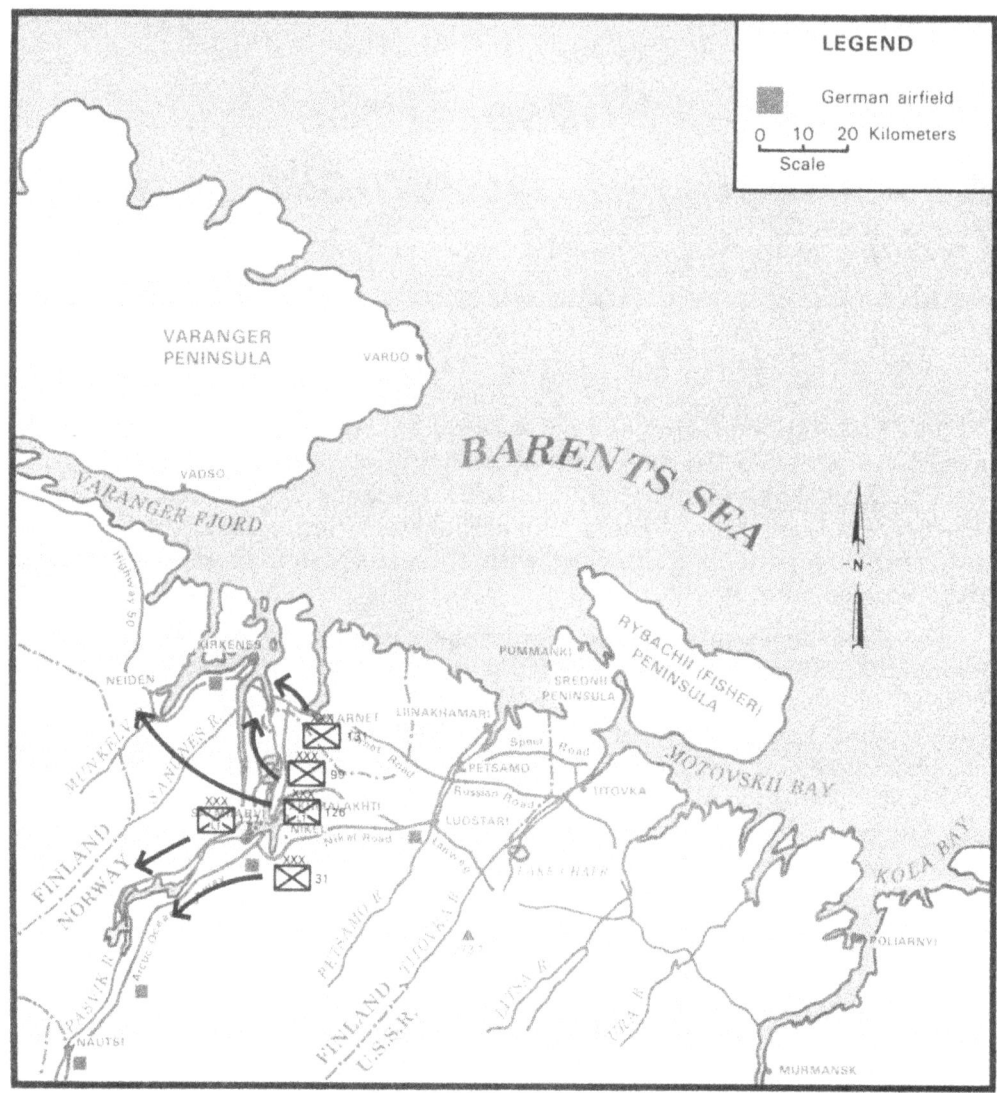

Map 9. 14th Army plan, phase three

launchers remained on the southern bank of Jar Fjord and joined the 14th Rifle Division attacking westward along the road.

On the 24th, the 14th Rifle Division fought its way forward to Bek Fjord at Elvenes, where the Germans had destroyed the trestle bridge. Attempts to cross the fjord using makeshift rafts failed. However, two companies of one rifle regiment made it across the water 1.5 kilometers south of Elvenes, where the width of the fjord was only 150 to 200 meters. In this two-day period, German artillery fired 45,000 rounds at the 131st Rifle Corps.[2]

In the 99th Rifle Corps sector to the south, the Soviets established small bridgeheads on the western shores of Lakes Klistervatn and Bjornevatn on

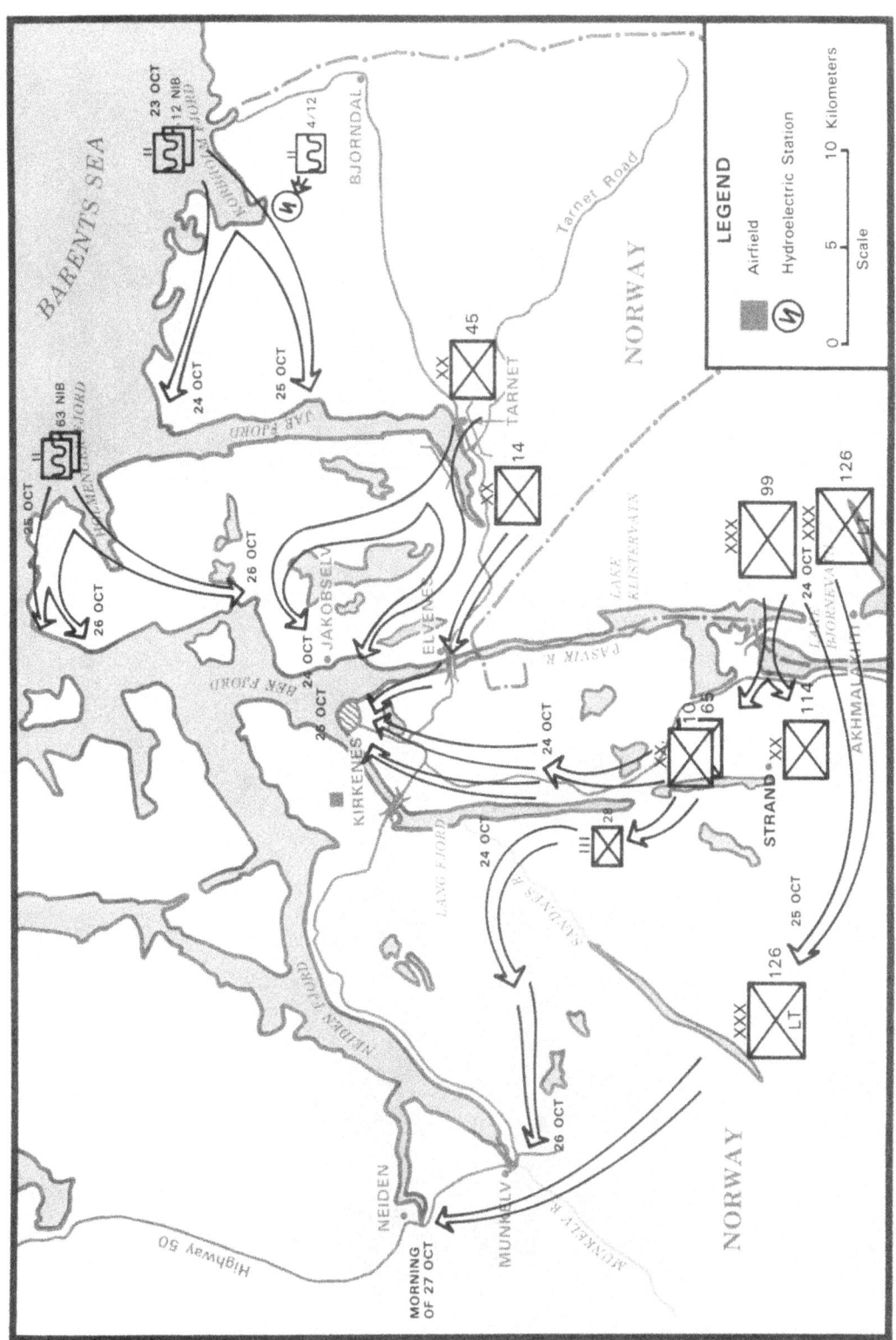

Map 10. 14th Army northern flank, 22—30 October 1944

The south side of the Tarnet-Kirkenes road. Soviet infantrymen attacked from the distant ridgeline to the hill in the right front of the photograph.

A hasty German defensive position east of Kirkenes, with a rock wall connecting two boulders

Debris from battle. German rifle shell casings as they were found at a position overlooking the road between Tarnet and Elvenes.

22 October and installed a pontoon bridge at Holmfoss. All the 99th Rifle Corps divisions crossed into Norway in rapid order. The 114th Rifle Division set up a screen line south of Strand, while the 65th Rifle Division and 10th Guards Rifle Division attacked northward. On the night of 23—24 October, the KV tanks and self-propelled guns accompanying the 10th Guards Rifle Division crossed into Norway on the pontoon bridge. By evening on 24 October, the 10th Guards attacking along the main road, and the 65th, to the right between the road and the Pasvik River, were only ten kilometers south of Kirkenes, fighting through the iron ore mines.

Meanwhile, a minor crisis had developed for the 126th Light Rifle Corps. On 23 October, this corps, which had been ordered to march cross-country to Munkelv to cut off the German escape route, was still concentrated near Akhmalakhti. It had exhausted its supplies of food and ammunition and could not move. On the afternoon of 24 October, Lieutenant General Shcherbakov, the 14th Army commander, reacting to this situation, ordered the 10th Guards Rifle Division commander, Major General Kh. A. Khudalov, to detach his 28th Rifle Regiment to fulfill the 126th Light Rifle Corps' mission.[3] The regiment had to traverse over thirty kilometers of difficult terrain laced with streams and rocks and then engage withdrawing German

A bridge destroyed by the Germans at Elvenes, southeast of Kirkenes

The bridge at Elvenes today

A German firing position dug into the rock, guarding the southwest approach to Kirkenes

The German forces used demolitions to destroy Kirkenes when they withdrew

Soviet male and female soldiers meet with Norwegian young people. The soldiers are holding mine probes. The vehicle in the background (at the arrow) is an American amphibian jeep.

units. At midnight on 24 October, when the regiment reached the high ground west of Lang Fjord, all communications with it were lost.

That same evening, Soviet air reconnaissance detected German columns leaving Kirkenes going west toward Neiden. In Kirkenes itself, the Soviets could see large explosions and fires, indicating destruction of the city and the supplies stockpiled there. Khudalov's 10th Guards Rifle Division troops were fighting in the southern outskirts of Kirkenes by 0300 on 25 October.[4]

At 0500 on 25 October, units of the 131st Rifle Corps attempted to cross Bek Fjord along a two-kilometer front at Elvenes. The German defenders withstood a twenty-minute Soviet artillery preparation and drove the Soviet troops back with strong direct and indirect fires. Forty minutes later, after a second barrage, Soviet units surged forward again and, this time, secured a small foothold. By 0900, the bulk of the corps had crossed the fjord either on amphibious vehicles or on makeshift rafts and logs and was approaching the southeast outskirts of Kirkenes.

Supported by tanks and self-propelled artillery, the 99th Rifle Corps units fought their way into Kirkenes from the south, as the 131st Rifle Corps closed in on Kirkenes from the southeast. Three Soviet rifle divisions, the 65th, 10th Guards, and 14th, supported by KV tanks, fought German rear guards in the streets of Kirkenes on 25 October and, by 1200, defeated the last organized resistance of the composite German force.⁵ On 26 October, the 10th Guards Rifle Division captured the airfield fifteen kilometers west of Kirkenes.

While the 14th Army ground forces were conducting their final assaults on the city of Kirkenes, naval infantry of the Northern Fleet landed unopposed in Holmenger Fjord before dawn on 25 October. These units swept the coastline westward and southward of German shore batteries and auxiliary units. On 27 October, this force reached the Jakobselv settlement, across the fjord east of Kirkenes. But by this time, the battle for Kirkenes was essentially over, and thus, the naval infantry had virtually no impact on its outcome.

By the morning of 26 October, the 28th Rifle Regiment of the 10th Guards Rifle Division reached Highway 50 at Munkelv.⁶ German units were still passing through the area moving westward. After a brief firefight, the Soviet troops blocked the road, thus forcing the Germans to exfiltrate northward to the fjord, where they escaped in boats.

After a 24-hour delay for logistic resupply, the 126th Light Rifle Corps marched cross-country from the Svanvik area toward Munkelv and Neiden

A German rock-lined trench in a hill overlooking Kirkenes

The last tactical engagement along Highway 50, the route of German withdrawal, was for this ridgeline. The Soviet infantry fought its way across the river and up the slope. The village of Neiden lies at the top.

on 25 and 26 October. Troops of the 3d Naval Rifle Brigade, 126th LRC, helped the 28th Rifle Regiment secure the Munkelv area by the evening of 26 October.[7] On 27 October, the entire corps moved up to the Neiden River, where German rear guards were preparing a hasty defense from the village of Neiden on the ridgeline north of the river on the opposite bank.

With the help of local fishermen, the corps crossed the river and captured Neiden. According to interviews with local Norwegian civilians who lived there in 1944, the Germans resisted strongly and, before withdrawing northward, burned or blew up every building except the wood-frame church.[8]

General Meretskov met with his military council to consider further pursuit. In light of the rugged terrain ahead and the approaching polar night, General Meretskov ordered the 14th Army troops in this sector to go over to the defensive on 29 October 1944.[9] Only a reconnaissance element of unspecified size from the 114th Rifle Division moved forward of Neiden, and on 13 November, it reached the Tana settlement 116 road kilometers northwest of Neiden and then halted.[10]

This church, built in 1902, was the only structure in Neiden not destroyed by the Germans during their withdrawal

Southward Pursuit

Having captured the village and mineworks at Nikel, units of the 127th Light Rifle Corps and 31st Rifle Corps awaited orders at the southern and eastern shores of Lake Kuetsiarvi on the night of 22—23 October. At 0520 on 23 October, the 31st Rifle Corps headquarters received a partial combat order to seize the airfield, attack and occupy a series of hills straddling Arctic Ocean Highway southwest of Lake Poroiarvi, and continue the attack southward along the road (see map 11).[11] The 127th Light Rifle Corps was to attack due westward, capture the two small settlements Menikko and Stenbakk, and then continue the attack in a southwestward direction on the Norwegian side of the Pasvik River.

On the assumption that the retreating Germans would demolish the road and employ a strong rear guard, the 31st Rifle Corps commander organized an aggressive pursuit along the road to deny the enemy time to establish an organized defense.[12] Major General Absaliamov planned to defeat the enemy by frontal attacks on the road in conjunction with flank and rear attacks by regiment- and battalion-size infantry detachments moving cross-country. Immediately behind the attacking troops, the engineers were to repair the road so that artillery could be brought up to support the pursuit. Combat units not required for the pursuit were to assist the engineers. Artillery with the greatest range was to engage in counterbattery fire, and if necessary, this artillery would be towed forward by tracked vehicles. Because of the severe mobility problems experienced with his armored vehicles in the previous days, Absaliamov parked his tanks and self-propelled guns, turning them back over to 14th Army control.[13] Finally, the corps commander asked Lieutenant General Shcherbakov, the 14th Army commander, to provide air support and air cover for the attacking force.

To implement this plan, Absaliamov gave the corps engineer control of all troops and vehicles in the corps second-echelon and reserve units that did not have a specific combat mission. An engineer reconnaissance team was formed to move with forward combat elements, assess the road damage, and communicate to the corps engineer the type and amount of support needed to push forward.

Absaliamov ordered the first-echelon 83d Rifle Division to detail one rifle regiment as the flanking detachment. At a moment's notice, it could maneuver off the road to the flank or rear of an enemy force attempting to defend from a delaying or intermediate position. As soon as this regiment was thus committed, another was to be prepared for commitment.

For better command and control, the division commander and key staff personnel were with the lead regiment. The deputy corps commander for logistics ensured that the flanking detachments had ration packets and reindeer to move bulk ammunition. Finally, the corps chief of staff and deputy commander for logistics established a control group to regulate traffic on the road.

As extensive as this planning might appear, it was not enough. The logistic support for the maneuver forces was poor. When large-scale combat operations resumed on 25 October, the 83d Rifle Division units experienced significant shortages in artillery and mortar ammunition and some food and forage commodities (see table 6). The 127th Light Rifle Corps had

Map 11. 14th Army southern flank, 23 October—2 November 1944

TABLE 6
Supply Status of Rifle Divisions of the 31st Rifle Corps

	On 20 Oct		On 25 Oct		On 31 Oct	
Ammunition (Units of Fire)	83d	367th	83d	367th	83d	367th
Rifle ammunition	1.1	1.4	1.1	1.4	1.4	1.5
Submachine gun ammunition	1.3	0.7	1.3	1.4	1.6	1.3
Antitank rifle shells	0.4	0.3	0.5	0.3	0.4	0.2
Hand grenades	0.7	0.6	0.6	0.5	0.7	0.5
82-mm mortar rounds	0.0	0.3	0.4	0.3	0.9	0.2
120-mm mortar rounds	1.0	0.4	0.2	0.4	0.6	0.7
45-mm antitank gun shells	0.6	0.5	0.2	0.5	0.4	0.4
76-mm (regimental artillery)	1.0	0.7	0.3	0.6	0.6	0.2
76-mm (divisional artillery)	0.7	0.1	0.2	0.2	0.3	0.16
122-mm howitzer shells	0.1	0.4	0.3	0.7	0.4	0.7
Provisions (Day's Supply)						
Rations for men	3.0	2.0				
Forage for animals	2.0	1.0				
Bread, flour			0.0	0.0	5.0	7.6
Biscuits			1.7	1.3	1.6	0.0
Canned meat			2.2	2.4	8.5	9.0
Groats			1.5	4.3	17.9	8.5
Potatoes, vegetables			0.0	0.0	0.5	0.9
Fat			11.0	24.0	6.0	18.0
Sugar			10.0	0.4	0.0	0.0
Salt			0.0	1.6	2.5	2.0
Tobacco			0.0	0.0	9.0	4.0
Forage			0.0	0.0	0.0	1.0
Petrolum, oils, and lubricants (in refuels)			0.5	0.5	2.0	1.1
Vodka (in liters)			200	500	2,095	1,630

NOTE: From 18 to 22 October 1944, the 367th Rifle Division was the first echelon of the 31st Rifle Corps, while the 83d Rifle Division repaired roads. On 23 October, these roles were reversed.

Source: Mikulskii and Absaliamov, *Nastupatel'nye boi,* 158.

received food supplies on 23 October from a German supply depot in Nikel, but only sufficient to last a few days.[14] These logistic shortcomings contributed to weakening the fighting strength of the combat units.

No amount of planning, however, could have prevented the retreating Germans' continued destruction of the road and bridges. By the evening of 23 October, the 127th Light Rifle Corps had crossed the two rivers at the southern end of Lake Kuetsiarvi. However, the main body of the 83d Rifle Division, moving along the road, was halted by the destroyed bridge and the absence of fording sites or bypasses. The rebuilding of the bridge was complicated because both approaches were in a swamp. Furthermore, the 14th Army's pontoon bridges and amphibious vehicles were deployed on the Kirkenes axis. Eventually, engineer battalions of both the 83d and 367th Rifle Divisions, a battalion of the 1st Motorized Combat Engineer Brigade, and two rifle battalions from a regiment of the 83d Rifle Division were dedicated to repairing this bridge and its approaches.[15] Even with all this effort, vehicular traffic did not pass this point until the morning of 25 October.

On the morning of 23 October, the 31st Rifle Corps commander brought forward troops of the 367th Rifle Division, and they crossed the Shuoniioki River on a foot bridge. Their task was to repair the road with hand tools. When traffic was finally able to move on the road, divisional and then reinforcing artillery had priority. One rifle regiment of the lead 83d Rifle Division was parceled out along the artillery column to assist in its movement. In sum, all on account of terrain and road conditions, four of the six rifle regiments of the 31st Rifle Corps now had engineer mobility tasks, and the corps had lost its armor support.

Meanwhile, the remaining two regiments moved cross-country without their artillery and support units. The 11th Rifle Regiment captured the airfield south of Nikel on 23 October, where the Germans had abandoned eight airplanes, numerous weapons, and large quantities of parts and supplies. The 26th Rifle Regiment, moving westward but south of the airfield, reached Arctic Ocean Highway by the evening of 23 October and engaged German rear guards. On the morning of 24 October, this regiment renewed the pursuit along the road.

By midafternoon, the 26th Rifle Regiment had advanced to the Laukkuioki River, beyond which lay Mount Kaskama and a strong German defensive position. The Soviet force brushed aside a small German outpost, but the Germans' strong, well-coordinated fires from prepared positions on the northern and northeastern slopes halted any further Soviet advance.[16] During the night of 24—25 October, on orders from the corps commander, the 83d Rifle Division commander went forward to the 26th Rifle Regiment command post and organized that unit for a bypass maneuver on the next day.

On the morning of 25 October, heavy vehicles were finally able to cross the Shuoniioki River southwest of Nikel. While additional infantry units and artillery moved up, the 26th Rifle Regiment, minus a battalion left in contact, began to maneuver around the German right flank. By 1530, the flanking detachment had infiltrated between two German positions and lodged itself on the road between Mount Kaskama and Lake Kaskama. If the Soviet forces north of Mount Kaskama had conducted a frontal attack, with the flanking detachment blocking the Germans' retreat, the German position would have collapsed. But the Soviets delayed, choosing instead to continue to prepare for an attack the next day.

An improvised log raft crossing the river, covered by a 7.62-mm Maxim machine gun

A Soviet 120-mm mortar crew

The Germans took advantage of this delay. They massed forces on the blocking position, counterattacked it several times, and finally, at around 1800, broke through. When Soviet troops swept over the top of the hill on the night of 25—26 October, the German defenders were gone. Many of them, according to Major General Absaliamov, escaped across the river to the west, where the 127th Light Rifle Corps should have engaged them.[17] But the 127th LRC had fallen behind some fifteen to twenty kilometers and was not able to block the 31st Rifle Corps right flank. Although the 127th LRC was supposed to be engaging the retreating Germans on the Norwegian side of the Pasvik River,[18] it had, in fact, stopped to replenish its extremely low food supply.[19] Thus, the 127th LRC did not influence the action at Kaskama.

The next morning, 26 October, the 83d Rifle Division, with two regiments on the road and one in the tundra to the east, continued to move southward pursuing the withdrawing Germans. These units pressed forward to Nautsi, their next objective, and, along the way, overran another airfield at Maiatolo. Here, the Germans had abandoned large quantities of petroleum products, munitions, and spare parts for airplanes and automotive equipment. The division halted south of the airfield on 26 October. That night, the 14th Army commander, Lieutenant General Shcherbakov, ordered the 31st Rifle Corps to seize Nautsi by the next morning. At 0600 on 27 October, he further ordered the corps to capture intact the hydroelectric station on the Pasvik River some twelve to thirteen kilometers southwest of Nautsi.

At midday, fire from German positions halted the 83d Rifle Division units just east of Nautsi. Through reconnaissance and observation, the

On 25 October 1944, Soviet troops crossed the Pasvik River at this site southwest of Nikel on scores of log rafts

Soviets determined that the Germans had established strong defensive positions along the road to the south and west. Therefore, the division commander spent the remainder of 27 October preparing for an attack the next morning. A portion of his artillery arrived on the scene that evening, having come forward thirty-five to forty kilometers that day over an extremely bad road. The remainder did not arrive until the morning of 28 October.

On the morning of 28 October, the 83d Rifle Division executed a frontal and flank attack against the German defenders, which drove the Germans back to a subsequent position. The Soviets spent another half-day reconnoitering this position and, at the same time, brought up more artillery. On 29 October, the 83d Rifle Division attacked and seized the hydroelectric station, which by now the Germans had demolished.[20]

On 30 October, the 14th Army commander ordered the 31st Rifle Corps to occupy defensive positions east of Lake Inari, with forward positions southeast of the lake at Mustola. On occupation of Mustola, a specially created detachment was to drive southward and make contact with the Finnish Army at Ivalo.[21] One attacking regiment fixed the German rear guards positioned astride the road at Virtaniemi, while two other regiments maneuvered cross-country over terrain the Germans believed impassable.[22] Understandably, the Soviet and German accounts differ as to who fought more skillfully, but the net outcome was the same. The German rear guards were driven out of their positions by nightfall on 31 October. Similar actions occurred on 1 and 2 November, resulting in the 83d Rifle Division seizing Mustola by midday on 2 November.

The main forces of the 31st Rifle Corps went over to the defense in positions specified in the 30 October order. A forward reconnaissance detachment pursued the withdrawing Germans as far as Ivalo where, on 5 November, it made contact with Finnish troops. The German forces then withdrew northwestward through Finnish territory back into Norway. In ten days of active pursuit operations (23 October—2 November), the 31st Rifle Corps had advanced approximately 150 kilometers.

Moscow saluted the men and units of the Karelian Front and Northern Fleet three times: on 15 October after the capture of Petsamo, on 25 October after the liberation of Kirkenes, and on 1 November after Pechenga (Petsamo) Oblast had been cleared of German troops.[23] Aided by Northern Fleet units, the Karelian Front had successfully concluded a joint and combined arms operation of unprecedented size on arctic terrain.

Northern Fleet Support of Ground Operations   5

The Northern Fleet was formally established in 1937 using the organization and assets of the Northern Flotilla.[1] In 1940, Admiral A. G. Golovko took command of the Northern Fleet.[2] Joining the Soviet Navy in 1925 and completing a commissioning school in 1928, he served in various surface vessel squadrons in the Black Sea, Baltic, and Pacific Fleets. In 1937—38, he was the Soviet adviser to the Spanish commander of the Cartegena Naval Base. While there, Golovko undoubtedly met Admiral N. G. Kuznetsov, senior Soviet naval adviser to Spain in 1936—37 and the commander in chief of the Soviet Navy in 1944. After a brief tour in the Northern Fleet as commander of a destroyer division and fleet chief of staff, Golovko commanded first the Caspian and then the Amur Flotillas. At the age of thirty-three, Golovko became the youngest fleet commander in the Soviet Navy.[3]

By the beginning of the war with Germany in 1941, the Northern Fleet consisted of units of submarines, destroyers, minesweepers, subchasers, and torpedo boats, with a modest ground-based air arm and, on the approaches to Murmansk and Belomorsk, antiaircraft and coastal artillery units.[4] From 1941 to 1944, the Northern Fleet's principal missions were to support the ground forces defending Murmansk against German ground attacks; to defend the internal and external sea lanes, including Allied convoys delivering supplies to Murmansk; and to disrupt German naval traffic along the northern Norwegian coast.[5]

By the fall of 1944, the Northern Fleet had grown significantly in both size and combat experience. Admiral Golovko now commanded a force of more than 25 submarines and almost 300 surface vessels,[6] including a significant number of small craft manufactured in the United States and delivered to the U.S.S.R. through lend-lease.[7] His air force numbered some 275 aircraft of all types.[8] On the Srednii and Rybachii Peninsulas were stationed two brigades of naval infantry, along with several separate numbered battalions (approximately 15,000 ground troops).[9]

In a directive issued on 31 March, *STAVKA* specified the following missions for the Northern Fleet in 1944:

- Operate jointly with the Karelian Front along its coastal flank with assault landings, artillery fire, and transporting of forces.

• Disrupt systematically the German shipping along the northern Norwegian coast and in the Varanger Fjord.

• Support the movement of convoys in cooperation with the Allies.

• Defend the region's naval bases, coastline, and internal shipping lanes against enemy operations.

• Conduct self-sustainment operations.[10]

Command Relationship

Admiral Golovko worked in a complicated command environment. It was common in the early years of the Great Patriotic War for a fleet to be subordinated to a Front commander for a particular operation.[11] But changes in the structure of the Soviet Navy's central command and control apparatus were introduced in the spring of 1944, which subordinated all naval forces to a navy commander in chief in Moscow who, at that time, was Admiral N. G. Kuznetsov.[12] As a result, in all subsequent strategic operations in which the navy participated, the General Staff, the commander in chief of the navy, and the Main Naval Staff examined all

A Higgins-Vosper patrol torpedo boat, manufactured in Bristol, Rhode Island, given to the U.S.S.R. in lend-lease and used by the Northern Fleet for surface, antishipping, and amphibious operations

A Douglas A-20 Boston, given to the U.S.S.R. in lend-lease and converted for use as a torpedo bomber for the naval air forces

missions in detail, and then they were approved by *STAVKA* (see figure 4 in chapter 1).[13] So, while Admiral Golovko was subordinated through the Main Naval Staff to Admiral Kuznetsov for purely naval matters, he also took orders from *STAVKA* whenever his fleet conducted joint operations.

The Petsamo-Kirkenes Operation fits this pattern. General Meretskov and Admiral Golovko first met in April 1944, two months after Meretskov assumed command of the Karelian Front. Despite Meretskov's seniority in age (forty-seven versus thirty-eight) and rank (one grade level), the two quickly established a close and friendly working relationship.[14] In late August or early September, when *STAVKA* issued planning instructions to General Meretskov, he quickly passed them on to Admiral Golovko.

In response to either these *STAVKA* planning instructions or to a *STAVKA* directive of 26 September, which specified the objectives of the offensive and the forces to be employed, Meretskov submitted a proposal that two brigades of naval infantry attack the German left flank at the same time as his ground forces' attack on the German right flank. Both the General Staff and the Main Naval Staff disapproved Meretskov's proposal. Together, Meretskov and Golovko developed another plan, which their superiors in Moscow accepted.

Notwithstanding the supporting role of the fleet, Golovko exercised overall direction of all naval forces participating in the operation, whether at sea or on land.[15] Clearly, Meretskov and Golovko were working in cooperation (*vzaimodeistviia*) with each other, subordinated through their respective chains of command to STAVKA.[16] Thus, although in a sense there was unity of command for this operation, it resided in STAVKA at the strategic level.

In the area of operations, General Meretskov could prevail on Admiral Golovko to act only within the parameters of the STAVKA-approved plan, and even that was not easily accomplished. According to Admiral V. I. Platonov, Golovko's chief of staff, no direct communications links existed between the fleet and Front forward command posts. All message traffic had to be routed through the fleet main command post at Poliarnyi, near Murmansk.[17]

Preparation

Preparation for naval support to the offensive began in the spring of 1944, coincident with the 31 March STAVKA directive and the April meeting between the two commanders. The Main Naval Staff sent out officers to work with Golovko's staff.[18] In early September, Golovko received an oral confirmation from Meretskov of the plan for the offensive and, in turn, issued directives to his own subordinate commands.[19] The two met at Golovko's fleet headquarters on 26 September[20] and coordinated the final plans in a subsequent meeting on 29 September at Meretskov's command post.[21] These two commanders agreed that the fleet's specific missions were to blockade the coastal area occupied by the Germans, permitting neither withdrawal nor reinforcement by sea; operate jointly with the 14th Army in penetrating enemy defenses and seizing ports; support the offensive of ground forces with coastal artillery and naval gunfire in coastal areas; participate actively in the land offensive by committing naval infantry across the Srednii isthmus and in amphibious landings; and aid in the logistic support of the 14th Army by transporting men and supplies from Murmansk.[22]

At about this same time, the Main Naval Staff in Moscow sent Golovko a dispatch suggesting that fleet units participate in reestablishing a Soviet naval base at Petsamo.[23] This suggestion, which Golovko perceived as an order, led to the planning and conducting of the amphibious landing at Liinakhamari on the night of 12—13 October.

In the days and weeks preceding the offensive, units of the fleet undertook a number of preparatory measures.[24] In the brief time remaining before the offensive, the hydrographic service was to conduct a photo reconnaissance of the entire coastal area from the Western Litsa River to Kirkenes and a geodesic survey of all Soviet shore battery firing positions; install shore markers to facilitate naval gunfire support of ground operations and navigational devices in port channels and on routes to fjord entrances or landing areas; establish a forward weather station to provide timely meteorological information to all fleet units; determine the precise locations of all German shore batteries that could affect planned amphibious landings; and identify and train harbor pilots to lead the amphibious landing force into Petsamo Bay and the Liinakhamari port.

All these tasks were accomplished. The results of aerial photo reconnaissance were made into charts, maps, and topographical training aids, all of which were used for target selection, landing site selection, and orientation of key personnel. The surveying of gun positions permitted the delivery of more accurate fire against known or suspected enemy targets. In prevailing arctic weather and light conditions, the navigational aids facilitated the safe operation of all fleet vessels and also ensured the accurate delivery of troops to their designated landing areas. Suspected German shore battery positions were lured into firing, then precisely located by specially instrumented patrol craft. Naval aviation was then called in to destroy the targets. Officers familiar with Petsamo Bay and the Liinakhamari harbor were sought out and detailed to the fleet landing force to guide the assault waves into Liinakhamari. Much of this work was accomplished specifically for the 9 and 12 October landings. But the effects certainly carried over to other landings as well.

A second aspect of the preparation for this operation was the training of troops in the 63d Naval Infantry Brigade, the unit designated to conduct the amphibious landings. They rehearsed loading and unloading troops, supplies, and equipment; actions ashore; and night combat. The reconnaissance detachments that participated in the raid on Cape Krestovyi were also selected and prepared. Also planned extensively was a demonstration landing in Motovskii Bay near the mouth of the Western Litsa River, which was intended to distract German attention from the main landing west of Srednii Peninsula.

On the night of 8—9 October, Admiral Golovko moved to a forward command post on Srednii Peninsula. At or near his command post were the rear admiral commanding the amphibious landings, the naval infantry major general commanding the ground and amphibious assault troops, the captain first rank commanding the brigade of torpedo boats, and the major general commanding the fleet air forces.[25] At this forward command post, Admiral Golovko did not have direct communication either with the Front commander, General Meretskov, or the 14th Army commander, Lieutenant General Shcherbakov.

Amphibious Landings

Forces of the Northern Fleet conducted five separate amphibious landings in support of the Soviet ground offensive. Table 7, which is keyed to map 12, provides an overview of all five landings and several points of analysis.

TABLE 7
Amphibious Landings

	Time and Date	Location of Landing	Unit	Size of Landing Force	Size of Support Force	Other Support Activities	Nature of Opposition	Actions Ashore	Enemy Response	Outcome
1	2330 9 Oct–0050 10 Oct	Maativuono Bay	1st, 2d, and 3d Bns, 63d Naval Inf Bde	2,750–3,000 3 waves	Mixture of 30 torpedo cutters and subchasers	Demonstration landing at Motovskii Bay; smoke screen; shore battery fire support	Illumination by searchlight; shore batteries; no enemy troops at water's edge	Attacked inland into flank and rear of German defenders	Heavy combat	Linked up with 12th Naval Inf Bde on 10 Oct; linked up with 14th Army on 13 Oct
2	2300–2400 12 Oct	Liinakhamari Harbor	Composite	660 3 waves	Mixture of 14 torpedo cutters and subchasers	Smoke screen; shore battery fire support; Krestovyi raid	Heavy shore battery; piers in harbor mined; enemy garrison	Seized port and settlement; attacked Petsamo from north	Heavy combat	Controlled port by late 13 Oct; attacked southward to envelop Petsamo
3	0650–0730 18 Oct	Suola-Vuono, Ares-Vuono	4th Bn, 12th Naval Inf Bde	485 2 groups	6 subchasers	Close air support when ashore	None at landing site; small garrisons of coastal installations	Attacked west to Norwegian border, defeating light opposition	Light to moderate opposition	Reached Norwegian border by late 19 Oct; linked up with ground forces of 368th Rifle Div
4	0600–0630 23 Oct	Kobbholm Fjord	3d Bn, 12th Naval Inf Bde; 125th Naval Inf Regt	625 2 groups	10 light craft	Close air support when ashore	None at landing site	Advanced on two separate axes, cleared coast of 75-mm antiaircraft and artillery batteries	Light opposition	Cleared zone; no significant impact
5	0455–0550 25 Oct	Holmenger Fjord	2d and 3d Bns, 63d Naval Inf Bde	835 3 waves	Mixture of 15 torpedo cutters and subchasers	3 cutters in overwatch	None at landing site	Advanced on two axes, clearing coastal installations	Light opposition	Reached Kirkenes vicinity on 27 Oct; little impact on outcome

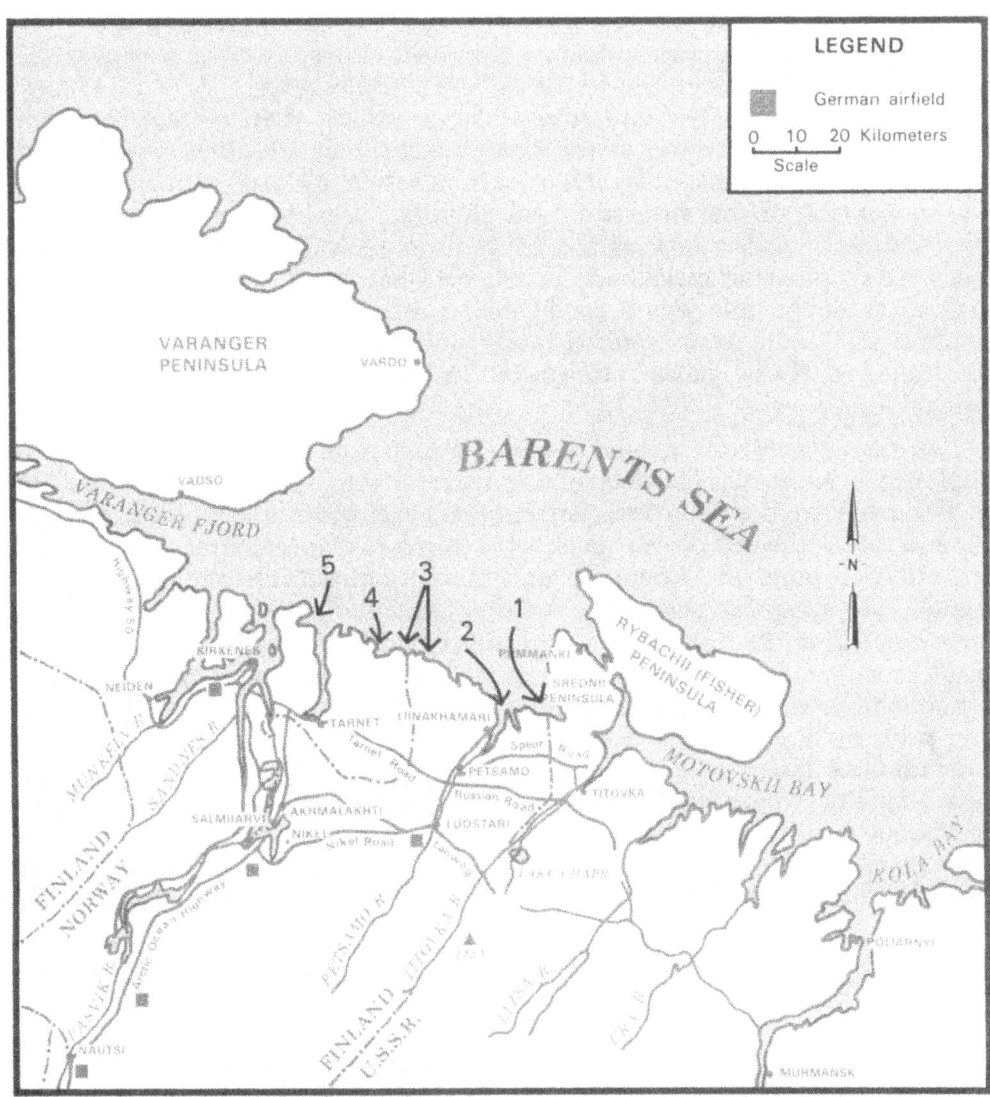

Map 12. Northern Fleet amphibious landings

The initial amphibious landing was by far the largest of all the landings in both men and support vessels. Also, it featured a demonstration landing on the opposite side of Srednii Peninsula at Motovskii Bay that consisted of two destroyer escorts firing against German shore installations, forty-four troops who went ashore in small boats, and other small patrol craft that fired torpedoes and guns and laid smoke screens.[26] Despite all these efforts, however, the Germans were not the least bit distracted by the demonstration, as indicated by this conversation recorded in the war diary of the German 20th Mountain Army:

> Chief of Staff, XIX Mountain Corps: "The enemy is conducting landings on both sides of Fisherhals [Rubachii Peninsula]."

> Chief of Staff, 20th Mountain Army: "The landing at the sea narrows is not of long-range significance; therefore, concentrate all your assets against the landing west of Fisherhals, in order to throw the enemy back."[27]

Significantly, at the point selected to go ashore, there were coastal batteries but no enemy troops at the water's edge. This situation existed in all landings save the one in Liinakhamari. Whether by design or accident, it was important to the success of the landing, because the naval infantry went ashore over the bow of the boats on long wooden planks. This relatively slow process of disembarking rendered both men and boats vulnerable to fire. No doubt, this was a consideration when Golovko's staff decided to conduct all landings at night. Finally, in both this landing and the one that followed, Soviet shore batteries on Srednii Peninsula conducted counterbattery fires.

At first glance, the second landing, which was at Liinakhamari, looks unplanned. After all, the bulk of the troops were "volunteers," scraped up at Poliarnyi from submarines, subchasers, and other units of the fleet on 10 and 11 October.[28] These men were hurriedly transported back to the embarkation point at Pummanki and then organized into the three detachments. The other 150-plus naval infantry and the leadership for the entire force came from two regular naval infantry units. All other signs, however, point to some careful planning for this landing. The hydrographic preparation, the preselecting and detailing of harbor pilots, and the designating and training of special units for the Krestovyi raid clearly indicate the fleet commander's intent to execute the landing. The failure of his staff to allocate adequate troops was compensated for by the courageous performance of the 500 hastily assembled men. Golovko's decision to carry out the plan with seemingly unprepared forces was vindicated by the results. The naval infantry captured the port and secured the northern flank of Petsamo.[29]

The third landing, at Suola-Vuono and Ares-Vuono, executed just before dawn on 18 October, was significant for three reasons. First, this force assembled and embarked at Petsamo, which only three days earlier had been taken from the Germans. Second, once it reached the Norwegian border, this force, with a rifle regiment of the 368th Rifle Division, was to clear the coastal zone to the west. Finally, on 22 October, this force captured intact the 3,000-kilowatt hydroelectric station at Kobbholm Fjord, which supplied electricity to the port of Kirkenes.[30]

The fourth landing was also executed from Petsamo, with forces going ashore unopposed on the west shore of Kobbholm Fjord on 23 October. One element of the landing force swept the coastline to the mouth of Jar Fjord, while the other element linked up with the naval infantrymen at the power station and marched toward the middle shore of Jar Fjord, north of Tarnet, arriving there on 25 October.

For the final landing, two battalions of the 63d Naval Infantry Brigade launched from Pummanki. This force went into Holmenger Fjord on 25 October, the same morning that army ground forces assaulted Kirkenes from the east and south. Advancing on two separate axes, one element

Senior Sergeant I. P. Katorzhnyi, who was awarded the title of Hero of the Soviet Union for his actions during the assault on Liinakhamari

swept the coastline to the west, while the other advanced southwestward toward Kirkenes. On 27 October, two days after Kirkenes was liberated, this force arrived at Jacobselvn, across the fjord from Kirkenes to the northeast. Both the 23 and 25 October landings can be viewed as clearing or mopping-up actions; neither was significant in the effort to capture Kirkenes.

Two additional landings were contemplated during the Petsamo-Kirkenes Operation. Sometime around 14—15 October, as sailors and soldiers closed in on Petsamo from the north and south, Admiral Golovko returned to his fleet headquarters at Poliarnyi. At that time, according to Golovko's chief of staff, Admiral Platonov, General Meretskov supported Golovko's idea for amphibious forces to seize the Norwegian ports of Vardo and Vadso on 17—18 October on Varanger Peninsula.[31] This bold plan, if executed successfully, would have resulted in the rapid collapse of the German defenses in front of Kirkenes, the interdicting of both land and sea routes of withdrawal, and tremendous troop and supply losses to the German XIX Mountain Corps. Platonov went to Pummanki the next day to organize the landing. A reconnaissance party had reported that the German defenses were vulnerable. A force of unspecified size embarked and informed the fleet headquarters at Poliarnyi as to its readiness to execute the landing. After a long delay, Admiral Golovko informed Platonov that Moscow would not support the plan.[32] The troops were then moved by boat to Petsamo and put ashore.

Perhaps one reason why Moscow did not support the plan was that the Main Naval Staff did not want to risk the personnel and equipment assets. The Germans, in spite of the rupture of their long-held positions on the Litsa front, had significant ground forces in the area between Kirkenes and Petsamo, as well as fortress battalions of the 210th Infantry Division at Vardo, Vadso, and Kirkenes. Still, it appears to be a case of too much caution. Both Golovko and Meretskov were prevented from possibly achieving a significant operational success.

A second attempt to put forces ashore on Varanger Peninsula was only partially successful.[33] A ten-man reconnaissance party parachuted into the hills southwest of Vardo on the night of 27 October, but the commander was killed and others of the group were injured as a result of strong winds. Radio contact with this group was lost immediately. On 29 October, three survivors of the ill-fated jump reached Soviet-controlled ports by motorboat. On the night of 30 October, the fleet headquarters reconnaissance detachment, commanded by Senior Lieutenant V. N. Leonov, went ashore twenty kilometers southwest of Vardo. This group established contact with survivors of the parachute jump, determined from contact with local civilians that the Germans had fled the area, and then moved by boat to Vardo. On the basis of this information, plans for a full-scale landing were canceled. Although the Germans had destroyed much of the port and its facilities at Vardo, they also had abandoned large stocks of food and other materiel, including small arms. Leonov and his men turned these supplies over to the Norwegians and returned to their base at Poliarnyi on 2 November.

Viewed in isolation from the 14th Army's ground offensive, the five major landings were significant accomplishments. Except for Leonov's reconnaissance detachment, fleet units were inexperienced in amphibious landings. The fleet had no amphibious landing craft and was forced to use patrol torpedo boats, minesweepers, submarine chasers, and other small craft to deliver landing forces and cargo. Under these circumstances, given the slowness and difficulty of putting large groups of men ashore, the fleet staff carefully selected landing sites that would minimize opposition to the landing force. When this was not possible, as in the case of Liinakhamari, the staff took other measures, such as the selection of harbor pilots and the Krestovyi raid, to protect the force. All landings were executed during darkness, either at night or in the early morning, and some were even covered by smoke screens. Shore-based artillery from Srednii Peninsula or naval close air supported all landings, and all landing forces successfully occupied beachheads and accomplished their tactical missions on land.

Viewed in the context of the ground offensive, however, only the first three landings were significant. The fault in the initial amphibious landing on the night of 9 October lay not in its execution, which was good, but in its timing. The operational objective of the naval amphibious and cross-isthmus attacks was to collapse the left flank of the XIX Mountain Corps and prevent withdrawal or reinforcement to the main axis. But the naval infantrymen came ashore about thirty hours after the German forces on that flank had been authorized to withdraw. The timing of this landing and the cross-isthmus attack that followed the next morning was not of Admiral Golovko's choosing. *STAVKA* had rejected General Meretskov's proposal to execute the naval infantry attacks simultaneously with his ground offensive on 7 October.

In the case of the Liinakhamari landing, it was mainly conducted with the objective of ensuring the rapid capture of Petsamo and of establishing a naval base there. That it, at the same time, closed off Petsamo Bay as an escape route for the German forces was not a justification for the landing, because a small force of patrol boats stationed off the entrance to the fjord could have accomplished the same goal. On the other hand, given the limited size and the composite nature of the force that executed the Liinakhamari landing, a more ambitious plan, such as a linkup with the light rifle brigade blocking Tarnet Road, would likely have failed.

The importance of the third landing to the ground offensive was that it cut off a portion of Kirkenes' electricity supply. However, the last two landings on 23 and 25 October did not affect, to even a small degree, the outcome of the ground offensive.

A reasonable explanation for the lack of coordination of all five landings with the land offensive is the structure of the Soviet command and control system. Unity of command existed at the *STAVKA* level, where strategy was translated into an operational plan. At the level where the operational plan was executed, at fleet and Front headquarters, there was a distinct absence of unity of command. This is clear from the descriptions of the command relationship between the two commanders and also from the fact that no direct communication between Meretskov's and Golovko's forward command posts existed. Nor is the use of liaison officers between the two headquarters mentioned in any source. Even if the two commanders had wanted to coordinate an amphibious landing with a land force maneuver, such coordination would have been difficult. Good personal relations between the two commanders notwithstanding, the operational ground and naval command relationship was ineffective.

Naval Air Operations

In the fall of 1944, the Northern Fleet had approximately 275 aircraft in its air arm for support of the Petsamo-Kirkenes Operation. The aircraft belonged to the 5th Torpedo, 14th Mixed, and 6th Interceptor Air Divisions and the 118th Reconnaissance Aviation Regiment. Between them, these aviation units controlled 55 bombers, 35 ground attack aircraft, 160 fighters, and an unspecified number of reconnaissance and utility aircraft.[34] Naval aviation was to support the naval infantry of the Northern Defensive Region in amphibious and ground operations and to destroy German shipping assets both in port and at sea.[35]

Close air support was crucial to the success of the naval infantry units' ground operations. Naval air supported the 9 October amphibious landings with strikes against German shore batteries and strongpoints. On 10 and

11 October, Northern Fleet aviation assets supported naval infantry forces attacking across the Srednii isthmus.[36] On 12 October, naval air strikes and supply deliveries ensured that the naval infantry reconnaissance force at Cape Krestovyi survived and was replenished, and on 13 October, naval air strikes supported the capture of Liinakhamari. Naval air also supported the amphibious landings of 18 and 23 October. Of the 8,907 total sorties flown by naval aviation during the operation, 1,127 were in support of the naval ground forces.[37] The other 6,000-plus sorties were against German naval traffic at sea. A careful examination of all Soviet sources does not reveal an instance where naval aviation supported the army ground forces.

Naval Support of Army Logistic Operations

In the preparatory phase and during the conduct of the Petsamo-Kirkenes Operation, units of the Northern Fleet provided important support for the 14th Army logisticians. Beginning on 6 September, fleet assets transported men, vehicles, and supplies across Kola Bay at Murmansk.[38] After the capture of Petsamo on 15 October and the reestablishment of a naval base there, troops and cargo were moved into Petsamo by sea, relieving some of the pressure on the overcrowded roads. On return trips, wounded troops were brought to the rear area medical treatment facilities. In table 8 are four Soviet sources that give somewhat disparate data on the overall scope of this support.

TABLE 8
Northern Fleet Support for 14th Army Logistic Operations

Source*	Description
Golovko	More than 25,000 troops, 24 KV tanks, 75 T-34 tanks, 19 self-propelled guns, 237 guns, 143 tracked prime movers, 271 vehicles, and a great quantity of provisions and ammunition
Shlomin	21,000 troops and approximately 20,000 tons of cargo
Egorov	5,719 troops; 118 tanks, armored cars, and self-propelled guns; 153 guns; 137 tracked prime movers; 197 wheeled vehicles; and 553,000 tons of ammunition and various types of cargo
Basov	More than 28,000 troops, 169 guns and mortars, 138 tanks and other armored vehicles, 361 trucks and tracked prime movers, and approximately 26,000 tons of ammunition and supplies

*For full citations, see note 38.

As is evident, there is general agreement on the number of vehicles, but little else. In itself, the ability of the Northern Fleet to ferry the heavy equipment across Kola Bay ensured that the 14th Army had tank and artillery support. Without naval support, the army could have moved the equipment, men, and supplies only by diverting scarce engineer assets from other critical tasks. Considering the time the engineers would have spent in constructing additional roads and bridges, this operation could never have been launched on 7 October without help from the Northern Fleet.

Definitely, the activities of the Northern Fleet were important to the overall success of the Petsamo-Kirkenes Operation. Northern Fleet units provided essential logistic support to the 14th Army by moving heavy equipment and supplies into the operations area before and during the offensive. Furthermore, despite the lack of close coordination between Golovko and Meretskov, ground combat units of the Northern Fleet engaged sizable German forces from 10 to 15 October along the coastal axis and prevented their withdrawal to reinforce another axis. Also, Northern Fleet air and naval units bombarded German units and installations and attacked German vessels at sea, fulfilling their mission to deny withdrawal or reinforcement by sea. All these actions contributed to the eventual success of 14th Army's ground operations.

Soviet Special Operations* 6

Both the Karelian Front and the Northern Fleet employed special-purpose detachments, so named because their special mission was to strike targets behind the German lines. Two special operations were conducted in support of the Petsamo-Kirkenes Operation, one by special-purpose troops of the 14th Army and the other by a composite detachment of naval infantrymen and sailors from the Northern Fleet.

Karelian Front Special-Purpose Forces

In July 1944, the Front commander, General Meretskov, ordered several special-purpose detachments from an assault combat engineer brigade to be formed and prepared for operations deep in the German rear.[1] The men came from various engineer units, including the 6th Separate Guards Battalion of Demolition Specialists (6th *OGBM***), the 64th and 222d Motorized Assault Combat Engineer Battalions, and the 168th Army Engineer Battalion.[2] Once formed, all detachments were subordinated directly to the Karelian Front engineer staff, which was responsible for their support, training, and operational deployment.

After their selection and designation, the special-purpose detachments lived and trained apart from other units.[3] The training program was designed to prepare the men both physically and psychologically for combat operations in the enemy rear.[4] Training included exercises in conducting platoon- and company-size ambushes, organizing a battalion march in mountainous and swampy terrain, and preparing a reconnaissance detachment to encircle and destroy an enemy strongpoint. The men also trained in coordinating actions between subunits, conducting reconnaissance, placing demolitions on roads and bridges, and learning to navigate by terrain reference without compasses. Men experienced in operations behind

---

*The descriptions of the combat actions in this chapter are much more detailed than in previous chapters, which generally avoided tactical-level discussions. Special-purpose forces, however, despite their strategic- and operational-level missions, are normally tactical in size and method of employment. Such is the case in this historical example. Additionally, well-documented accounts of Soviet special operations from World War II are rare in the Western military press. These actions, therefore, merit the fullest possible exposure and discussion.

**Otdelnyi gvardeiskii batalon minerov.*

German lines were chosen to be the Communist Party and Komsomol leaders in companies and platoons. Their task was to ensure that each soldier was psychologically prepared to operate away from friendly forces, to endure physical and mental stress, and to be prepared for any sacrifice in order to accomplish the mission. Physical conditioning emphasized carrying heavy loads and fighting in hand-to-hand combat. In essence, all training exercises attempted to foster teamwork and comradeship among the soldiers.

In early September, Meretskov met with his chief of engineer troops, Lieutenant General A. F. Khrenov, and approved a plan for using special-purpose detachments to support the 14th Army's offensive.[5] The plan called for inserting three special-purpose detachments into the German rear before the offensive was launched (see map 13). These detachments were to reconnoiter the route of the follow-on light rifle corps, conduct uninterrupted reconnaissance of the enemy and terrain, and gain control over the roadnet. On initiation of the offensive, special-purpose troops would assist the main attack by disrupting enemy command, control, and communications; destroying men and equipment; mining roads; and demolishing bridges. Lieutenant General Khrenov personally approved the combat actions plan of each detachment.[6]

The first detachment to deploy was the 6th *OGBM*, minus one company, commanded by Guards Major A. F. Popov.[7] Most of the 133 men in the 6th carried submachine guns, four basic loads (600 rounds) of ammunition, and hand grenades. Additionally, the detachment carried 3 light machine guns, 3 sniper rifles with 600 rounds for each, explosives and fuses, 130 antitank mines, 10 delayed-action mines, 2 radios with 2 supplies of batteries for each, flare guns, medical supplies, and individual rations for 17 days. The average equipment load for each soldier in the detachment was 42 kilograms (92 pounds).

Popov's detachment departed its assembly area behind the Soviet 14th Army's left flank at 1400 on 18 September and began the long march around the German right flank. Popov used a reinforced platoon for his advance guard, a squad per company for flank guards, and a platoon for the rear guard. He and his command group marched at the front of the main body. Communication between companies was maintained by runners and light signals, within companies and platoons by voice and flags. The formation moved two kilometers per hour over the swampy and rocky tundra, halting for ten minutes each hour to rest. Until they reached the Titovka River, the men moved during the day and rested at night.

On the fourth day, at 1300 on 21 September, the detachment crossed the Titovka River. Moving now at night to avoid detection, Popov and his men waded across the icy cold, chest-deep, fifty-meter-wide Petsamo River. On the night of 23–24 September, they reached Nikel Road, along which flowed a steady stream of German traffic. At 0400 on 24 September, the detachment rapidly rushed across this dangerous obstacle and moved quickly to the north. Popov led his men to a small stream in a wooded

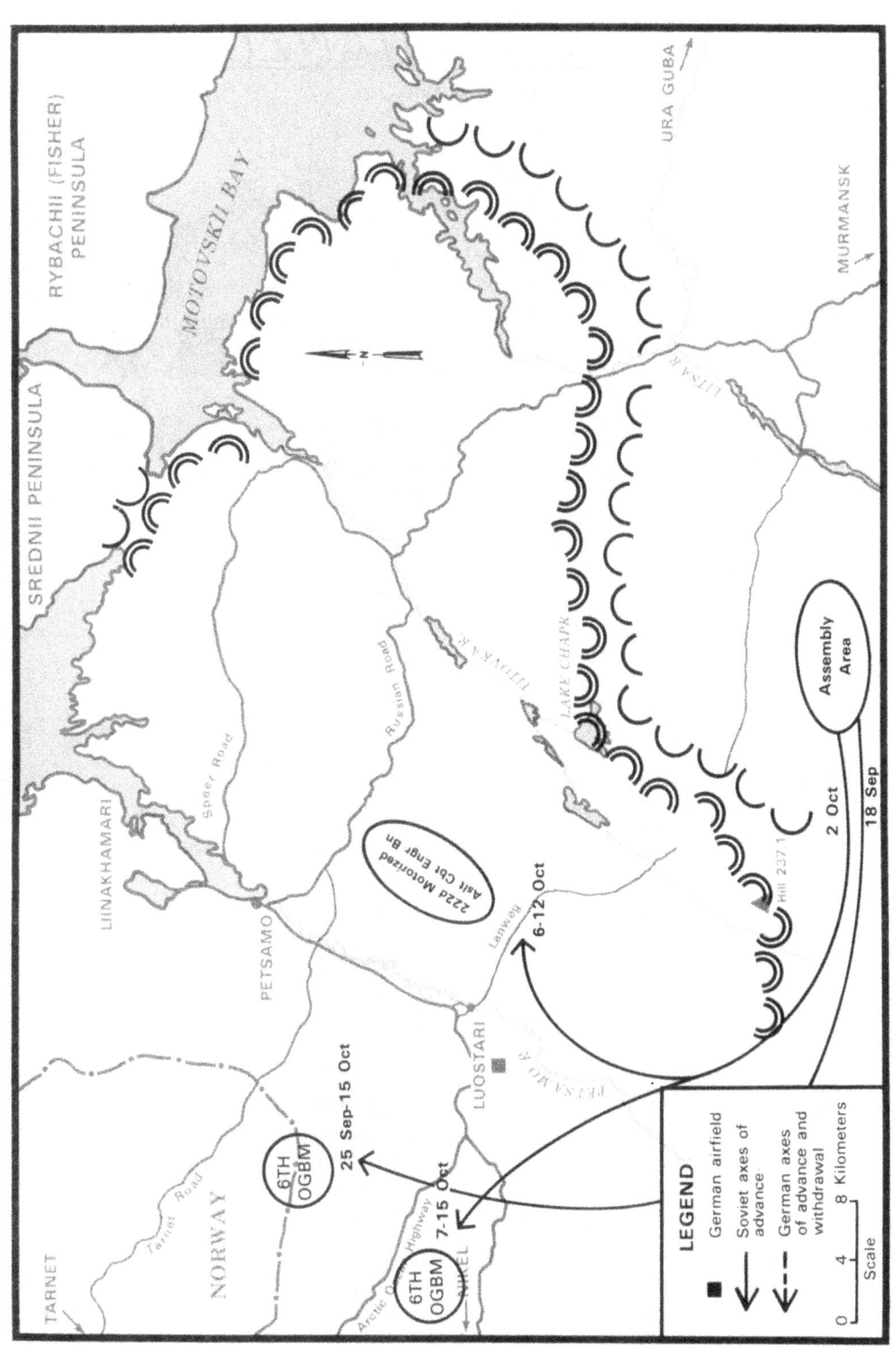

Map 13. 14th Army special-purpose actions

RUSSISCHER TARNANZUG

Russian Camouflage Suit

View of the hood with
the facial covering removed

Color: Olive green
    a) Camouflage tufts made from twigs
    b) Green mosquito net

A Soviet arctic camouflage suit, probably worn by Soviet snipers

Tarnet Road, built by Soviet prisoners of war in 1943

area near the Norwegian border, arriving on the morning of 25 September, and reported their arrival to Front headquarters by radio.

From this position, Popov's men conducted reconnaissance out as far as twenty-five kilometers, principally to Tarnet Road, Nikel Road, and Arctic Ocean Highway between Luostari and Akhmalakhti. His men studied traffic patterns and selected targets and ambush sites for subsequent combat actions. In the base camp, strict noise and light discipline was enforced. Not long after his arrival, Popov, to conserve rations, reduced portions to 50 percent. The frequent rain and snow showers kept the men wet and cold, which posed hazards to their health.

While Popov's detachment executed its reconnaissance mission, the remaining company of the 6th *OGBM* departed its assembly area on 2 October and moved toward its objective area northeast of Nikel. Led by Popov's deputy, Captain A. P. Kononenko, the 49-man detachment reached its operating base on the night of 7—8 October and established communications with the battalion's main force.

A third detachment, 108 men of the 222d Motorized Assault Combat Engineer Battalion, commanded by Major G. A. Gradov, also departed its assembly area on 2 October and, on 6 October, reached its objective area between Luostari and the Titovka River in the rear of the 2d Mountain

Division. This detachment of five platoons deployed along Lanweg and Russian Road.

Several hours before the 14th Army's attack on 7 October, all three special-purpose detachments received orders by radio to begin combat actions. A platoon of Gradov's 222d Battalion struck the first blow, attacking an isolated outpost of the 2d Mountain Division at 1900 on 6 October, fourteen kilometers east of Luostari on Lanweg.[8]

Popov's detachment also went into action quickly. His first priority was to destroy the wire communications between the German rear area and frontline units, thus forcing the enemy units to use the radio and, under the intense pressure of combat, use noncoded text. Second, he was to destroy the bridges on all three roads controlled by his battalion. On the night of 6—7 October, Popov's detachment deployed in three groups, one to each road, and destroyed communications wire, blew up bridges, and planted mines. After all three groups had returned to base by dawn on 7 October, Major Popov reported to Front headquarters and then moved his base camp several kilometers to the west.

The cold, rainy weather and rough terrain were extracting a heavy toll on Popov's men. Weakened by exhaustion, hunger, and cold, forty could no longer fight and were sent back toward Soviet lines. The remaining ninety-plus men continued their nightly raids. A sabotage group blew up the bridge at Kilometer 28 of Tarnet Road, destroying one truck, and damaged a bridge and destroyed several power-line poles at Kilometer 486 (west of Luostari before the road fork) of Arctic Ocean Highway.[9]

On the night of 7—8 October, Captain Kononenko's unit made its first raid along the road several kilometers east of Nikel. In this attack, his troops took out several hundred meters of telephone line and planted mines that later destroyed two German fuel trucks. By 10 October, the Twentieth Army headquarters had identified Major Popov's battalion and knew its general location. Recorded in a German war diary are reports of the "employment of a 150—200 man element with a sabotage mission in the area between the Eismeer Strasse [Arctic Ocean Highway] and the Tarnet-Kirkenes road," which succeeded in disrupting traffic along the main supply routes in the area. The diary later specifically identified one sabotage group as an element of the "6th Independent Guards Detachment (Sabotage)."[10]

Major Gradov and his five platoons of the 222d Battalion continued to attack isolated German units and positions in front of the advancing 99th and 131st Rifle Corps, rejoining the main force on 12 October, the day Luostari was captured. In six separate attacks, Gradov's men destroyed 3,600 meters of telephone line, blew up two bridges, and killed over 150 German soldiers; Gradov's unit suffered only three lightly wounded.[11]

Major Popov's 6th *OGBM* continued its operations against retreating German columns. On the nights of 11—14 October, low-flying aircraft delivered urgently needed supplies of food, ammunition, and warm clothing to Popov's men. As the encirclement of the German right flank and the capture of Luostari on 12 October began to force the Germans to withdraw

Wreckage of a German staff car along Tarnet Road

into Norway toward Tarnet, Popov increased his attacks along Tarnet Road. His men stopped traffic at numerous defiles and streams with mines and demolitions and, on more than one occasion, directed air strikes against concentrations of German units. General Jodl, commander of the XIX Mountain Corps, recorded that, on 13 October, the 6th Mountain Division had to deploy combat elements against the Soviet 6th Guards Special Engineer Detachment, which had occupied a sector of road.[12]

After a final successful attack along Tarnet Road on 15 October, in which his troops expended all their ammunition, Major Popov led his entire battalion back into Soviet positions, which by then were west of Petsamo and Luostari. In eight days of active combat, Popov's battalion had destroyed more than eleven kilometers of telephone wire, four bridges, and large amounts of German equipment and troops. His battalion's losses were only four wounded and two missing in action.[13]

In analyzing the Karelian Front's employment of special-purpose units, it is important to realize that the use of sabotage troops behind German lines was nothing new or extraordinary. Soviet troops had been conducting raids and reconnaissance in German rear areas since the first weeks of the war back in 1941. By mid-1944, the Soviet unconventional war against the German Army was extremely well organized and played a significant role in all major Soviet offensive operations. However, the employment of special-purpose detachments for rear area combat was distinctly different in the arctic region. The weather and terrain were severe; the terrain provided almost no cover and concealment; and no indigenous civilians were available to provide logistic, intelligence, or partisan support.

The combat experience of the 6th *OGBM* and the 222d Motorized Assault Combat Engineer Battalion in special operations prior to autumn 1944 is unknown. However, that they were engineer-based units and reported to the Front chief of engineer troops, not the intelligence staff, is significant. Since they were trained to strike enemy troops and installations, their reconnaissance skills were important, but mainly for acquiring targets for immediate destruction. Engineer troops, more so than the infantry, were likely to have the individual and collective skills and equipment necessary for demolitions work. Furthermore, ordinary engineer units could have provided a plentiful supply of trained manpower for special-purpose units.

Not only were these special-purpose detachments well trained, but their plan of action was well executed. The method of insertion—walking—although slow, was probably the most secure, and it served the additional purpose of reconnoitering a route for the important follow-on force, the 126th Light Rifle Corps. The selection of an operating base adjacent to Norwegian territory and continuous reconnaissance and combat activities on Norwegian territory *prior to* 18 October, when Meretskov received permission to send conventional forces across the border into Norway, indicates that military requirements for unconventional warfare took precedence over political sensitivities. It cannot be determined from available sources if the Karelian Front commander had to gain approval from *STAVKA* to deploy special-purpose forces into Norway.

Disregarding the time required for the deepest-penetrating detachment to reach its position (Major Popov's group), the Soviet special-purpose units were functioning forty to fifty kilometers deep in German-occupied territory for twelve days before the main offensive. Although the Soviet troops moved about only at night and hid during the day, they reported their actions to Front headquarters by regular radio transmissions, two per day before 7 October and every two hours thereafter. That the Soviets avoided German detection for such a long period of time in terrain known for its lack of cover says much about the Soviets' excellent camouflage and movement security and also about the poor German rear area security. To be willing to place 133 men so deep behind enemy lines almost two weeks before an offensive attests to the Front headquarters' confidence in their military skills and their political reliability, which was just as important for soldiers of the special-purpose units.

In terms of depth, the special-purpose detachments operated in a broad zone that extended from the German regimental rear to corps rear, from eight to fifty kilometers behind the front line. Their reconnaissance and combat activities were directed more at communications and transportation facilities and targets than at combat forces. However, if they did come upon an unsecured artillery battery, the special-purpose troops would not hesitate to attack. Also, on a few occasions, these detachments would occupy a piece of key terrain and then would repulse a German unit seeking to use the same terrain without first conducting its own reconnaissance.

The employment of special-purpose forces in support of the ground offensive was extremely effective. In terms of their mission, they reconnoitered the route for the 126th Light Rifle Corps and conducted continuous reconnaissance of the enemy and terrain. Their control of the roadnet was never total but certainly adequate considering the hardships imposed by cold, wet weather; rough terrain; and a formidable enemy. German war diary accounts do not contain sufficient evidence to validate or refute the claims made in Soviet sources about the quantities of German troops, equipment, and installations killed or damaged. But that reports of Soviet special-purpose force actions appeared at all in Twentieth Army records is testimony to the German commanders' concern for this unanticipated and unwelcome battle in their rear area.

Two Soviet commanders praised the special-purpose units highly. Lieutenant General Khrenov, the chief of engineer troops in the Karelian Front, wrote the following in 1982:

> Of course, these forms of combat behind the front line did not determine the success of the offensive. But I have considered it my duty to write about the sapper-scouts in order to more fully expose this little-known type of activity of engineer troops, which demanded special moral-combat qualities and permitted the inflicting on the enemy of great losses with small forces.[14]

Marshal Meretskov, the Karelian Front commander, expressed similar thoughts:

> From these detachments was gained valuable information, which kept the command informed of changes that were occurring in the enemy's defenses. In addition, the sappers controlled the roads, blew up bridges, and destroyed telephone lines, causing disorder in the work of German rear services. Finally, on more than one occasion, they directed our close air and bomber aviation to concentrations of enemy troops.[15]

Naval Special Operations

During the planning for Northern Fleet support to the 14th Army's ground offensive, the Main Naval Staff in Moscow ordered Admiral Golovko to reestablish a Soviet naval base at Petsamo.[16] Pursuant to this order, Golovko's staff began to plan an amphibious landing at Liinakhamari, the small port north of Petsamo on the west shore of Petsamo Bay. A battery of four German 150-mm guns, positioned on the northern shore of Cape Krestovyi, controlled the entrance to the bay (see map 14). For the main landing force to succeed, these guns had to be neutralized.

To accomplish this task, the fleet assembled a composite force of naval infantrymen and sailors from the Northern Defensive Region reconnaissance detachment, commanded by Captain I. P. Barchenko-Emelianov, and the Northern Fleet reconnaissance detachment, commanded by Senior Lieutenant V. N. Leonov. An experienced naval infantryman, Barchenko-Emelianov had

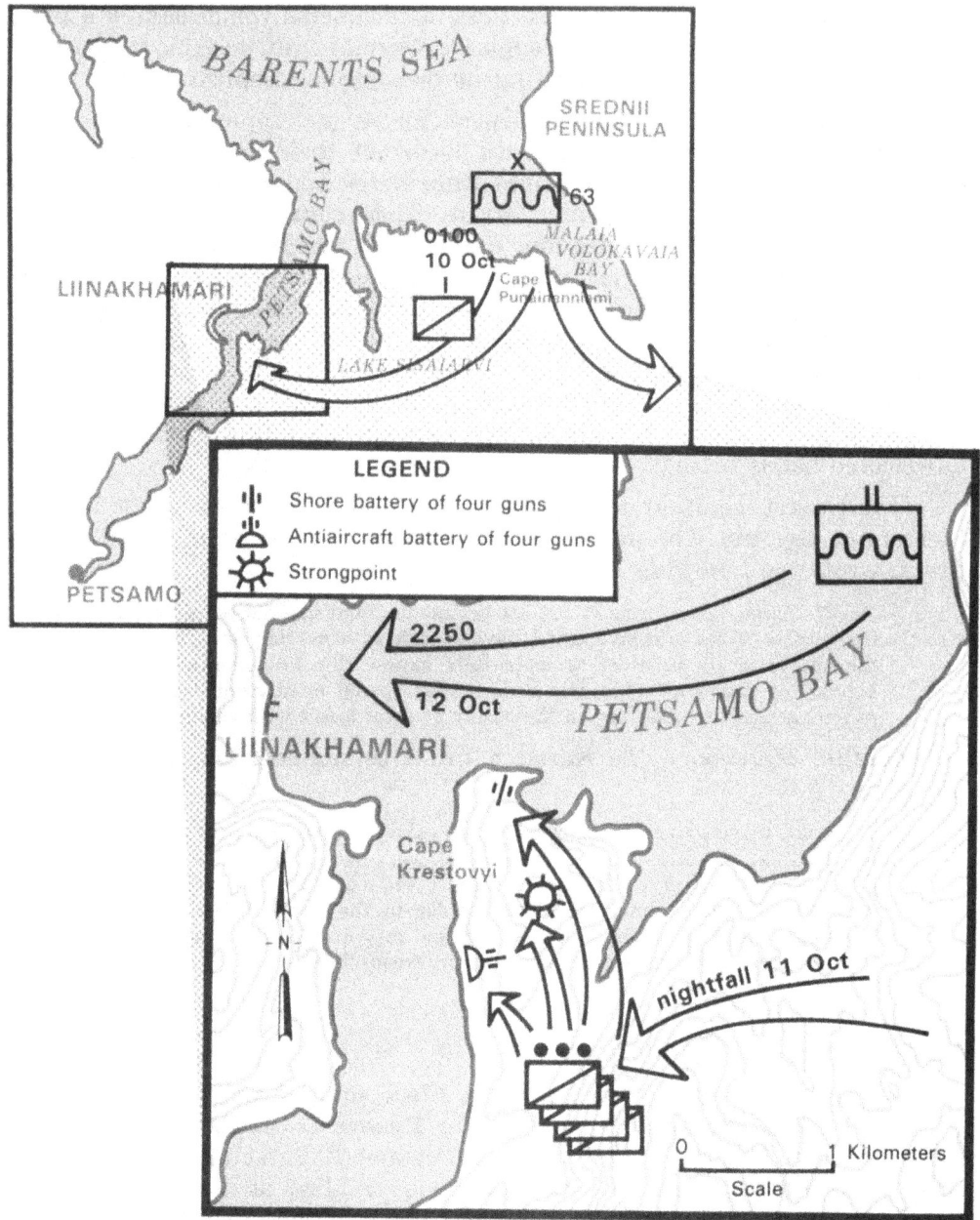

Map 14. Krestovyi raid, 11—12 October 1944

served in reconnaissance units of the 12th Naval Infantry Brigade in the Murmansk area since November 1941. In June 1943, he took command of the Northern Defensive Region reconnaissance detachment, a collection of naval infantrymen who were veteran scouts of many reconnaissance and raid operations against German units and positions along the coast of occupied Finnish and Soviet territory.[17]

Hero of the Soviet Union, Captain I. P. Barchenko-Emelianov, commander of the reconnaissance detachment of Headquarters, Northern Defensive Region

Leonov, on the other hand, and most of his detachment were sailors, volunteers from the several surface and submarine units of the Northern Fleet. Having participated in many operations behind German lines on Soviet, Finnish, and Norwegian territory, the detachment had a distinguished combat record dating back to its creation in July 1941 by Admiral Golovko.[18] Leonov, himself a veteran of submarine service, came to the detachment in the late summer of 1941. Courage and leadership displayed in battle earned him a promotion to officer rank in late 1942 and to commander of the detachment in late 1943.[19]

As commander of the composite detachment, Barchenko-Emelianov received his first specific mission statement on 11 September when Leonov and his men joined the composite unit.[20] Other attachments included a team of artillerymen from the 113th Separate Artillery Battalion, a group of combat engineers from the 338th Separate Combat Engineer Battalion, and an unspecified number of medics and radio operators—a total strength of 195 men. For the next four weeks, the composite detachment trained and rehearsed its mission at Rybachii Peninsula, which had terrain similar to Cape Krestovyi's. The detachment's final preparations included coordinating with the naval aviators who would later support them.

Twice Hero of the Soviet Union, Senior Lieutenant V. N. Leonov, commander of the reconnaissance detachment of Headquarters, Northern Fleet (shown here after his first award)

On the evening of 9 October, the composite detachment boarded two small subchasers and a torpedo cutter. This raiding party, as part of a larger force of approximately 30 vessels and 2,800 men, approached the German-held southern shore of Malaia Volokovaia Bay. While the main force, the 63d Naval Infantry Brigade, landed and attacked to the south and east, the composite detachment of raiders were to land and march to the southwest. After breaking off from the main force, these three small ships reached Cape Punainenniemi, their designated landing area, at 0100 on 10 October. Under cover of darkness and a smoke screen, and despite enemy shore battery fire aided by searchlights, the detachment got ashore with no personnel casualties and the loss of only one of its five radios. Once established on shore, it reported its status to fleet headquarters and then began the cross-country march (see map 14).

Moving undetected was difficult because the terrain in this region was sparsely vegetated, rocky, mountainous, and interspersed with streams and lakes. Elevations of over 1,000 feet were found 2 to 3 kilometers inland from the Barents Sea. On the night of 9—10 October 1944, during and after the landing, the temperature hovered around freezing, with a strong wind blowing in from the sea. The group moved inland that night in a snowstorm that had turned to rain by morning. So as not to be detected easily and to blend in with the grey-brown surroundings, the men removed their white camouflage smocks.

All day on 10 October, the men hid in rock caves and only moved again at dusk. At daybreak on 11 October, Captain Barchenko-Emelianov hid his men in a growth of bushes at the southern end of Lake Sisaiarvi. In eighteen hours, they had marched just fifteen kilometers. After a rest period, they continued to move at twilight. By nightfall, they had reached a spur on Petsamo Bay, from which they could observe the silhouette of their target, Cape Krestovyi. Beyond the cape, they could see the port of Liinakhamari across the bay. The men were standing at the top of a vertical cliff, from which their descent took six hours.

The plan for the Cape Krestovyi assault was simple (see map 14). Leonov's 95-man group would assault the battery of four 88-mm antiaircraft guns sited on a gentle slope on the southern portion of the cape. Two of Barchenko-Emelianov's platoons would attack and seize the strongpoint located 300 meters north of the flak battery. This position in the center of the cape guarded the landward approaches to the 150-mm coastal battery. His remaining platoon would storm the four-gun shore battery located at the water's edge on the northernmost shore of the cape.

After a brief leaders' orientation, which included an oral order, the three elements moved off into the darkness to await the attack signal. It is unclear whether the attackers or the startled German defenders fired the signal rocket that triggered the assault.[21] In either case, the Soviets had the element of surprise. Leonov's men were crawling through the barbed wire forty to fifty meters from the 88-mm guns when the rocket went up, followed by German-fired illumination. Leonov and his men quickly breached the barbed wire and assaulted the bunkers and, in hand-to-hand combat, killed or drove off the crews, seizing the four-gun battery. Leonov's detachment spent the rest of the night fending off numerous German counterattacks, his attached artillerymen firing the captured guns.

Platoons commanded by two naval infantry lieutenants also quickly overwhelmed the German defenders in the strongpoint. German survivors from both the flak battery and strongpoint positions withdrew singly and in groups northward along the cape into the 150-mm battery positions. While Barchenko-Emelianov was establishing his command post in the strongpoint position, his remaining platoon was assaulting the by-now fully alerted 150-mm shore battery position. Well-dug-in Germans in bunkers and trenches behind barbed wire repulsed Soviet attempts to take the battery from the landward side. The Soviets sent an element around the western flank to attack along the rocky shore, but this group was driven back by the incoming tide. According to one Soviet source, the besieged Germans began to destroy their own guns, while Leonov contends that these same guns were firing against his men in support of a German counterattack.[22] Unable at this time to either capture or destroy the guns, Barchenko-Emelianov reported the situation to his headquarters.

At dawn on 12 October, the Germans remaining on the cape regrouped and launched a counterattack. According to German war diary entries, as well as Soviet sources, these counterattacks were supported by German troops sent across the harbor in assault boats.[23] All available German indirect-fire support assets were also directed against the Soviet raiding force, thus resulting in serious casualties. Outnumbered and unable to hold the flak battery positions, Leonov withdrew his men to a nearby hill. To render the 88-mm guns inoperable, the artillerymen removed and took the breechblocks with them.

As the counterattacking Germans approached the strongpoint position where Barchenko-Emelianov and his detachment were holding out, on-call Soviet naval aviation assets came in and restored the situation. In the course of four hours, Northern Fleet pilots delivered ten air strikes and several parachute containers of ammunition and provisions.[24] In addition, Soviet ground artillery from Srednii Peninsula conducted counterbattery fire throughout the day, helping to defeat several German counterattacks.

By midday on 12 October, the Soviet positions in the center of the cape were secure enough for Barchenko-Emelianov to give Leonov one platoon plus two squads to bolster Leonov's position overlooking the flak battery. With these reinforcements, Leonov and his men counterattacked. By dusk, they had retaken the position and the adjacent shore, depriving the Germans of the ability to reinforce on that flank.[25] Some isolated groups of Germans were captured, while others found their way northward to the shore battery position. By nightfall, except for an occasional burst of gunfire, the area was quiet.

At about 2000, Barchenko-Emelianov received a radio message that an amphibious landing force would assault the Liinakhamari harbor in three hours. Between 2250 and 2400 on 12 October, approximately 600 men landed in three waves from eight torpedo cutters and six subchasers.[26] By all accounts, this landing force was detected, illuminated, and fired on by several German shore batteries. The key battery on Cape Krestovyi did not engage the amphibious landing force, either because its guns had been destroyed or it was preoccupied with Barchenko-Emelianov's renewed assaults. All Soviet accounts credit the success of the landings in the harbor to the raiders' actions.[27]

During the night of 12—13 October, the raiders were reinforced by a company from the 63d Naval Infantry Brigade that had participated in the night landing of 9—10 October. These men came in overland from the east. An additional platoon came ashore from a disabled cutter. Before dawn on 13 October, Barchenko-Emelianov selected a German officer from among his prisoners and sent him into the shore battery position with a surrender demand. After some delay, the garrison of seventy-eight officers and men surrendered.

The detachment spent the day of 13 October looking after the prisoners and captured equipment. That night, the entire detachment was taken across the bay into Liinakhamari to assist in the mopping-up actions, which were completed by midday on 14 October. In three days of battle for Krestovyi and Liinakhamari, the detachments of Senior Lieutenant Leonov and Captain

Leonov with his men after the raid on Cape Krestovyi

Barchenko-Emelianov lost fifty-three men killed and wounded, or 27 percent of their 195-man force. Barchenko-Emelianov, Leonov, and two enlisted men were awarded the gold star and title of Hero of the Soviet Union.

The raid by naval special-purpose forces against the German positions on Cape Krestovyi was not an unusual event. Both reconnaissance detachments that combined to execute the Krestovyi raid were experienced, having conducted similar attacks on other enemy objectives throughout 1941—44.

Several aspects of the mission are worth noting, however. The two units came together, along with their attachments, about thirty days prior to their commitment. They trained and rehearsed on terrain specially chosen for its similarity to the objective. The insertion of the force onto the enemy shore was cleverly masked by the much larger brigade-size landing to the east. The composite detachment walked the extremely difficult route to the objective area. Although physically demanding and time-consuming, this was perhaps the only way to reach the target and maintain the advantage of surprise.

Often, in special operations, small-unit commanders have only as much information as they need to accomplish their immediate tasks. Barchenko-Emelianov undoubtedly knew that an amphibious landing was planned at Liinakhamari, but his superiors communicated to him the actual time of the amphibious assault only three to four hours before it occurred. Had the raid failed and he or Leonov been captured, the Germans would have gained little of immediate intelligence value from them.

The chain of command from Barchenko-Emelianov to the fleet commander passed through a single intermediate headquarters, the Northern Defensive Region, commanded by Major General E. T. Dubovtsev. This headquarters was responsible for the raiders' artillery support. The aerial resupply and close air support, meanwhile, came from the Northern Fleet commander's assets. Admiral Golovko personally monitored the progress of the raid and met with the surviving members of the composite detachment in the dock area of Liinakhamari on the day after that small port village was captured.

The raid on Cape Krestovyi was the last combat action of the war for Barchenko-Emelianov's naval infantry reconnaissance detachment. Leonov and his men made a final journey to Varanger Peninsula in the closing days of October, where they were welcomed as liberators. The Krestovyi raid remains an outstanding example of the maturity in planning, training, organizing, and executing of special operations by Soviet naval personnel in the latter stages of World War II.

Conclusions 7

Strategic and Operational Planning

At the strategic level, Soviet sources do not indicate that the Petsamo-Kirkenes Operation was timed to coincide with any other offensive being conducted on the Soviet-German front. The rationale for the timing of this offensive seems to be related primarily to events occurring in this somewhat isolated theater of war, beginning with the spring 1944 Soviet decision to attack the Finnish Army. Having thus committed the bulk of the maneuver units of the Karelian Front to the offensive in southern Karelia in June, General Meretskov could not have hoped to begin a large-scale offensive anywhere else in his Front until troops became available again. For this reason, given the time required to reposition forces from southern Karelia to the Murmansk area, the Petsamo-Kirkenes Operation could not have begun much earlier than 7 October.

General Meretskov could have waited until winter when the ground would be frozen and perhaps more suitable for cross-country maneuver. However, given the presence of so many water obstacles and the nature of the soil and topography, it is questionable whether winter weather would have made the terrain any more trafficable. Also, with harsh winter weather came other problems, namely, the survivability of the force in subzero temperatures and the continuous limited visibility due to the polar night.

Whether *STAVKA* or General Meretskov considered these problems is not known, but it is certain they looked at the political and military situation. Although Meretskov did not know the intentions of the German command after Finland's exit from the war, he believed that, sooner or later, Germany would have to withdraw its forces from northern Finland. It was his desire that these forces not depart "unpunished," and so, he wanted to attack them as soon as possible.[1] *STAVKA*, on the other hand, perhaps not aware of German plans to withdraw into Norway under Operation Nordlicht, was convinced that the Germans intended to remain in the Petsamo area and, therefore, could reinforce XIX Mountain Corps for another push toward Murmansk.[2] In addition, the Soviet government had the desire, though unstated, to occupy that portion of Finnish territory adjacent to Norway, which the Germans had used in 1941 as a springboard into Soviet territory. This strip included the port of Petsamo, as well as the strategically important nickel mine to the southwest.

In all the strategic considerations, it does not appear that the Soviet government gave any serious forethought to the occupation of Norwegian territory. The Soviets' subsequent occupation seems to have been undertaken primarily for the military objectives. The designation of the Arctic Ocean Highway and Nikel Road area as the main axis in phase two and that Soviet forces left Norway in October 1945 of their own volition, leaving the border as it had been for the past 140 years, support this conclusion.

N. M. Rumiantsev, the author of an in-depth study of the Petsamo-Kirkenes Operation, labeled it as "a Frontal operation of strategic significance," citing the isolation of the arctic axis, as well as the combined employment of air, ground, and fleet forces.[3] In a 1963 review of Rumiantsev's book, Marshal Meretskov agreed with this assessment.[4] That Soviet military historians still consider this to have been an operation of strategic significance was made manifestly clear in 1986—87 when *Voenno-istoricheskii Zhurnal* (Military History Journal), the Soviet Ministry of Defense's official historical publication, published a series of articles defining "strategic" operations of the Great Patriotic War.[5] Though challenged by readers, the editors of the journal affirmed this operation as strategic, stating that "important military-political and strategic goals were accomplished as a result of its conduct." The editors also emphasized the importance of the use of naval forces.[6]

This labeling of the operation as strategic is more than a petty argument among historians. Given the current and future importance of both the military and economic infrastructures in the Murmansk area and the proximity of Norway, a NATO partner, any future military operations in the Murmansk area will be strategically important and will be planned and controlled at the Soviet government's highest level. Without question, naval as well as land forces will be involved.

STAVKA also influenced the planning for this offensive at the operational level. The principal weakness of the Soviet operational plan was the *STAVKA*-imposed delay of the initial amphibious landing and cross-isthmus attack of the Northern Fleet's ground forces. Meretskov originally had proposed that these naval infantry attacks be conducted simultaneously with his land offensive. As it turned out, the naval ground forces' entry into the battle came approximately thirty hours after German units on that flank were given permission to withdraw. This operational plan prevented Golovko's naval infantry from encircling the German left flank.

Also, the operational plan made no provision for pursuing the German forces into Norway, which was an entirely foreseeable event. It is to Meretskov's credit that he and his subordinate army and corps commanders were able to react quickly to the developing situation and divert three corps toward Kirkenes in the second and third phases of the operation. And while he made no plan to pursue German forces into Norway, Meretskov did not hesitate to allow his special-purpose units to use Norwegian territory for their activities. This was consistent with the Soviet practice of sending naval ground reconnaissance groups into Norway as far back as 1941 to reconnoiter German installations and naval vessel movement.

Notwithstanding these faults, the operational plan was exceptional in concentrating overwhelming combat power on a narrow breakthrough sector.[7] Lieutenant General Shcherbakov, the 14th Army commander, had two rifle corps, with a total of four divisions in their first echelons, attacking against a single German division. This German division was defending a zone fifteen kilometers wide with a single regiment forward of the Titovka River and the second regiment behind the river. In effect, each German battalion along the strongpoint line was defending against a Soviet force of greater than division strength. With this kind of superiority, it is no surprise that the Soviets achieved a breakthrough so quickly.

According to Rumiantsev, the plan's designation of a single breakthrough sector had several advantages. It facilitated joint operations with the Northern Fleet's ground forces, targeted the enemy's weakness, and provided the shortest path to the enemy's lines of communication. The allocation of a rifle corps with two divisions to the army second echelon allowed for the possibility of a major counterattack to the Soviet right flank by the 6th Mountain Division, as well as the retention of a relatively fresh force that could be committed after the breakthrough.[8]

At corps level, evidence suggests that corps commanders and staffs without experience in arctic combat initially developed unrealistic plans. For example, Lieutenant General Mikulskii's 99th Rifle Corps had arrived in the Murmansk area straight from combat in the forests of southern Karelia just days before the offensive began. By Mikulskii's own admission, he and his staff did not understand how the arctic terrain could affect operations. Consequently, they planned to employ tanks and artillery just as they would have on ordinary terrain.[9] The lesson here is that commanders who are earmarked for arctic deployment should study arctic war experience or, even better, conduct terrain walks or staff rides on arctic terrain.

Soviet Command and Control

The Soviet command and control system was extremely complex. Meretskov, a former chief of staff of the Red Army, who had commanded an active Front throughout the entire war and whom Stalin personally regarded as a reliable and competent general, still had to have *STAVKA* approve his operational plan. Admiral Golovko operated in two chains of command. He received operational guidance and orders from *STAVKA* and also administrative support and orders from the Main Naval Staff in Moscow. General Sokolov, the 7th Air Army commander, also worked for two bosses. His operational orders came from his immediate superior, General Meretskov, and his administrative guidance and orders on training, personnel, maintenance, and other support issues came from the Main Air Staff in Moscow. To further complicate matters, at Front and below, there were both common and special staffs whose tentacles reached down into subordinate staffs at each level, wielding considerable authority.

Since this complex system had been developed over time and had been tested and proven in battle, it functioned rationally. In fact, the command and control of large-scale offensives, much larger than the Petsamo-Kirkenes Operation, had reached a high level of proficiency by this stage in the war. Even the difficulties imposed by the arctic terrain and weather did not severely degrade the ground operational command and control of this battle. The glue that held the whole system together and made it effective was the personal trust of patrons (the Soviet commanders) and clients (their subordinate commanders and staff officers). This trust had developed over many years, with personal relationships often dating back to the Russian Civil War (1918—22). Meretskov, for example, surrounded himself with commanders and staff officers he had served with when he commanded the 7th Army during the war with Finland in 1939—40 and the Volkhov Front in 1942—44.

Meretskov, as an energetic Front commander, established his forward command post on 7 October only fifteen kilometers behind the lead elements of the attacking forces on the main axis. During the battle, he frequently visited corps or division command posts to check on the execution of his plans and orders. Consequently, this tendency to personally supervise subordinates traveled down the chain of command. Lieutenant General Shcherbakov, the 14th Army commander, moved his command post to the main axis and transmitted oral or written orders to his subordinates on the average of one every twenty-four to forty-eight hours. Corps command posts were located within the sound of the battle, generally six to twelve kilometers behind the battle area, and corps commanders gave daily oral orders to division commanders, either in person or over the telephone, followed later by written orders. Division observation posts were well forward, often with the lead rifle regiment. This close proximity of senior commanders to the battle enabled them to see the terrain on which their units were advancing, ascertain the physical status of their units, and judge the effectiveness of their plans and orders.

In sharp contrast, the command post of Lieutenant General Degen, commander of the 2d Mountain Division, was on the west side of the Titovka River, several kilometers behind his division's forward edge. General Jodl, the XIX Mountain Corps commander, ran the battle from his command post at Petsamo, some thirty kilometers distant from the most threatened sector. Colonel General Rendulic, the Twentieth Army commander, visited the battlefield only once, about a week into the offensive, and then only to meet with his corps and division commanders. The edge in generalship clearly belonged to the Soviets.

Even though the Soviet command and control system was complex, it repeatedly demonstrated adaptability and flexibility. For example, at Front level, the operational plan rapidly changed to accommodate pursuit of German forces into Norway. At army level, Shcherbakov, on 8 October, abandoned his plan to have engineers construct a road on the axis of each rifle corps in the main attack and ordered that a single road be built to connect existing Soviet and German roads. Frequently, in reaction to either the enemy situation or to higher orders, commanders at corps level changed the task organizations of divisions and special units, such as engineer and armored forces. Examples include the 8 October exchange of rifle divisions between the 99th and 131st Rifle Corps, the breakup of Group Pigarevich on 15 October and resubordination of its combat elements to other corps, the redirection of armored units from a single axis to three axes after 15 October, and the substitution of a rifle regiment for the 126th Light Rifle Corps' mission on 23—24 October.

Not discussed in any Soviet source is the one major command change that occurred during the operation. On 23 October, as the 131st Rifle Corps approached Kirkenes from the Tarnet area, Major General Alekseev was replaced by one of his division commanders.[10] His corps, which had performed well in the breakthrough, was on the army secondary axis. Its advance toward Kirkenes from the east was not unduly slow considering the stiff opposition and the difficult terrain. It is noteworthy that, even though the change occurred, the 131st, along with the 99th Rifle Corps, successfully pressed its attack and captured Kirkenes on 25 October.[11]

Unreliable communications and inaccurate maps also created serious command and control problems that often contributed to disorder and uncoordinated actions at both the operational and tactical levels. Once the offensive was launched, wire communications were largely abandoned, and radios had to be used. Unfortunately, because of atmospheric interference, radios frequently did not work. According to Rumiantsev, radio messages were transmitted in uncoded text, using a map reference point system, instead of a preplanned complex system of codes. Because of the uncertainty of radio communications, army headquarters could not always communicate with one or both of the light rifle corps, and conventional rifle corps headquarters could not always communicate to subordinate divisions.[12] The lack of accurate maps frequently interfered with operations by not correctly reflecting the terrain. This prevented units from pinpointing their precise location in reports to higher headquarters and further led to difficulties in adjusting air and artillery fire support and in coordinating cross-country maneuvers and attacks by flanking detachments.

To mitigate these problems, the Soviet commanders attempted to place themselves as close to their subordinate commanders and units as possible. Other obvious remedies to these problems would have been to establish redundant communications systems and to ensure that map rooms were stocked with the most recent and accurate maps available.

Combat Forces

Given the tremendous hardships imposed on the Soviets by the terrain and weather, the performance of Soviet combat units was generally good. Regular infantry units were employed in frontal assaults up steep slopes defended by entrenched German mountain troops, while other Soviet regiments attacked the same positions from the flank or rear. In this way, Soviet tactics mirrored the operational scheme of maneuver, wherein large formations conducted a frontal attack while light rifle corps and naval infantry units attacked from the flanks and rear. On the third day of the battle, as the forces on the main axis crossed the Titovka River, the infantrymen fought with less and less ammunition and fire support against German units whose lines were shortening. Soviet units frequently moved or attacked at night on terrain that was difficult to traverse even in daylight.

Of all the Soviet units, the light infantry had the most difficult task—to advance on axes without roads carrying all their food and ammunition as well as heavy weapons on pack animals. In all three phases of the operation, both light rifle corps were assigned similar missions—move around the flank of a German unit or position, block the main supply route, and hold it until the main force arrived. The 126th Light Rifle Corps successfully executed this mission from 7 to 12 October, blocking Arctic Ocean Highway behind the 2d Mountain Division west of Luostari. However, when the main force arrived in the area, the 126th Light Rifle Corps was split, and one brigade was sent northward to block Tarnet Road west of Petsamo.

The 127th Light Rifle Corps was less successful than the 126th during the first phase of the offensive. The 70th Naval Rifle Brigade, after an exhausting several-day trek over exceedingly difficult terrain, arrived in the objective area too weak to accomplish its mission. When the brigade finally approached Tarnet Road on 12 October, its troops had neither the physical strength nor the combat power to block the road. To survive, these men were forced to eat captured German supplies and their own animals.

Many questions about the 127th Light Rifle Corps remain unanswered. Where was the 69th Naval Rifle Brigade during 11—15 October? Was it available and employed against Tarnet Road, or did it remain in the Luostari area? Was an attempt made to resupply the 127th Light Rifle Corps by air, as was done with the 126th Light Rifle Corps? Was there any effort to employ close air support in conjunction with the ground attacks against Tarnet Road? Hopefully, these questions will be answered by the future publication of additional Soviet source materials. Even without these answers, it can be said with certainty that the failure of the two light infantry brigades to seal off Tarnet Road, when coupled with the planned delay of the amphibious landing and cross-isthmus attack by Northern Fleet forces, led to the failure of Soviet forces to encircle and destroy the XIX Mountain Corps, as was their goal.

In the second phase of the operation, an element of the 127th Light Rifle Corps, operating on the southern flank of the 31st Rifle Corps, reached the German main supply route southwest of Nikel. However, this element was destroyed because it had insufficient combat power to survive against a more mobile and powerful enemy. In the third phase of the operation, both light rifle corps were delayed due to logistic problems, and both were unable to coordinate their subsequent movement with the units they were to support in the main attacks.

Soviet light infantry units proved to be highly mobile, but the same mobility often took them out of the range of their supporting heavy artillery. It placed them in fighting positions where their lightness in combat power became a liability. The enemy was able to maneuver reserves quickly to counterattack or simply to apply greater force at the critical point.[13] In all phases of the operation, the cumulative effects of physical exhaustion, brought on by continuous movement and combat, and the inability to provide logistic sustainment seriously degraded the combat effectiveness of both light rifle corps.

Soviet analysts today recognize that helicopters and all-terrain vehicles have changed the way light forces will move, fight, and resupply on arctic terrain.[14] But even if the vehicles of war have changed since 1944, arctic weather and terrain have not. Proponents of light forces must always keep in mind these forces' inherent limitations, which over time considerably lowered their combat effectiveness in this operation.

Important to both the regular and light infantry was artillery support. According to the 29 September Front order, the artillery's first mission was to defeat the enemy's artillery, most of which was deployed on the reverse slopes of the 2d Mountain Division's strongpoints or in firing positions east of the Titovka River. The 2-hour and 35-minute artillery preparation was only partially effective in accomplishing this mission. Soviet sources attribute this failure to low weapons system density (only ninety-five guns and mortars per kilometer of breakthrough sector), poor reconnaissance of targets, and problems in observation and adjustment of fire caused by inclement weather. As a result, in some sectors, German artillery survived the Soviet artillery preparation, thus delaying the success of Soviet infantry attacks.[15]

Another artillery mission was to support the breakthrough and then the crossing of the Titovka River. Although Lieutenant General Mikulskii indicated an insufficiency of heavy artillery for this task, it was indeed accomplished from initial firing positions.[16] Also, the mix of artillery calibers was a problem. Over half of the approximately 2,100 tubes supporting the operation were mortars, and only 20 percent of the total was in calibers of 122-mm and above. Mortars were good at reaching reverse slopes and for supporting cross-country flanking movements, but their bursting effect was reduced by the soil type. Their shells could not penetrate the rocky soil and exploded harmlessly in swampy soil. In addition, their range was limited.

The most difficult mission for Soviet artillery units, not only early in the offensive but also in its latter two phases, was to support the infantry's attack into the intermediate German positions. Contributing to this problem was a shortage of accurate maps of the area of operations.[17] Also, due to unreliable communications, control and adjustment of fires was often poor. In many cases, because of a lack of trained observers in infantry units, area fire, rather than adjusted fire, was employed. To solve this problem, artillery commanders sent officers with their own radio sets out to supported units. In the closing phase of the operation, the Soviets also used small spotter planes to adjust fires.

However, the most serious obstacle to good artillery fire support to the infantry was mobility, both for the weapons systems and for the resupply of ammunition. Soviet artillery units did not displace from their initial firing positions until late on the third day of the offensive and, after crossing the Titovka River, were still unable to disperse across the width of the attack zone, all on account of the restricting terrain and the limited road network. Although terrain management (that is, the efficient use of ground suitable for multiple uses) became less of a problem after the capture of Petsamo, it remained extremely difficult to move gun units and ammunition because the retreating Germans had destroyed the roads.

Given the Soviets' experience in operating on this same terrain during the Soviet-Finnish War of 1939—40, it is difficult to understand why they did not foresee these terrain-related problems and plan for them. Equally difficult to rationalize is the Soviet predisposition for high tube densities. They attempted to compensate for lack of accuracy with mass, quantity replacing quality. Instead, the Soviets should have used fewer artillery pieces and organized, controlled, and supplied them more efficiently. In essence, in designing artillery packages to support combat on arctic terrain, artillery planners should seek to achieve some optimum balance between mobility of weapons systems, range, maximum target effect, and ammunition support.

The Soviet employment of armored vehicles in this operation did not have a great impact on the final outcome of the offensive, even though the Germans had no armored force. Tanks and self-propelled guns did not enter combat until 11 October, which was four days after the infantry had crossed the Titovka River. During the second and third phases of the offensive, armored units were employed on three separate road axes. But restricting terrain and the roads' poor condition limited armored units to an infantry support role in which they could advance on a frontage of only one or two vehicles.

Armored units suffered high combat and mobility losses, a reflection both of the German antitank defenses and the terrain. Due to the hardness of both the soil and the German positions, these units expended a higher than normal rate of main gun ammunition. Thanks to overwhelming Soviet air superiority, Soviet armored units were not particularly vulnerable to air attack as normally would be the case on arctic terrain. Despite these problems, current Soviet doctrine and force structure continue to reflect the employment of tanks in arctic regions. Although tanks can be employed in the Arctic, their value as a combat multiplier can be nullified by an opposing force physically and psychologically trained and equipped to fight against tanks.

Combat Support Operations

Lieutenant General Khrenov, commander of engineer troops in the Karelian Front, best expressed the Soviet attitude toward engineer support of offensive combat in special terrain conditions: "Absolutely untrafficable terrain does not exist. The degree of trafficability depends on the quality of engineer support."[18] Despite this attitude, however, and an enormous effort on the part of Soviet engineers, Lieutenant General Mikulskii, the 99th Rifle Corps commander, stated that "engineer support was the weakest aspect in the planning and preparation of the corps offensive."[19] This criticism can fairly be extended to the operation as a whole.

Much of the engineer work of developing the road network and preparing assembly areas in the area of operations was to have been accomplished during the summer of 1944. While the bulk of this work was indeed completed, Mikulskii recalls that, on 6 October, his men had to construct their own primitive shelters in their divisional and regimental assembly areas.[20]

In addition to constructing roads and assembly areas, engineer troops were to assist the infantry forces in the initial assault on German defensive positions. During the preparatory period, engineer units aided in the reconnaissance of the terrain by helping to determine the nature and strength of the fortifications, suitable terrain for the future construction of roads and paths, and possible crossing sites on the Titovka River. Again, according to Mikulskii, at least in his corps sector, these tasks were not performed well.

> Reconnaissance and study of the enemy defenses and terrain ... turned out to be inadequate. Data on the enemy, and especially about the character of his defensive works and their disposition on the terrain, was incomplete and inaccurate, as was made clear in the course of the battle.[21]

On the main axis, engineer troops were also to support the rapid forcing of water obstacles. Equipped with both light and heavy bridge sets and two battalions of amphibious vehicles, the Soviet engineers were generally able to construct or organize a crossing at any major obstacle, first for dismounted troops and then for vehicles. As the operation progressed, however, and the bridging equipment was consumed, Soviet engineers had to rely more on the use of amphibious vehicles and bridges made of wood. Timber, especially in the thicknesses required to construct heavy bridging, was in short supply. Some delays occurred at bridging sites, especially late in the operation, which slowed the tempo of the advance.

By far the most difficult task for engineer troops was the construction, repair, and maintenance of the roadnet. The 14th Army commander quickly abandoned his overly ambitious road construction plan and, instead, concentrated all engineer efforts on completing a single road through the breakthrough zone. In the first phase of the operation, a pattern was established that was repeated throughout the operation: second-echelon infantry units, up to division in strength, along with uncommitted artillery units, were used for engineer tasks.

During the second and third phases of the offensive, the principal engineer tasks were to clear and restore roads, tedious work considering the degree of destruction caused by German demolitions, the soil composition, and the lack of specialized equipment. According to Major General Absaliamov, the 31st Rifle Corps commander, this work proceeded at a rate of one kilometer of road per engineer battalion per 24-hour period.[22] In this offensive, the aggregate accomplishments of the Soviet engineer units, with significant infantry support, were considerable. Soviet engineers built 15 kilometers of road suitable for wheeled vehicles, 210 kilometers of tracks and paths, 33 temporary bridges of various lengths with a capacity of up to 16 tons, 20 bridges with a capacity of up to 60 tons, and 2 pontoon bridges and 3 assault bridges; organized 4 assault crossings; constructed 30 fords for armored vehicles; and cleared and restored nearly 500 kilometers of road, removing nearly 16,000 explosive devices totaling more than 50 tons of explosives.[23]

Despite these herculean efforts, the engineer forces were not able to sustain the tempo of the offensive. So many other aspects of the operation depended on the engineers. Armored vehicles could not keep pace with the infantry, towed artillery could not displace to new firing positions, and logistic vehicles could not make timely supply deliveries. Even the Soviets' allocation of two or three times the normal ratio of engineer units to maneuver units did not suffice.[24] In the Arctic, engineer units must also have special equipment and training for working on rough and difficult terrain.

During the course of the operation, Soviet air forces of the ground forces flew approximately 6,750 sorties.[25] Although a general Soviet air superiority of 6 to 1 did not guarantee local air superiority in every circumstance (due to the difference in weather patterns over respective airfields), close air support and air reconnaissance were important to the success of the ground offensive. On some days, when attacking infantry forces were out of range of their supporting artillery, close air support units were the infantry's only fire support.[26] On several occasions, the Soviet air forces also air-dropped ammunition and provisions to special-purpose and light infantry units and later provided supplies to the main force by landing at the captured Luostari airfield. Additionally, on return trips, almost 1,000 wounded soldiers were evacuated to Murmansk.[27]

Bad weather frequently hindered air operations. According to Absaliamov, "meteorological conditions severely limited the utilization of our aviation. This permitted the enemy to conduct an unobstructed retreat and to organize defenses at intermediate positions."[28] However, other problems existed as well. As the offensive moved westward, Soviet airfields became more distant from the battle, reducing time over target for close air support units. In addition, atmospheric electromagnetic disturbances interfered with radios and other electrical equipment, affecting navigation and command and control. Finally, the combination of topography and prevailing weather and light conditions greatly complicated visual orientation for flight crews. All these adverse conditions demanded special skills and experience in pilots and crews.

Given the developments since World War II in navigation, fire control, and communications systems, air operations are likely to play an even larger role in arctic operations now than in the past. But the problems of forward airfield construction, visual orientation, and reduced target effects due to soil composition remain. In the end, the side with air superiority will have not only an important combat multiplier but also a greater ability to employ helicopters for moving troops and supplies.

Soviet logistic support to the offensive was, despite Soviet claims to the contrary, poorly executed. Units began to run out of small-arms ammunition on the third day of the offensive and were forced to abandon a hard-won position, a situation that subsequently repeated itself several times. Moving artillery ammunition forward became more vexing with each day's advance, and as well, the problem of supplying ammunition and provisions to the light rifle corps operating away from road axes was never satisfactorily solved.[29]

The logistic problems resulted from both a shortage of transportation assets and the limited road network. For example, between the two rifle divisions in the 31st Rifle Corps, there were only sixty-two worn-out trucks. Of these, according to the corps commander, 20 to 30 percent were constantly down for repairs.[30] The situation at 14th Army was no better. Although there were enough trucks to haul twice the daily required rate of 800 tons, these vehicles were frequently down for repairs. Both the cold weather and the extremely bad roads caused engine failures or axle and suspension problems. One Soviet source calculates that one-third of the truck fleet underwent some type of repair during the operation.[31]

The road network, inadequate to begin with, was shared by both tracked and wheeled vehicles. Logistic and tactical units shared the same road. Each kilometer of westward advance added two kilometers to the round trip of a supply column. The distance from the 14th Army main supply point to forward units grew from 80 to 100 kilometers on 7 October to nearly 200 kilometers by 22 October.

The road problem also affected medical evacuation, since nearly all of 14th Army's casualties were transported to the rear by wheeled vehicles. Accordingly, as a result, 53 percent of the wounded arrived at a medical treatment facility six to twenty-four hours after being wounded, and 17 percent arrived after twenty-four hours.[32]

Also hampering logistic operations in this arctic offensive was the sparse civilian population from which to requisition large quantities of food, construction materials, petroleum products, or vehicles. The Soviet experience in the Petsamo-Kirkenes Operation clearly demonstrates that the degree of success or failure of military operations on arctic terrain will, in large part, be determined by the ability of logistic planners and operators to sustain the combat force.

Conclusion

According to General Meretskov's Front order, the mission of the 14th Army in phase one (7–15 October 1944) was to encircle the XIX Mountain Corps. Only Rumiantsev directly addresses why the 14th Army did not accomplish its mission: the 99th Rifle Corps' advance was too slow, mobility problems caused a lack of fire support and logistic support, units fighting in crucial sectors suffered severe ammunition shortages, close air support and reserves were unable to reinforce heavily committed units, and Group Pigarevich was delayed in pursuing the 6th Mountain Division.[33]

Two additional significant problems contributed to the failure to encircle and destroy the XIX Mountain Corps. The 29 September Karelian Front operational plan was flawed in that the initial amphibious landing and cross-isthmus attack by naval infantry was delayed until the 14th Army achieved an operational breakthrough. Responsibility for this planning flaw belongs to *STAVKA*, which disapproved Meretskov's original proposal for a simultaneous attack by the 14th Army and Northern Fleet ground and amphibious forces. Also, the light rifle corps failed to block Tarnet Road on 12—15 October, thus allowing the XIX Mountain Corps to withdraw into Norway. The 14th Army operational planners overestimated the combat power of their light rifle units, and the logistic planners underestimated the supply requirements for these same units.

These two flaws in planning, coupled with the performance problems mentioned by Rumiantsev, enabled the German units to avoid total encirclement and to escape into Norway. Even though the 14th Army failed to destroy the XIX Mountain Corps, its accomplishments in the Petsamo-Kirkenes Operation were still significant. Soviet forces inflicted over 9,000 casualties on the Germans, at a cost to themselves of approximately 16,000, a loss rate of approximately 16 percent on both sides. This is not a bad exchange for an attack against a prepared defense.[34]

In addition to "punishing" the withdrawing Germans, as was Meretskov's personal goal, the Soviet forces liberated Soviet territory and a part of Norwegian territory from German occupation, occupied the strip of Finnish territory that had been used as a bridgehead for the 1941 invasion and that included valuable mineral resources and a useful port, and secured the land flank of the vital sea route to Murmansk. Truly, these strategic gains were significant.

Since 1964, the Soviet military press has published over fifty journal articles, twenty of them since 1984, pertaining to the Petsamo-Kirkenes Operation. Because it was such a unique operation as to the size and type of forces on arctic terrain, it has given the Soviet armed forces valuable experience in arctic warfare. This recent interest is not just history for history's sake. Soviet military historians continue to study and write about the battle in order to gain and pass along important lessons to their forces.

In the past, the U.S. Army has conducted only small-scale operations on arctic terrain. Units that have been designated in their contingency or mobilization plans for deployment to arctic regions have had little historical experience to study to improve their understanding of the peculiar problems of combat and combat support activities in this inhospitable environment. This Leavenworth Paper has made available the information contained in a large body of Russian-language materials, which until now has been nearly inaccessible. It should be used to stimulate wide-ranging discussions of the many problems facing commanders and staff officers of units that may some day fight on similar terrain.

Epilogue

The 45th Rifle Division of the 131st Rifle Corps remained in Kirkenes and assisted the local population in preparing for the coming winter. A Norwegian military mission arrived in Murmansk on 9 November and went to Kirkenes the following day.[1] Over the next several months, small detachments of Norwegian soldiers from England and Sweden arrived in Murmansk and were subordinated to the 14th Army for operations on Norwegian territory. The exiled government of Norway was allowed to send naval vessels into Kirkenes harbor in early December. By the end of January 1945, the number of troops reached 1,350 and, by the war's end in May, 2,735. Soviet forces withdrew from Norwegian territory in October 1945, leaving the border as it had stood since 1807.

Combat experience gained in the Petsamo-Kirkenes Operation was quickly exploited when, in late 1944 and early 1945, many Soviet commanders, staffs, and units were transferred to other fronts. Army General Meretskov was promoted to marshal in November 1944 and, in the spring of 1945, transferred to Khabarovsk in eastern Siberia to command the 1st Far Eastern Front in the campaign against Japanese forces in Korea and Manchuria. His entire Front staff and the commander of the 7th Air Army, Lieutenant General Sokolov, preceded him. In August and September 1945, Meretskov's forces operated on extremely difficult coastal terrain, coordinating their actions with amphibious operations by naval infantry units of the Pacific Fleet.

The 20th Svirsk Assault Combat Engineer Brigade was also transferred to the 1st Far Eastern Front, where its units conducted conventional and special operations against Japanese forces. Under the leadership of Lieutenant Colonel D. A. Krutskikh, who had organized and trained the special-purpose units of the Karelian Front, special-purpose soldiers of the 20th Svirsk, on 9 August, neutralized an important Japanese position blocking the army on the Front's main axis. Later in August, the same units participated in air-landing operations against the Japanese garrisons in Harbin and Girin.[2] In 1982, Krutskikh was a general officer and chief of staff of civil defense of the R.S.F.S.R. (Russian Republic).

The 126th and 127th Light Rifle Corps appeared in southern Poland in February 1945 as the 126th and 127th Mountain Rifle Corps, with the same commanders and numbered brigades. Both corps fought through the mountains of north-central Czechoslovakia with the 4th Ukrainian Front and finished the war against Germany east of Prague.[3] The 72d Naval Rifle Brigade of the 126th Light Rifle Corps, replenished with healthy young men from other units, deployed to the Far East in the summer of 1945.[4] In January and February of 1945, the 10th Guards, 65th (renamed 101st Guards), and 114th (renamed 102d Guards) Rifle Divisions of the 99th Rifle Corps (renamed 40th Guards) and the 14th Rifle Division of the 131st Rifle Corps were all sent to the 19th Army in East Prussia.[5] The 19th participated in combat operations along the Baltic coast as part of the 2d Belorussian Front and finished the war near the German island of Rugen, northeast of Rostock. One corps from this army occupied the Danish island of Bornholm.[6]

Senior Lieutenant Leonov and over forty men of his fleet reconnaissance detachment went to the Pacific Fleet in May 1945.[7] Leonov became commander of the reconnaissance detachment of Headquarters, Pacific Fleet, and his "northerners" assumed leadership positions in the detachment. In August 1945, Leonov's new command distinguished itself in four landing operations against Japanese-held Korean ports, earning "guards" status. On 14 August 1945, Leonov earned his second Hero of the Soviet Union award for heroism and courage. He retired from active service in 1956 and now lives in Moscow.

Many officers who participated in the Petsamo-Kirkenes Operation remained in service after the war and reached positions of great responsibility. For example, Major P. S. Kutakhov, who was the commander of a fighter regiment in the 7th Air Army that supported the offensive, became the commander in chief of the Air Forces of the U.S.S.R. in 1969 and held that post until his death in 1984.[8] Lieutenant Colonel N. V. Ogarkov, who was the deputy chief of the operations section of the Karelian Front engineer staff, became chief of the General Staff of the Armed Forces of the U.S.S.R. in 1977, a post he held until 1984.[9] Lieutenant Colonel G. E. Peredelskii, who in October 1944 commanded the divisional artillery regiment of the 367th Rifle Division of the 31st Rifle Corps, was named the commander in chief of Rocket Forces and Artillery of Ground Forces in 1969, a post he held until 1983.[10] He died early in 1988. Colonel S. L. Sokolov, a senior staff officer in the Directorate of Tank and Mechanized Forces of the Karelian Front in 1944, became the minister of defense of the U.S.S.R. in 1984 and held that post until his retirement in mid-1987 after the Mathais Rust incident.[11]

After the war, Marshal Meretskov commanded several military districts in turn, including the Moscow Military District. In 1955, he became the deputy minister of defense for higher military-academic institutions. He entered the General Inspectorate in April 1964 and died in December 1968.[12]

In April 1946, Admiral Golovko became the deputy and, in February 1947, the chief of staff of the Main Naval Staff in Moscow. In 1950—52, he was chief of the Naval General Staff and first deputy of the naval minister. From 1952 to 1956, Golovko commanded the 4th and Baltic Fleets and then returned to Moscow to become the first deputy to the commander in chief of the Soviet Navy. Golovko died in 1962 at the age of 56.[13]

Lieutenant General Shcherbakov remained in the European theater and, after the war, commanded the Baltic and Archangel Military Districts (1945—49). From 1949 to 1953, he commanded the Gorkii Military District and then went to the Voronezh Military District to be the deputy commander until his retirement in 1957. He died in 1981.[14]

The Petsamo-Kirkenes area today is quiet. The border is marked by both Soviet and Norwegian posts, and on the Soviet side, there is a fence to prevent the migration of caribou. On the Norwegian side of the border, small guard towers look out over the barren landscape. Norwegian soldiers concern themselves both with activities across the border and with the summer migration of European tourists, who would remove Soviet border markers. A single border crossing point just west of Tarnet is used to pass an occasional logging truck from the U.S.S.R. into Norway. Sensitive to the security concerns of the Soviet Union, the government of Norway does not allow NATO forces to train or terrain walk in this area.

On the Soviet side of the border, the former German airfields at Luostari and Salmiiarvi are now military airfields. Forces permanently stationed in the area include the 45th Rifle Division, the 63d Kirkenes Naval Infantry Brigade, an artillery brigade, air assault units, and other unidentified formations, all of which are trained and equipped for arctic combat.[15]

Appendix A

From the Directive of the Commander, Karelian Front,
29 September 1944,
on the Conduct of an Offensive Operation
to the Commander of the 14th Army

I. The enemy's 19th Mountain Corps "Norway" is defending on the Murmansk axis, covering the approaches to Petsamo, Luostari, and the region of nickel deposits. During September, the enemy, in order to secure the extraction of the main body of the 20th Lapland Army to northern Norway, has conducted regrouping of forces and means of the 19th Mountain Corps, having reinforced the Luostari axis. . . .

The possibility is not ruled out that part of the forces and means of the southern corps of the 20th Lapland Army, which are retreating into Norway, may be incorporated into the operational reserve of the enemy in the Petsamo-Luostari region.

II. I [General Meretskov] order:

1. The 14th Army to clear the enemy from the Petsamo region. The main effort will be conducted from the region Lake Chapr, Hill 237.1, Lake Mareiarvi in the general direction Luostari, Petsamo, with the mission to defeat the enemy's 2d Mountain Division and to seize the Luostari-Petsamo area by a frontal attack in conjunction with a bypassing maneuver of a light corps, and, screened on the Salmiiarvi axis, to destroy the enemy forces that are located in the Titovka region and to the southeast.

Immediate mission is to break through the enemy's defenses in the sector Lake Chapr, Hill 237.1, to cross the Titovka River (Valasioki River) and, simultaneously bypassing the right flank of the enemy's 2d Mountain Division with the 126th Light Rifle Corps, to defeat the Hitlerite 2d Mountain Division and gain the line Lake Chapr-Lake Kuosmeiarvi-Lake Khiriiarvi-Lake Keiniaiarvi, Mount Silgia Tunturi-Petsamoioki River.

The subsequent mission is to orient the main forces from the Luostari region for the quickest possible seizure of Petsamo and to gain

Source: Colonel I. V. Iaroshenko and Colonel L. I. Smirnova, comps., "Osvobozhdenie sovetskogo Zapoliar'ia" [Liberation of the Soviet polar region], *VIZh*, June 1985:35—36.

the line Lake Khiriiarvi, Petsamo, Lake Niasiukkiaiarvi, Lake Liuppeiarvi, Lake Pilguiarvi, Lake Kalloiarvi.

After that, keep in mind the possible rapid seizure of the line Iso Tunturi-Porovara-Trifona, and, while being screened on the line Lake Niasiukkiaiarvi-Lake Liuppeiarvi-Lake Pilguiarvi-Lake Kalloiarvi, defeat the forces that remain in the Titovka region and to the southeast. Upon fulfillment of the stated mission, be prepared to move to the south as far as the national border.

2. In the event of a sudden retreat of the enemy, quickly go over to the pursuit with the forces of the [14th] army on hand, operating in such a manner as to prevent the main forces of the 19th Mountain Corps in the Petsamo region and beyond from reaching the border of northern Norway for a junction with the main forces of the 20th Lapland Army.

3. The operational formation of the army will be two echelons.

The first echelon will consist of two rifle corps made up of five rifle divisions, a light [rifle] corps, two tank regiments, one tank brigade, and artillery reinforcement.

The second echelon will consist of one rifle corps of two rifle divisions and one light corps of two rifle brigades.

For the defense of the sector Bolshaia Zapadnaia Litsa inlet, set aside not more than one rifle division, one rifle brigade, and one fortified region.

4. Keep in mind to utilize the light [rifle] corps in the course of the operation on the enveloping flank of the army to facilitate the development of the frontal breakthrough with a bypassing maneuver into the flank and rear of the enemy that is defending on the Luostari axis.

The second echelon of the army should be used, depending on the situation, either in the direction of Salmiiarvi, in the event of the appearance of powerful enemy forces from the south and from the Kirkenes direction, protecting the left flank of the army, or for defeat of the enemy forces that are located in the Titovka region.

III. On the right are the Northern Fleet and the Northern Defensive Region, at existing lines and bases.

With forces of not less than one rifle brigade, the Northern Fleet is attacking from the Srednii Peninsula from the Kutovka region to the south, with the mission to prevent the regrouping of the 503d Airfield Brigade.

On the left, the 19th Army is pursuing retreating enemy units of the 36th Army Corps in the direction of Kuoloiarvi. Army boundaries remain as before.

IV. Artillery and mortars. The primary mission of artillery is to suppress artillery-mortar groupings and to defeat the enemy defenses on the Luostari axis, thus supporting the attacking units' breakthrough of the enemy defenses, the forced crossing of the Titovka River, and the penetration to the Luostari-Petsamo region.

Artillery preparation is two hours and thirty-five minutes. The order of artillery preparation: five-minute barrage on the enemy's defenses, artillery and mortar batteries, headquarters, communications centers, and reserves; thirty minutes of controlled fire for registration and on targets and on "final" reconnaissance of the enemy; a sixty-minute period of methodical destruction of defensive works and partial suppression of targets and trenches in the depth of the defense and strikes against enemy artillery and mortars; thirty-minute period of suppression of targets at the forward edge and in the tactical depth of the enemy defense by aviation and artillery and mortars and thirty-minute period of suppression of enemy defenses by artillery and mortars and volleys of [multiple] rocket [launcher] fire. The infantry attack will be accompanied by the method of successive concentration of fire to support the rapid seizure of strongpoints on the forward edge and in the immediate tactical depth by infantry and tanks.

On the main axis, an artillery-mortar density of not less than 150 tubes per kilometer (excluding 45-mm guns) will be created.

Aviation. The 7th Air Army of the Front, consisting of three mixed, two bomber, and one interceptor air division, is supporting the operation of the 14th Army.

The primary mission of the aviation is close cooperation with the artillery to break open the defensive zone of the enemy, to disorganize his troop command and control, to suppress artillery-mortar groupings, to restrict the maneuver of the enemy's operational and tactical reserves, and to defeat them on the approaches to the battlefield. Aviation support will also provide to the forces of the army a quick and decisive fulfillment of the mission of breaking through the defense of the enemy on the Luostari axis and the defeat of his forces in the Petsamo region.

Considering the mountainous relief of the terrain and the hardness of the enemy defensive fortifications (stone and granite), arm the bomber aviation with high-explosive bombs in weights of 100, 250, and 500 kilograms.

Destroy the crossings over the Titovka River in the middle of its course so as to deny the enemy the ability to maneuver reserves and to retreat from the Bolshaia Litsa area to the west to the Petsamo region.

Destroy the enemy's aviation on his airfields.

In the course of the offensive, accompany the infantry and tanks on the battlefield, not permitting a planned retreat of the enemy to intermediate lines. Disrupt the counterattacks of his reserves and destroy communications centers, command posts, and means of mobility that could be used for the purpose of inflicting blows on the flank and seams of the attacking forces.

Cover the tanks and motorized infantry during the development of the operation and the development of pursuit operations against the retreating enemy.

Engineer support. The primary mission of engineer troops is to prepare assembly areas for the attacking army, to ensure the rapid and organized crossing of water obstacles on the Luostari axis (Titovka River, Petsamoioki River), to support the maneuver of attacking forces after the breakthrough of the enemy defensive zone and consolidation of occupied positions.

In supporting the maneuver of the attacking forces, pay special attention to the organization of direct, immediate accompaniment of the troops during the development of the offensive, the clearing of obstacles from the tactical and operational zone, and the covering by our own obstacles of the flanks of the army and attacking units and formations.

The command post of the [14th] army will be in the area of Lake Nozhiarvi. The axis of communications of the army is Luostari.

Commander, Karelian Front
General of the Army
/s/ Meretskov

Member, Front Military Council
Lieutenant General
/s/ Shtykov

Front Chief of Staff
Lieutenant General
/s/ Krutikov

Appendix B

To the Commander, 31st Rifle Corps,
Partial Combat Order No. 0046/HQ, 14th Army (8644-1) 172350 October 1944
Map 1:100,000 1936

1. Having suffered a defeat in the battle for Petsamo, the enemy has begun to withdraw remnants of defeated units from the Petsamo area into northern Norway. In order to support the withdrawal of remnants of the 19th Mountain Corps, the enemy has deployed units of the 163d Infantry Division from the Rovaniemi area. These forces will attempt to prevent the penetration of our forces into the region Akhmalakhti-Salmiiarvi-Nikel.

2. The 14th Army, developing the offensive to the west and southwest along the international boundary with Norway, is destroying remnants of units of the 19th Mountain Corps and units of 163d Infantry Division and is clearing the enemy from the Petsamo region in sector Vuoremi (4616), Lake Vuoremiiarvi (2018), Border Post No. 360 (3488), and Salmiiarvi in preparation for developing the offensive to Nautsi and Ivalo.

3. The 31st Rifle Corps (83d and 367th Rifle Divisions) [is to be] with the 89th Separate Tank Regiment, 339th Separate Self-Propelled Artillery Regiment, 471st Heavy Gun Regiment, 989th Mountain Artillery Regiment, 633d Corps Artillery Regiment, 535th and 482d Mortar Regiments, 44th and 64th Guards Mortar Regiments [multiple rocket launchers], and 1st Motorized Combat Engineer Brigade (minus 168th Battalion).

Immediate mission is to defeat the enemy on the line Hill 339.0 (0606)—Hill 466.3 (0404)—lakes in grid square 0204. By the end of the day, 19 Oct 44, the corps is to seize the line from the unnamed hill in grid 0802, to Hill 349.8 (0602), to Hill 636.6 (0000) and, subsequently, to attack toward Nikel and the road junction in grid square 0684.

On the right, the 99th Rifle Corps is attacking along the road to Akhmalakhti, Salmiiarvi. The boundary with them is Luostari, the fork in the road in grid square 0614, Hill 276.0 (0610), the unnamed hill in grid

Source: S. Mikulskii and M. Absaliamov, (*Nastupatel'nye boi 99-go i 31-go strelkovykh korpusov v zapoliar'e (Oktiabr' 1944g)* [Offensive battles of the 99th and 31st Rifle Corps in the polar region (October 1944)] (Moscow: Voenizdat, 1959), 154—55.

squares 0802—5, Hill 173.1 (0890), and the bridge in grid square 0886. All points, except Luostari and the fork in the road in grid square 0614, are for the 99th Rifle Corps exclusively.

On the left, the 127th Rifle Corps, supporting the 31st Rifle Corps from the south, is attacking south of the Luostari-Nikel road and in a bypassing maneuver from the south will seize the Nikel area by 21 Oct 44 and hold it until the arrival of our units.

4. Artillery.

Be prepared by 18 Oct 44.

Duration of artillery preparation: 45 minutes.

Missions:

a. Ensure a firm defense for the army's right flank on the line Hill 292.5 (3024), Hill 258.7 (2220), and unnamed hill (1618).

b. Suppress and destroy the firing positions and troops on Hills 332.9 (1606), 312.7 (1200), 318.0 (1000), 313.0 (1002), 282.5 (1098), 339.0 (0606), 349.8 (0602), 466.3 (0404), 496.0 (0202), and 636.6 (0000).

c. Suppress the enemy's artillery in the area of Hill 273 (1602), Hill 312.7 (1202), and Hill 266.7 (1498).

d. Prevent the approach of reserves from Kuvernerinkoski and Nikel along roads going east.

e. Prevent counterattacks from the area of Hill 273.0 (1604) in the direction of the hut (1204) and from the area of Hill 466.3 (0404) in an eastward direction.

f. Prevent the enemy's withdrawal of troops and equipment along the roads to Kuvernerinkoski and Nikel.

5. Aviation.

Missions:

a. Cover the shock group of the army against air strikes.

b. Coordinate closely with units of the 99th Rifle Corps, 31st Rifle Corps, and 126th and 127th Light Rifle Corps. Assist their movement, destroying and suppressing enemy strongpoints, artillery, and troops with groups of ground attack aircraft [*shturmoviki*].

c. Prevent the approach of reserves and the withdrawal of the enemy along the roads Luostari-Akhmalakhti-Elvenes; Luostari-Akhmalakhti-Salmiiarivi-Nautsi; Luostari-Nikel-Nautsi.

d. Suppress and destroy enemy aviation assets with strikes on his airfields.

e. Exhaust the enemy troops in their assembly areas by night-bombing operations; suppress artillery and mortars in firing positions.

6. Be prepared by 182400 Oct 44. H-hour will be announced by a special message.

7. The command post of the army is in grid square 0424. The axis of its movement is Luostari-Akhmalakhti-Salmiiarvi.

8. Required reports:
   a. Preparedness of troops for the fulfillment of the mission.
   b. Occupation of jumping off position for the attack.
   c. Beginning of attack and subsequently every two hours.

Commander, 14th Army
Lieutenant General
/s/ Shcherbakov

Member, Army Military Council
Major General
/s/ Sergeev

Chief of Staff, 14th Army
Major General
/s/ Gerasev

Appendix C

Excerpt From Combat Order No. 0039, HQ 31st Rifle Corps
181530 October 1944
Map 1:100,000 1936

Paragraphs 1, 2, and 3 contain the contents of the corresponding paragraphs of the order of the commander, 14th Army No. 0046 from 17 Oct 44 [see appendix B].

4. The 31st Rifle Corps is pursuing the retreating enemy along the Luostari-Nikel road, with 367th Rifle Division in the first echelon and 83d Rifle Division in the second echelon. Attacking with mobile groups along the road and bypassing the flanks of the enemy with supporting detachments operating off the road, the corps must get into the enemy's rear; cut off his path of retreat, surround, destroy, and capture the enemy troops; and seize his equipment.

5. The 367th Rifle Division with 89th Independent Tank Regiment, 339th Separate Self-Propelled Artillery Regiment, 989th Mountain Artillery Regiment, 64th Guards Mortar Regiment (M-8) [multiple rocket launchers], and 535th and 482d Mortar Regiments are to continue the pursuit of the retreating enemy along the road in the direction of Nikel. Operating along the road with mobile detachments, which are reinforced by engineers, tanks, and self-propelled artillery, and by aggressive dismounted maneuver off the road, the division must get into the flanks and rear of the enemy *with the immediate mission* to encircle and destroy retreating enemy units. By end of day 18 Oct, reach the line of Hills 300 (0802), 349.8 (0602), and 636.6 (0000).

Subsequently, developing aggressive pursuit, by the end of day 19 Oct 44, seize Nikel. Forward detachments are to seize a crossing at Salmiiarvi and the road junction three kilometers southwest of it.

6. 83d Rifle Division by 182000 Oct is to be concentrated in the sector 0414, 0214, 0212. *Mission of the division*: following in the second echelon,

Source: S. Mikulskii and M. Absaliamov, *Nastupatel'nye boi 99-go i 31-go strelkovykh korpusov v zapoliar'e (Oktiabr' 1944g)* [Offensive battles of the 99th and 31st Rifle Corps in the polar region (October 1944)] (Moscow: Voenizdat, 1959), 156—58.

be prepared after the seizure by 367th Rifle Division of the Nikel region and road junction three kilometers southwest of Salmiiarvi to develop the attack along the road Salmiiarvi-Nautsi.

7. Artillery. Long-range artillery of 31st Rifle Corps is 471st Heavy Gun Regiment and 633d Corps Artillery Regiment; the commander is the commander of the 471st Heavy Gun Regiment.

Missions:

a. Suppress enemy artillery in the corps zone of attack.

b. Prevent the approach of reserves from the Nikel area and an enemy withdrawal to the west.

c. Prevent enemy counterattacks from the areas of Hills 349.8, 466.3, 496.0, 441.4, and 636.6.

Rocket launcher group of the 31st Rifle Corps is 44th Guards Mortars Regiment. Be prepared to fire volleys upon my signal into the area of Hills 349.8, 466.3, 496.0, 441.4, and 636.6.

Infantry support group.

Missions:

a. Suppress infantry and enemy firing points in the corps zone of attack using all calibers of artillery and mortars.

b. Support rifle subunits by fire and by towed guns in direct fire.

c. Prevent enemy counterattacks from the area of Hills 349.8, 466.3, and 466.6.

d. Prevent enemy withdrawal to the west.

e. Support the movement of advance guard battalions by the creation of a mobile group of artillery and mortars.

8. 1st Motorized Combat Engineer Brigade (minus 168th Battalion) is at my disposal.

Missions:

a. Conduct uninterrupted engineer reconnaissance in the corps zone.

b. Follow behind the combat formations of first-echelon units, conduct continuous mine clearing of the roadbed, and clear a zone of fifty meters to the sides of the road.

c. Restore destroyed roadbeds and bridges for the passing of heavy artillery and tanks.

d. Attach one platoon of engineers each to the 89th Separate Tank Regiment and the 339th Separate Self-Propelled Artillery Regiment for support of mobility of tanks and *SAU* [self-propelled artillery].

9. Air defense. Antiaircraft units and interceptor aviation are covering the basic group of artillery and combat infantry formations according to the army plan.

To the commanders of formations and units:

a. Strengthen air defense by your own means, designating in each rifle company one squad with light machine guns and in each rifle battalion one platoon with heavy machine guns and antitank rifles.

b. Strengthen the camouflage and operational security [*maskirovka*] of your combat formations during the pursuit and, in areas of deployment, have trenches and shelters for infantry and horses.

10. Antitank defense. Be prepared to repel enemy tanks from the direction of Nikel, having in your combat formations antitank guns and antitank rifles.

11. Command post is in grid square 0618-9. Axis of relocation is grid square 0212-1, Hill 441.4.

12. Reports are required every two hours.

Commander, 31st Rifle Corps
Major General
/s/ Absaliamov

Corps Chief of Staff
Colonel
/s/ Polukarov

Appendix D

2d Mountain Division Division Headquarters 12.9.1944
   Commander

               Soldiers of the 2d Mountain Division!

Although the enemy has not launched any major attacks against us this year, he has forced Finland to lay down its arms and now threatens to extend his grasp to Petsamo.

In front of our strongpoint front, the 31st Ski Rifle Brigade for days has been preparing an attack. Additional forces are probably arrayed behind it. We will permit the enemy to hurl himself against our diligently and solidly built strongpoints and then destroy him through a counterattack.

All advantages are on our side.

The strongpoint garrisons should know that behind them all available battalions and batteries of the 2d Mountain Division are ready for action. The counterattack reserves know what to do when the enemy bloodies himself on the withering defensive fire of our strongpoints.

Above all, I know that the fighting spirit of the 2d Mountain Division is more mature, that every infantryman, every gunner, every engineer soldier will do his best, that none of you will let down the honor of our proud division.

It is ordered that we, in spite of the political changes in Finland, must hold our front. All of you know why this must be so: because we need the nickel and copper from the Kolosjoki works, whose ovens will soon be smoking again, because we must here show the Russian that there is still one front on which their hunger for territory will not be satisfied.

Soldiers of the 2d Mountain Division! The homeland is looking to you! I put my trust in you! We will master every situation, no matter how and when it may develop.

                                       Hail the Führer!
                                           /s/ Degen
                                       Generalleutnant
                                       Commander, 2d Mountain Division

This order is to be issued by 14 September to all soldiers at roll call or in bunkers by the unit commander or strongpoint commander.

Source: Germany, Heer, 2. Gebirgs-division [Germany, Army, 2d Mountain Division], Kriegstagebuch nr. 1 [War diary no. 1], microfilm series T-315, roll 109, frame 00823, National Archives and Records Administration, Washington, DC.

Appendix E

Equipment and Troop Strength of 99th Rifle Corps and Reinforcing Units on 7 October 1944

Formations and Units	Rifle Battalions	Men	Rifles	Submachine Guns	Machine Guns		Antiaircraft	Mortars				Artillery						Total	Total Guns/Mortars	Tanks	Amphibians
					Light	Heavy		82-mm	107-mm	120-mm	Total	45-mm	Regimental 76-mm	Divisional 76-mm	122-mm	150-mm	152-mm	Total			
65th Rifle Div	9	6,641	2,689	2,154	187	74	—	44	—	12	56	26	9	18	10	—	—	63	119	—	—
38th Rifle Regt	3	1,536	600	633	50	24	—	12	—	4	16	5	3	—	—	—	—	8	—	—	—
60th Rifle Regt	3	1,535	616	576	55	23	—	12	—	4	16	6	3	—	—	—	—	9	—	—	—
311th Rifle Regt	3	1,568	632	526	53	23	—	12	—	4	16	6	3	—	—	—	—	9	—	—	—
6th Gds Arty Regt	—	669	133	58	3	—	—	—	—	—	—	—	—	18	10	—	—	28	—	—	—
114th Rifle Div	9	6,418	2,781	2,216	212	56	3	62	—	20	82	42	12	20	12	—	—	86	168	—	—
363d Rifle Regt	3	1,815	891	672	90	27	—	—	—	—	—	12	4	—	—	—	—	16	—	—	—
536th Rifle Regt	3	1,318	408	645	61	14	—	—	—	—	—	10	4	—	—	—	—	14	—	—	—
763d Rifle Regt	3	1,341	523	508	60	14	—	—	—	—	—	8	4	—	—	—	—	12	—	—	—
405th Arty Regt	—	906	513	48	—	—	—	—	—	—	—	—	—	20	12	—	—	32	—	—	—
368th Rifle Div	9	6,098	2,831	1,998	188	76	5	40	—	16	56	42	12	19	12	—	—	85	141	—	—
Total in Divisions	27	19,157	8,301	6,368	587	206	8	146	—	48	194	110	33	57	34	—	—	234	428	—	—
Corps Units																					
1236th Arty Regt	—	—	—	—	—	—	—	—	—	—	—	—	—	—	12	—	12	24	—	—	—
471st Arty Regt	—	—	—	—	—	—	—	—	—	—	—	—	—	—	—	16	—	16	—	—	—
Reinforcing Units																					
149th Arty Regt	—	(not present 7 Oct: did not participate in breakthrough)																				
989th Arty Regt	—														—	24	—	—	24	—	—	—
275th Mortar Regt	—							—	—	36	36										
535th Mortar Regt	—							—	—	36	36										
620th Mortar Regt	—							—	—	36	36										
173d Mortar Regt	—							—	36	—	36										
905th Mt Arty Regt	—														24	—	—	24	—	—	—
7th Gds Tank Bde	—	(not present 7 Oct: did not participate in breakthrough)																		37	—	
89th Sep Tk Regt	—																			18	—	
339th Sep SP Regt	—																			17	—	
284th Sep Bn OSNAZ	—																					94
Total in Corps and Reinforcements	—	—	—	—	—	—	—	146	36	156	338	110	33	81	70	16	12	322	660	54	94

Source: S. Mikulskii and M. Absaliamov, *Nastupatel'nye boi 99-go i 31-go strelkovykh korpusov v zapoliar'e (Oktiabr' 1944)* [Offensive battles of the 99th and 31st Rifle Corps in the polar regions (October 1944)] (Moscow: Voenizdat, 1959), 12–13.

Appendix F

Equipment and Troop Strength of 31st Rifle Corps and Reinforcing Elements on 18 October 1944

Formations and Units	Men	Submachine Guns	Light Machine Guns	Heavy Machine Guns	Antitank Rifles	Mortars 82-mm	Mortars 120-mm	Multiple Rocket Launchers	Guns 45-mm	Guns 76-mm	Guns 122-mm	Guns 152-mm	Anti-Aircraft Heavy Machine Guns	Anti-Aircraft 76-mm	Horses	Wheeled Vehicles and Prime Movers Light	Wheeled Vehicles and Prime Movers Cargo	Wheeled Vehicles and Prime Movers Special
31st Rifle Corps HQ	699	39	10	—	—	—	—	—	—	—	—	—	—	—	58	5	30	—
83d Rifle Div	5,761	1,509	145	66	75	48	12	—	34	31	—	—	12	—	912	3	59	9
11th Rifle Regt	1,551	468	59	27	28	17	4	—	12	3	—	—	—	—	188	—	—	—
26th Rifle Regt	1,158	475	47	21	19	15	4	—	12	4	—	—	—	—	187	—	—	—
46th Rifle Regt	1,451	416	36	18	12	16	4	—	10	4	—	—	—	—	188	1	—	—
588th Arty Regt	724	37	—	—	9	—	—	—	—	20	12	—	—	—	264	—	4	9
367th Rifle Div	5,971	1,670	220	76	119	59	18	—	30	31	12	—	9	—	1,025	—	53	—
1217th Rifle Regt	1,436	515	69	27	34	18	6	—	6	4	—	—	—	—	193	—	—	—
1219th Rifle Regt	1,385	512	65	26	24	18	6	—	6	4	—	—	—	—	185	—	—	—
1221st Rifle Regt	1,250	417	50	20	30	17	6	—	6	4	—	—	—	—	183	—	—	—
928th Arty Regt	782	33	8	—	16	—	—	—	—	19	12	—	—	—	318	—	—	—
Corps Total	12,431	3,218	375	142	194	107	30	—	64	62	24	—	21	—	1,995	9	142	9
Reinforcing Units																		
51st Cannon Arty Regt	data not available																	
633d Corps Arty Regt	481	105	8	—	16	—	—	—	—	—	—	18	—	—	—	—	41	—
989th How Arty Regt	623	226	12	—	24	—	—	—	—	—	24	14	—	—	—	—	60	10
535th Mortar Regt	543	107	—	—	36	—	36	—	—	—	—	—	—	—	—	—	60	6
482d Mortar Regt	501	60	—	—	30	—	34	—	—	—	—	—	—	—	—	—	56	4
44th Gds Mortar Regt	632	182	18	—	10	—	—	24	—	—	—	—	—	—	—	—	106	—
64th Gds Mortar Regt	data not available							24										
325th Sep AAA Bn	—	—	—	—	—	—	—	—	—	—	—	—	3	11	—	—	—	—
1st Motorized Cbt Engr Bde	998	759	30	0	8	—	—	—	—	—	—	—	—	—	—	—	34	41
Total in Reinforcing Units	—	—	—	—	—	107	70	48	—	—	24	32	3	11	—	—	—	—
Total on the Axis	—	—	—	—	—	107	100	48	64	62	48	32	24	11	—	—	—	—

Source: S. Mikulskii and M. Abesliamov, *Nastupatel'nye boi 99-go i 31-go strelkovykh korpusov v zapoliar'e (Oktiabr' 1944)* [Offensive battles of the 99th and 31st Rifle Corps in the polar regions (October 1944)] (Moscow: Voenizdat, 1959), 83–85.

Appendix G

Formations and Units That Received Specific Honorific Titles for the Liberation of Pechenga (Petsamo) and Kirkenes

Pechenga

10th Guards Rifle Division, Major General Kh. A. Khudalov; 14th Rifle Division, Major General F. F. Korotkov; 45th Rifle Division, Major General I. V. Panin; 368th Rifle Division, Major General V. K. Sopenko; 3d Separate Naval Rifle Brigade, Colonel A. G. Kaverin; 12th Naval Infantry Brigade, Colonel V. V. Rassokhin; 69th Separate Naval Rifle Brigade, Lieutenant Colonel E. G. Evmenov; 70th Separate Naval Rifle Brigade, Colonel A. V. Blak.

284th Separate Motorized Battalion *OSNAZ* (*osobogo naznacheniia*), Lieutenant Colonel V. S. Korshunov.

89th Separate Tank Regiment, Lieutenant Colonel E. A. Suchkov.

104th Cannon Artillery Regiment (Navy), Lieutenant Colonel N. I. Kavun; 471st Army Cannon Artillery Regiment, Colonel I. A. Maniakin; 901st Mountain Artillery Regiment, Major A. I. Lebedev; 989th Howitzer Artillery Regiment, Colonel V. N. Perlov; 1066th Corps Artillery Regiment, Major I. V. Fetisov; 1236th Army Cannon Artillery Regiment, Major F. F. Doludenko; 1942d Corps Artillery Regiment, Major F. S. Goluker; 41st Guards Mortar Regiment, Major P. S. Eresko; 172d Army Mortar Regiment, Major I. N. Kozhin; 275th Army Mortar Regiment, Lieutenant Colonel V. S. Shepel; 297th Army Mortar Regiment, Lieutenant Colonel Iu. S. Shapiro; 535th Army Mortar Regiment, Lieutenant Colonel P. A. Rogovyi.

40th Antiaircraft Artillery Division, Colonel I. V. Khramov; 156th Army Antiaircraft Artillery Regiment, Lieutenant Colonel P. F. Goltykhov; 487th Separate Antiaircraft Artillery Battalion, Major P. I. Vakurov.

1st Separate Motorized Engineer Brigade, Lieutenant Colonel A. G. Zakharov; 30th Separate Motorized Pontoon Bridge Battalion, Lieutenant Colonel N. N. Demianenko.

Brigade of Torpedo Patrol Boats, Captain First Rank A. V. Kuzmin; 2d Guards Battalion Naval Antisubmarine Patrol Boats, Captain Second Rank S. D. Ziuzin.

6th Fighter Aviation Division (Navy), Major General of Aviation N. T. Petrukhin; 122d *PVO* Fighter Aviation Division, Colonel F. A. Pogreshaev; 2d Guards Fighter Aviation Regiment (Navy), Lieutenant Colonel D. F. Marenko; 46th Close Support Aviation Regiment (Navy), Major G. V. Pavlov.

Kirkenes

24th Guards Rifle Regiment (10th Guards Rifle Division), Lieutenant Colonel V. F. Lazarev; 28th Guards Rifle Regiment (10th Guards Rifle Division), Major A. R. Pasko; 95th Rifle Regiment (14th Rifle Division), Lieutenant Colonel N. N. Tsypyshev; 155th Rifle Regiment (14th Rifle Division), Lieutenant Colonel Ia. N. Povarenkov; 253d Rifle Regiment (45th Rifle Division), Lieutenant Colonel I. K. Kopyl; 63d Naval Infantry Brigade, Colonel A. M. Krylov; 60th Rifle Regiment (65th Rifle Division), Lieutenant Colonel Ia. P. Pidust.

Brigade Large Subchasers, Captain First Rank M. S. Klevenskii.

51st Army Cannon Artillery Regiment, Lieutenant Colonel M. V. Iusov; 149th Corps Artillery Regiment, Lieutenant Colonel S. Petrov; 1411th Antiaircraft Artillery Regiment, Lieutenant Colonel P. F. Staroverov.

5th Mine-Torpedo Aviation Division (Navy), Major General of Aviation N. M. Kidalinskii; 9th Guards Mine-Torpedo Aviation Regiment (Navy), Major A. I. Fokin; 20th Fighter Aviation Regiment (Navy), Lieutenant Colonel D. A. Petrov; 80th Bomber Aviation Regiment, Lieutenant Colonel G. P. Starikov; 114th Guards Long-Range Bomber Aviation Regiment, Major A. N. Volodin; 118th Reconnaissance Aviation Regiment (Navy), Lieutenant Colonel S. K. Litvinov.

Source: F. F. Viktorov, ed., *Istoriia ordena lenina leningradskogo voennogo okruga* [History of the order of Lenin Leningrad Military District] (Moscow: Voenizdat, 1974), 571.

Notes

Introduction

1. Quoted by Marshal of the Soviet Union K. A. Meretskov in his memoir, *Na sluzhbe narodu* [In service to the people] (Moscow: Voenizdat, 1983), 373, hereafter cited as Meretskov, *Na sluzhbe*.

2. See, for example, S. Golikov, *Vydaiushchiesia pobedy Sovetskoi Armii v Velikoi Otechestvennoi voine* [The greatest victories of the Soviet Army in the Great Patriotic War] (Moscow: Gosudarstvennoe izdatel'stvo politicheskoi literatury, 1954), 198—201.

3. See, for example, V. K. Shamshurov, *Inzhenernoe obespechenie boia v osobykh usloviiakh* [Engineer support of combat in special conditions] (Moscow: Voenizdat, 1985), 192—234; and S. N. Dudarev and B. V. Shipov, *Artilleriia v osobykh usloviiakh* [Artillery in special conditions] (Moscow: Voenizdat, 1970), 85—119.

4. Brian Garfield, *The Thousand Mile War: World War II in Alaska and the Aleutians* (Garden City, NY: Doubleday and Co., 1969), chaps. 16 and 17.

5. See Richard Goldhurst, *The Midnight War: The American Intervention in Russia, 1918—1920* (New York: McGraw-Hill Book Co., 1978).

6. Edward M. Coffman, "The Intervention in Russia, 1918—1921," *Military Review* 68 (September 1988):60—71.

7. See, for example, Allen F. Chew, *Fighting the Russians in Winter: Three Case Studies*, Leavenworth Papers no. 5 (Fort Leavenworth, KS: Combat Studies Institute, U.S. Army Command and General Staff College, December 1981), 7—19.

8. U.S. Department of the Army, Field Manual 100—5, *Operations* (Washington, DC, May 1986), 84—85.

9. U.S. Department of the Army, Field Manual 90—11, *Cold Weather Operations*, Preliminary Draft (Fort Leavenworth, KS: Doctrinal Literature Management Office, U.S. Army Command and General Staff College, 30 November 1988).

10. Dennis M. Egan and David W. Orr, "Sea Control in the Arctic: A Soviet Perspective," *Naval War College Review* 61 (Winter 1988):51—80.

11. Carl von Clausewitz, *On War*, edited and translated by Michael Howard and Peter Paret (Princeton, NJ: Princeton University Press, 1976), 170—71.

12. U. S. Department of the Army, Pamphlet no. 20—271, *The German Northern Theater of Operations, 1940—1945*, by Earl F. Ziemke (Washington, DC: U.S. Government Printing Office, 1959), 303—8, hereafter cited as DA Pam 20—271.

13. Earl F. Ziemke, *Stalingrad to Berlin: The German Defeat in the East*, Army Historical

Series (Washington, DC: Office of the Chief of Military History, United States Army, 1968), 397—401.

14. S. Mikulskii and M. Absaliamov, *Nastupatel'nye boi 99-go i 31-go strelkovykh korpusov v Zapoliar'e (Oktiabr' 1944g)* [Offensive battles of the 99th and 31st Rifle Corps in the polar region (October 1944)] (Moscow: Voenizdat, 1959), hereafter cited as Mikulskii and Absaliamov, *Nastupatel'nye boi*.

15. Nikolai M. Rumiantsev, *Razgrom vraga v Zapoliare (1941—1944gg): Voenno-istoricheskii ocherk* [The defeat of the enemy in the polar region (1941—1944): A military-historical outline] (Moscow: Voenizdat, 1963), hereafter cited as Rumiantsev, *Razgrom vraga*.

16. Peter DeLeon, "Emerging Security Considerations for NATO's Northern Flank," *RUSI, Journal of the Royal United Services Institute of Defence Studies* 130 (June 1985):35; the journal is hereafter cited as *RUSI*. See also General Fredrik Bull-Hansen, "Norway, NATO's Strategic Pivot?," *RUSI* 132 (September 1987):13—18; and Sir Geoffrey Howlett, "Concepts and Future Capabilities in NATO's Northern Region," *RUSI* 133 (Autumn 1988):13—18.

Chapter 1

1. M. I. Semiriaga, ed., *Istoriia vtoroi mirovoi voiny 1939—1945* [History of the Second World War, 1939—1945] (Moscow: Voenizdat, 1978), 9:19, hereafter cited as Semiriaga, ed., *Istoriia*).

2. Sergei M. Shtemenko, *The Soviet General Staff at War, 1941—1945* (Moscow: Progress Publishers, 1986), 2:372—77, hereafter cited as Shtemenko, *Soviet General Staff*.

3. P. N. Pospelov, ed., *Great Patriotic War of the Soviet Union, 1941—1945* (Moscow: Progress Publishers, 1974), 258—60.

4. Waldemar Erfurth, "The Last Finnish War (1941—1944)," Foreign Military Studies no. MS C-073 (Historical Division, U.S. Army, Europe, 1952), 34, hereafter cited as MS C-073. Erfurth's study was published in German under the title *Der Finnische Krieg, 1941—1944* (Wiesbaden/Munich: Limes-Verlag, 1950). See also Alex Buchner, "Attack in the Tundra," *Military Review* 36 (April 1956):98—109.

5. The best account in English of the activities of the German Army in this theater is DA Pam 20—271. See also U.S. Department of the Army, Pamphlet no. 20—269, *Small Unit Actions During the German Campaign in Russia* (Washington, DC: U.S. Government Printing Office, July 1953), chap. 4.

6. For a detailed explanation of Operation Birke, see DA Pam 20—271, 276—78, and chap. 14.

7. Ibid. 300—302.

8. "The Petsamo Region," *Geographical Review* 34 (July 1944):409. Tundra is defined in *Webster's Ninth New Collegiate Dictionary* (Springfield, MA: Merriam-Webster, 1983) as "a level or undulating treeless plain that is characteristic of arctic and subarctic regions, consists of black mucky soil with a permanently frozen subsoil, and supports a dense growth of often conspicuously flowering dwarf herbs."

9. The disposition of the XIX Mountain Corps units is shown to battalion level on a map at annex 15 to Germany, Heer, 20. Heer [Headquarters, 20th German Army], Kriegstagebuch nr. 5 [War diary no. 5], entry for 11 September 1944, microfilm series T-312, roll 1062, frame 9264296, National Archives and Records Administration, Washington, DC, hereafter cited as Germany, 20th Army, KTB 5, and the National Archives is hereafter cited as NARA. A detailed description of the defensive positions of 2d Mountain Division is con-

tained in that unit's records. See Germany, Heer, 2. Gebirgs-division [Germany, Army, 2d Mountain Division], Kriegestagebuch nr. 1 [War diary no. 1], microfilm series T-315, roll 109, NARA, hereafter cited as Germany, 2d Mt Div, KTB 1.

10. *Hiwi (hilfswilligen)* [volunteer auxiliary], frequently foreign nationals organized and equipped for combat service support tasks.

11. Data for table 1 was obtained from various documents in folder 65635/14 in Germany, 20th Army, "Zustandbericht" [Status reports], 1 July–30 September 1944, microfilm series T-312, rolls 1064 and 1065, NARA. The total personnel strength figure of 56,000 is as of 1 July 1944 (frame 9266849), and the corps total weapons data is as of 13 August 1944 (frames 9266626–27). Personnel and equipment levels of corps units are from unit status reports dated 1 September 1944.

12. DA Pam 20–271, 304.

13. A detailed description of all strongpoints in the 2d Mountain Division's sector is in Germany, Heer, Gebirgsjagerregiment 137 [Mountain Rifle Regiment 137], "Gefechtsbericht ueber die Kampfhandlungen am 7. u. 8.10.44 im Abschnitt Isar" [Combat report of the battle action on 7 and 8 October 1944 in Sector Isar], in Germany, 2d Mt Div, KTB 1, microfilm series T-315, roll 109, NARA.

14. Several Soviet sources describe the German defensive system in detail. See, for example, Rumiantsev, *Razgrom vraga*, 129–37. See also P. V. Terekhov, *Boevye deistviia tankov na severo-zapade v 1944g* [Combat operations of tanks in the northwest in 1944] (Moscow: Voenizdat, 1965), 113–14, hereafter cited as Terekhov, *Boevye deistviia tankov*.

15. "Soldaten der 2. Gebirgsdivision!" [Soldiers of the 2d Mountain Division!] in Germany, 2d Mt Div, KTB 1, microfilm series T-315, roll 109, NARA, frame 000823.

16. "Divisionsbefehl fur die Umgliederung des Unterabschnitts Isar zur Stellungsfront" [Divisional order for the reorganization of Subsector Isar into a strongpoint front], Germany, 2d Mt Div, KTB 1, microfilm series T-315, roll 109, NARA, frames 000753–62.

17. Meretskov, *Na sluzhbe*, 343.

18. Stalin is quoted in Meretskov, *Na sluzhbe*, 343. The date of the meeting is from Shtememko, *Soviet General Staff*, 2:372.

19. Meretskov, *Na sluzhbe*, 351–52.

20. Ibid., 349. For a biographical sketch of Shcherbakov, see *Sovetskaia voennaia entsiklopediia* [Soviet military encyclopedia] (Moscow: Voenizdat, 1980), 8:552; the encyclopedia is cited hereafter as *SVE*.

21. According to Rumiantsev, *Razgrom vraga*, 142, troop units repaired or improved over sixty kilometers of road, built eighty bridges and culverts, and constructed over fifty kilometers of new road.

22. Units that came from the Svir-Petrozavodsk Operation, which ended on 7 August, were the 127th Light Rifle Corps headquarters; the 3d, 69th, and 70th Naval Rifle Brigades; the 99th Rifle Corps headquarters; the 114th and 368th Rifle Divisions; the 20th Motorized Combat Engineer Brigade; the 275th and 284th Separate Motorized Special-Purpose Battalions (Amphibians); the 7th Guards Tank and 89th Tank Regiments; and the 339th and 378th Self-Propelled Artillery. See Terekhov, *Boevye deistviia tankov*, 87–111. The 31st Rifle Corps headquarters and the 45th, 83d, and 367th Rifle Divisions came from the 26th Army on the Kandalaksha axis, having concluded combat operations there on 27 September. See A. I. Babin, *Karel'skii front v Velikoi Otechestvennoi voine 1941–1945* [Karelian Front in the Great Patriotic War, 1941–1945] (Moscow: Izdatel'stvo "Nauka," 1984), map in chap. 8, hereafter cited as Babin, *Karel'skii front*. The 65th Rifle Division came to the Karelian Front in early 1944 from the Volkhov Front. The origin of other tank, engineer, and artillery reinforcements cannot be determined on the basis of available evidence.

23. Kh. A. Khudalov, *U kromki kontinenta* [At the edge of the continent] (Moscow: Voenizdat, 1974), 124, hereafter cited as Khudalov, *U kromki*.

24. The 72d Naval Rifle Brigade was one of twenty-five such brigades created in the fall of 1941. After its formation in the Siberian Military District, it was assigned to the Karelian Front, where it remained until January 1945. See Captain First Rank V. Shlomin, "Dvadtsat' piat' morskikh strelkovykh" [Twenty-five naval rifle], *Voenno istoricheskii zhurnal* [Military history journal], July 1970:96—99, hereafter cited as Shlomin, "Dvadtsat' piat'." The journal is hereafter cited as *VIZh*.

25. *Eto bylo na Karel'skom fronte* [It was on the Karelian Front] (Petrozavodsk: Izdatel'stvo "Karelia," 1985), 190; and Babin, *Karel'skii front*, 316.

26. Both of these brigades were also created in the fall of 1941 in the Siberian Military District. They were assigned to the 7th Separate Army of the Leningrad Front and came to the Karelian Front in 1944. The formation and activities of the 70th Naval Rifle Brigade from 1941 to 1944 are described in the memoir of a former member of the brigade staff, S. A. Pestanov, *Soldaty morskoi pekhoty* [Soldiers of the naval infantry] (Petrozavodsk: "Karelia," 1976), hereafter cited as Pestanov, *Soldaty*.

27. Ibid., 96. Based on the interrogation of a prisoner, a similar description of the organization of one of these brigades is found in a German source. See Klaus Brockelmann and Hans Roschmann, "Small Unit Tactics, Combats in Taiga and Tundra," Foreign Military Studies no. MS P-060m (Historical Division, U.S. Army, Europe, 1952), 148—49, hereafter cited as MS P-060m.

28. Meretskov, *Na sluzhbe*, 351.

29. N. Rumiantsev, "Primenenie olen'ego transporta v 14-i armii karel'skogo fronta" [Utilization of reindeer transport in the 14th Army of the Karelian Front], *VIZh*, November 1972:90, hereafter cited as Rumiantsev, "Primenenie."

30. Babin, *Karel'skii front*, 292, n. 20.

31. Pestanov, *Soldaty*, chap. 3, describes the encirclement of the 70th Naval Rifle Brigade during the Tuloksinsk landing. His brigade had a strength of approximately 3,000 persons in October (p. 101).

32. In October 1944, the average rifle division strength in the 99th Rifle Corps was 6,350 and, in the 31st Rifle Corps, 5,860. See appendixes E and F.

33. Babin *Karel'skii front*, 316; and *Eto bylo na Karel'skom fronte*, 189.

34. Babin, *Karel'skii front*, 317.

35. *SVE*, 6:332.

36. Shtemenko, *Soviet General Staff*, 2:374; and Meretskov, *Na sluzhbe*, 371.

37. The Russian term is *ukreplennyi raion*, which is "standard troop formation, designated for the fulfillment of a defensive mission." Such a formation routinely consisted of several artillery battalions and combat support and logistic units. *SVE*, 8:185.

38. A. G. Golovko, *Vmeste s flotom* [Together with the fleet] (Moscow: Voenizdat, 1979), 224, hereafter cited as Golovko, *Vmeste*.

39. Meretskov's proposal and the 29 September order were published in Colonel I. V. Iaroshenko and Colonel L. I. Smirnova, comps., "Osvobozhdenie sovetskogo Zapoliar'ia" [Liberation of the Soviet polar region], *VIZh*, June 1985:33—36.

40. Mikulskii and Absaliamov, *Nastupatel'nye boi*, 26. These more specific missions are further corroborated in an article by Marshal of Artillery G. Peredelskii, "Boevoe primenenie artillerii v Petsamo-Kirkenesskoi operatsii" [Combat employment of artillery in the Petsamo-Kirkenes Operation], *VIZh*, October 1984:17, hereafter cited as Peredelskii, "Primenenie artillerii."

41. This data was extracted from charts in Mikulskii and Absaliamov, *Nastupatel'nye boi*, 12—13 and 83—84. Translations of the charts are at appendixes E and F.

42. Ibid.; and Rumiantsev, *Razgrom vraga*, 157 n.

43. Peredelskii, "Primenenie artillerii," 17.

44. Peredelskii, "Primenenie artillerii," 17; Rumiantsev, *Razgrom vraga*, 157; and Mikulskii and Absaliamov, *Nastupatel'nye boi*, 27. Peredelskii, who wrote his article in 1984, probably took these figures from Rumiantsev, who wrote his study in 1963. A plausible explanation for the discrepancy between Rumiantsev and Mikulskii is that Mikulskii, the former 99th Rifle Corps commander, could have used personal notes, while Rumiantsev used archival documents.

45. Mikulskii and Absaliamov, *Nastupatel'nye boi*, 28.

46. Ibid., 29.

47. Rumiantsev, *Razgrom vraga*, 158. The Russian is *instrumental'naia razvedka*, used with the verb *zacekat'/zacech'*, which means "to determine by intersection."

48. Peredelskii, "Primenenie artillerii," 18.

49. Rumiantsev, *Razgrom vraga*, 159—60; Peredelskii, "Primenenie artillerii," 19; and Mikulskii and Absaliamov, *Nastupatel'nye boi*, 42—43.

50. In the Russian, *posledovatel'noe sosredotochenie ognia*. For a detailed explanation, see A. I. Averianov, "Posledovatel'nogo sosredotochenie ognia" [Subsequent concentration of fire], *SVE*, 6:467.

51. Peredelskii, "Primenenie artillerii," 20.

52. Self-propelled guns are included in this discussion because they were used only in direct-fire roles and were always attached to tank units.

53. Meretskov, *Na sluzhbe*, 376.

54. Rumiantsev, *Razgrom vraga*, 170; and Terekhov, *Boevye deistviia tankov*, 120—21.

55. Terekhov, *Boevye deistviia tankov*, 118—19; Rumiantsev, *Razgrom vraga*, 160—61; and Mikulskii and Absaliamov, *Nastupatel'nye boi*, 33.

56. Colonel E. I. Maikov, "Inzhenernoe obespechenie boevykh deistvii voisk v Zapoliar'e (Petsamo-Kirkenesskaia operatsiia)" [Engineer support of the combat operations of the troops in the polar region (Petsamo-Kirkenes Operation)], a chapter in *Inzhenernye voiska Sovetskoi Armii v vazhneishikh operatsiiakh Velikoi Otechestvennoi voiny* [Engineer troops of the Soviet Army in the most important operations of the Great Patriotic War], compiled by V. P. Andreev, D. S. Borisov, and A. F. Evtushenko (Moscow: Voenizdat, 1958), 178, hereafter cited as Maikov, "Inzhenernoe obespechenie." This source further defines the mission to prepare assembly areas for the army as "to provide for the concealed (*skrytnoe*) concentration of forces on the main axis."

57. Rumiantsev, *Razgrom vraga*, 161; Mikulskii and Absaliamov, *Nastupatel'nye boi*, 34—35, 81—82; and Colonel General A. F. Khrenov, *Mosty k pobede* [Bridges to victory] (Moscow: Voenizdat, 1982), 315, hereafter cited as Khrenov, *Mosty k pobede*. Another source indicates that the Karelian Front also reinforced 14th Army with fifteen battalions of various types of highway troops. See Colonel V. V. Ovsiannikov and Lieutenant Colonel V. V. Shmidt, "Tylovoe obespechenie 14-i armii v Petsamo-Kirkenesskoi operatsii" [Rear area support of 14th Army in the Petsamo-Kirkenes Operation], *VIZh*, October 1985:84, hereafter cited as Ovsiannikov and Shmidt, "Tylovoi obespechenie." Highway troops, by definition, include traffic control, road construction, and bridge construction units. See "Dorozhnye voiska" [Highway troops], *SVE*, 3:251—52.

58. Rumiantsev, *Razgrom vraga*, 160. Textual and photographic evidence suggests that the 275th was equipped with 2½-ton amphibious trucks, and the 284th was equipped with

¼-ton amphibious jeeps. See Terekhov, *Boevye deistvii tankov*, photograph on 91 and text on 92 and 104.

59. Mikulskii and Absaliamov, *Nastupatel'nye boi*, 12.

60. Rumiantsev, *Razgrom vraga*, 161—62; and Maikov, "Inzhenernoe obespechenie," 179.

61. Rumiantsev, *Razgrom vraga*, 162; Maikov, "Inzhenernoe obespechenie," 182; and Mikulskii and Absaliamov, *Nastupatel'nye boi*, 36.

62. Maikov, "Inzhenernoe obespechenie, 179, 181; Rumiantsev, *Razgrom vraga*, 161; and Mikulskii and Absaliamov, *Nastupatel'nye boi*, chart on 35—36.

63. Rumiantsev, *Razgrom vraga*, 162—63; and Maikov, "Inzhenernoe obespechenie," 181.

64. Information pertaining to air support was compiled principally from four Soviet journal articles: Lieutenant Colonel N. Komarov, "Voiska PVO strany v Petsamo-Kirkenesskoi operatsii" [Troops of national air defense in the Petsamo-Kirkenes Operation], *VIZh*, October 1974:28—33, hereafter cited as Komarov, "Voiska PVO"; and three articles by Lieutenant Colonel I. G. Inozemtsev, "Udari po aerodromam protivnika na severnom i severo-zapadnom napravleniiakh (1941—1944gg)" [Strikes against enemy airfields on the northern and northwestern axes (1941—1944)], *VIZh*, December 1974:17—24, hereafter cited as Inozemtsev, "Udari"; "Sovetskaia aviatsiia v Petsamo-Kirkenesskoi operatsii (Oktiabr 1944g)" [Soviet aviation in the Petsamo-Kirkenes Operation (October 1944)], *Istoriia SSSR* [History of the U.S.S.R.], February 1975:101—10, hereafter cited as Inozemtsev, "Sovetskaia aviatsiia"; and "Osobennosti boevogo primeneniia aviatsii v Zapoliare" [Features of combat utilization of aviation in the polar region], *VIZh*, November 1976:20—28.

65. Inozemtsev, "Sovetskaia aviatsiia," 102.

66. General Sokolov was born in 1900, joined the Red Army in 1918, and transferred from the cavalry to the air force in 1929. He was the chief of staff of an aviation brigade in the 1939—40 Soviet-Finnish War, then chief of staff of an aviation division of the 14th Army, and finally chief of staff of the air forces of the Karelian Front. He took command of the Karelian Front's air forces in June 1942 and, in November, the 7th Air Army. See *SVE*, 7:435.

67. Terekhov, *Boevye deistviia tankov*, 120.

68. Rumiantsev, *Razgrom vraga*, 165.

69. Ibid., 102; and Komarov, "Voiska PVO," 28.

70. Information pertaining to logistic support is derived primarily from four sources: Rumiantsev, *Razgrom vraga*, 168—70; Colonel N. Maliugin, "Tyl 14-i armii v Petsamo-Kirkenesskoi operatsii" [The rear services of the 14th Army in the Petsamo-Kirkenes Operation], *VIZh*, February 1973:97—102, hereafter cited as Maliugin, "Tyl"; Colonel General (Reserve) I. Volkotrubenko, "Obespechenie voisk boepripasami v operatsii po razgromu vraga v Zapoliare" [The supplying of ammunition to the forces in the operation for the defeat of the enemy in the polar region], *VIZh*, October 1984:81—82, hereafter cited as Volkotrubenko, "Obespechenie voisk"; and Ovsiannikov and Shmidt, "Tylovoe obespechenie," 82—87.

71. Rumiantsev, *Razgrom vraga*, 168.

72. Maliugin, "Tyl," 97.

73. In Russian *boevoi komplekt*, which is the estimated quantity of ammunition required per day to sustain operations for a single weapon system or unit, based on both expenditure experience and system carrying capacity. The closest NATO equivalent is "required supply rate."

74. Maliugin, "Tyl," 99; and Ovsiannikov and Shmidt, "Tylovoe obespechenie," 85, both citing the same archival source.

75. Ibid.

76. Maliugin, "Tyl," 100, gives the number of reindeer as 532, and Ovsiannikov and Shmidt, "Tylovoe obespechenie," 85, gives 572. Load capacities for horses and reindeer are from Volkotrubenko, "Obespechenie voisk," 87. For a detailed discussion of using reindeer as draft animals in the 14th Army, see Rumiantsev, "Primenenie," 86—90.

77. Khudalov, *U kromki*, 122; and Ovsiannikov and Shmidt, "Tylovoe obespechenie," 86.

78. Maliugin, "Tyl," 102; and Ovsiannikov and Shmidt, "Tylovoe obespechenie," 87.

79. Volkotrubenko, "Obespechenie voisk," 87.

80. Rumiantsev, *Razgrom vraga*, 167. The 14th Army chief of rear services was Major General N. A. Shabanov. The identity of the Karelian Front chief of rear services is not known.

81. Meretskov, *Na sluzhbe*, 343, 354.

82. For a thorough discussion of this very complex command and control system, see "Upravlenie voiskami" [Troop control], *SVE*, 8:203—4; M. M. Kirian, ed., *Fronty nastupali: po opytu Velikoi Otechestvennoi voiny* [Fronts attacked: According to the experience of the Great Patriotic War] (Moscow: "Nauka," 1987), 178—79; and R. Portugalskii and N. Fomin, "Nekotorye voprosy sovershenstvovaniia struktury organov upravleniia fronta i armii" [Some questions about the improvement of the structure of the command and control organs of the Front and army], *VIZh*, August 1978:33—41.

83. Khrenov, *Mosty k pobede*, 236.

84. A. I. Babin, *Na volkhovskom fronte 1941—1944gg* [On the Volkhov Front, 1941—1944] (Moscow: "Nauka," 1982), 341.

85. Babin, *Karel'skii front*, 313.

86. This process is described in detail in Mikulskii and Absaliamov, *Nastupatel'nye boi*, 37—38.

87. Rumiantsev, *Razgrom vraga*, 171.

Chapter 2

1. This quotation is an excerpt from Lieutenant General Degen's proclamation to the soldiers of 2d Mountain Division on 12 September 1944. See Germany, 2d Mt Div, KTB 1, microfilm series T-315, roll 109, frame 00823, NARA. A translation of the proclamation is at appendix D.

2. Terekhov, *Boevye deistviia tankov*, 121.

3. Mikulskii and Absaliamov, *Nastupatel'nye boi*, 50.

4. Ibid., 24—25.

5. Khudalov, *U kromki*, 144. General Khudalov's 10th Guards Rifle Division was on the left flank of the 131st Rifle Corps' first echelon.

6. Mikulskii and Absaliamov, *Nastupatel'nye boi*, 48—49.

7. Ibid., 50; and Germany, 20th Army, KTB 5, Air operations daily and morning report for 7—8 October 1944, microfilm series T-312, roll 1063, frame 9265044, NARA.

8. Khudalov, *U kromki*, 147.

9. Ibid., 151.

10. Rumiantsev, *Razgrom vraga*, 177.

11. A. Pavozkov, "Reid korpusa polkovnika solov'eva" [The raid of Colonel Solovev's corps], in *Eto bylo na Krainem Severe*, 208—14, hereafter cited as Pavozkov, "Reid."

12. Germany, 20th Army, KTB 5, entry for 1000, 8 October 1944, roll 1061; and Anlage 13 to 8 October entry, roll 1063, frames 9265095—96; both in microfilm series T-312, NARA.

13. Pestanov, *Soldaty*, 99.

14. Germany, 20th Army, KTB 5, entry for 1300, 8 October 1944, microfilm series T-312, roll 1061, NARA.

15. Ibid., entry for 1645, 8 October 1944. General Ferdinand Jodl was General Alfred Jodl's (of the *OKW*) nephew.

16. Ibid., Anlage 11 to 8 October entry, microfilm series T-312, roll 1063, frame 9265093, NARA.

17. Ibid., Anlage 13 to 8 October entry, microfilm series T-312, roll 1063, NARA.

18. Rumiantsev, *Razgrom vraga*, 178.

19. Mikulskii and Absaliamov, *Nastupatel'nye boi*, 56—57.

20. Ibid.

21. Rumiantsev, *Razgrom vraga*, 179.

22. Long-distance conversation between the German 20th Army chief of staff, General Holter, and commander, XIX Mountain Corps. Germany, 20th Army, KTB 5, entry for 1600, 9 October 1944, microfilm series T-312, roll 1061, NARA.

23. Rumiantsev, *Razgrom vraga*, 268.

24. Ibid., 180; and Germany, 20th Army, KTB 5, Daily air operations report for 8—9 October 1944, microfilm series T-312, roll 1061, frame 9265086, NARA.

25. Germany, 20th Army, KTB 5, entries for 1145 and 1600, 9 October 1944, microfilm series T-312, roll 1061, NARA.

26. In various Soviet sources, the size of this landing force ranges from 2,751 to 3,000. For a complete description of all the amphibious landings, see chapter 5.

27. Disoriented by German searchlights and their own smoke screen, several vessels landed their troops at points other than those specified in their plans and orders, resulting in confusion that lasted until morning. See S. I. Kabanov, *Pole boiia-bereg* [The battlefield is the shore] (Moscow: Voenizdat, 1977), 297—99, hereafter cited as Kabonov, *Pole boiia*.

28. Germany, 20th Army, KTB 5, entries for 2245 and 2400, 9 October 1944, microfilm series T-312, roll 1061, NARA.

29. The German defenses along the isthmus are described in greater detail in Kabanov, *Pole boiia*, 293—95.

30. Rumiantsev, *Razgrom vraga*, 191—92; and Kabanov, *Pole boiia*, 300—302.

31. Pavozkov, "Reid," 211.

32. Pestanov, *Soldaty*, 104—05.

33. Rumiantsev, *Razgrom vraga*, 188; and Mikulskii and Absaliamov, *Nastupatel'nye boi*, 59.

34. Mikulskii and Absaliamov, *Nastupatel'nye boi*, 59; and Khudalov, *U kromki*, 156.

35. Germany, 20th Army, KTB 5, entry for 1630, 9 October 1944, conversation between chiefs of staff, 20th Army and XIX Mountain Corps, microfilm series T-312, roll 1061, NARA.

36. The approach march of this division and its combat actions for 11—15 October are described in an article by Major Iu. Kuzmichev, "S marsha v boi" [From the march into battle], *VIZh*, November 1974:48—55, hereafter cited as Kuzmichev, "S marsha v boi."

37. Germany, 20th Army, KTB 5, entries for 1345 and 1600, 10 October 1944, microfilm series T-312, roll 1061, NARA.

38. Mikulskii and Absaliamov, *Nastupatel'nye boi*, 61.

39. Ibid., 60—61; and Khudalov, *U kromki*, 160.

40. Mikulskii and Absaliamov, *Nastupatel'nye boi*, 60; and Khudalov, *U kromki*, 159.

41. Soviet sources differ in explaining the naval infantry's failure to closely pursue the retreating German force. See Admiral of the Fleet G. Egorov, "Severnyi flot v Petsamo-Kirkenesskoi operatsii" [Northern Fleet in the Petsamo-Kirkenes operation], *VIZh*, October 1974:19—26, hereafter cited as Egorov, "Severnyi"; and Kabanov, *Pole boiia*, 306. The former commander of the 12th Naval Infantry Brigade neatly avoided discussing this problem in his brief memoir of the offensive. See Major General (Reserve) V. V. Rassokhin, "Ikh podvig v pamiati narodnoi" [Their feat is in the national memory], in *V boiakh-morskaia pekhota* [Naval infantry in battles], compiled by S. I. Polozov and V. P. Zagrebin (Murmansk: Knizhnoe Izdatel'stvo, 1984), 35.

42. Inozemtsev, "Sovetskaia aviatsiia," 106. Unfortunately, the German air operations report for this date could not be found to support or refute the Soviet account. In another article, Inozemtsev claims that Soviet air forces flew a total of 371 sorties against German airfields in October. Inozemtsev, "Udari," 23—24.

43. Pestanov, *Soldaty*, 106. So desperate was this unit for food that it ambushed a German supply truck and carried off the provisions.

44. Germany, 20th Army, KTB 5, entry for 0001, 12 October 1944, microfilm series T-312, roll 1061, NARA.

45. MS P-060m, 106.

46. Rumiantsev, *Razgrom vraga*, 187.

47. Pestanov, *Soldaty*, beginning on 107. It cannot be determined precisely where or when the 70th Naval Rifle Brigade reached Tarnet Road. Pestanov's memoir lacks a map, uses place names that do not appear on other maps, and does not contain any dates between 7 and 14 October. Since he personally participated in this action, however, and describes it in some detail, his account must be considered. Rumiantsev, *Razgrom vraga*, sketch 13, 184, shows the 70th Naval Rifle Brigade to the west and south of Tarnet Road on 13 and 14 October and does not mention that the 70th cut the road. This aspect of the battle needs additional research in Soviet sources not yet available.

48. Khudalov, *U kromki*, 165—66.

49. Germany, 20th Army, KTB 5, entries for 1500 and 2105, 13 October, microfilm series T-312, roll 1061, NARA.

50. Ibid., Morning report (Anlage 3) and Daily report (Anlage 1) for 14 October 1944, microfilm series T-312, roll 1061, frames 9265196, 9265202—3, NARA. Pestanov, *Soldaty*, beginning on 108, indicates that the 70th Naval Rifle Brigade of 127th Light Rifle Corps finally seized positions straddling Tarnet Road on the morning of 14 October, cutting the path of retreat. This does not agree with other Soviet accounts or with German records.

51. Rumiantsev, *Razgrom vraga*, 210. This estimate is probably low.

52. Ibid., 198.

53. Concerning German personnel losses on 7—15 October, three Soviet sources use the figure 18,000: Rumiantsev, *Razgrom vraga*, 199 ("up to 18,000 killed"); Mikulskii and Absaliamov, *Nastupatel'nye boi*, 78 ("18,000 killed and wounded"); and Lieutenant General (Reserve) Kh. A. Khudalov, "Petsamo-Kirkenesskaia operatsiia" [The Petsamo-Kirkenes Operation], *VIZh*, October 1969:116 ("18,000 killed") citing an archival source. The author's estimate of 6,000 is based on an analysis of XIX Mountain Corps reports and records. The after-

action reports of the 136th and 137th Mountain Rifle Regiments, 2d Mountain Division, indicate that the 2d Mountain Division suffered at least 1,858 casualties, approximately two-thirds of the division's 2,954 casualties for the whole of October. Since XIX Mountain Corps' losses for the month of October were between 8,000 and 9,000 men, the 2d Mountain Division casualty ratio of two-thirds equates to 5,300 to 6,000 casualites across the entire corps for 7—15 October. See Germany, 2d Mt Div, KTB 1, microfilm series T-315, roll 109, folder 77653, NARA. Total German casualties for the period are indicated in Message to Major Benze, *OKW* staff, from Operations group, Commander Nordfinnland, no. 1494/44, dated 8 November 1944, in Germany, 20th Army, KTB 5, microfilm series T-312, roll 1063, frame 9265810, NARA.

Chapter 3

1. Germany, 20th Army, KTB 5, entries for 15 and 16 October, microfilm series T-312, roll 1061, NARA. Ziemke discusses the 15 October meeting in DA Pam 20-271, 306—7.

2. Maliugin, "Tyl," 101; and Rumiantsev, *Razgrom vraga*, 207.

3. Location and missions of Soviet units are discussed in Rumiantsev, *Razgrom vraga*, 201—2; and Mikulskii and Absaliamov, *Nastupatel'nye boi*, 79, 89.

4. Several Norwegian civilians interviewed by the author during a field research trip to the Kirkenes area in October 1987 both heard and saw "Stalin's organs" between Tarnet and Kirkenes during 22—25 October.

5. Rumiantsev, *Razgrom vraga*, 207.

6. Meretskov, *Na sluzhbe*, 380. As justification for crossing the Norwegian border, the Soviets cite an agreement signed with the Norwegian government in exile in London on 16 May 1944. See Admiral V. Alekseev, "Severnyi flot v osvobozhdenii sovetskogo Zapoliaria i severnoi Norvegii" [The Northern Fleet in the liberation of the Soviet polar region and northern Norway], *Morskoi Sbornik* [Naval proceedings], No. 10—1974:65, hereafter cited as Alekseev, "Severnyi." A text of the agreement is contained in *Vneshniaia politika Sovetskogo Soiuza v period Otechestvennoi Voiny* [Foreign policy of the Soviet Union during the Patriotic War] (Moscow: Politizdat, 1946), 2:135.

7. Mikulskii and Absaliamov, *Nastupatel'nye boi*, 82.

8. The tank regiment had sixteen operational vehicles, with three being repaired at unit level. The self-propelled artillery regiment had only four operational systems, with three being repaired at unit level and ten at Front level. Ibid., chart on 85.

9. Ibid., 82.

10. Rumiantsev, *Razgrom vraga*, 204; and Mikulskii and Absaliamov, *Nastupatel'nye boi*, 79.

11. Rumiantsev, *Razgrom vraga*, 205.

12. Kare Kristensen, interview with author, Elvenes, Norway, 15 October 1987. A second, unnamed civilian verified this in an interview at his home on Jar Fjord, 16 October 1987.

13. The degree of coordination between the 368th Rifle Division and naval infantry units cannot be ascertained from available Soviet sources. The source that was most likely to address this important issue, but did not, is the history of 368th Rifle Division. See *Ot Tiumeni do Kirkenesa* [From Tiumen to Kirkenes] (Sverdlovsk: Sverdlovsk-Uralskoe knizhoe izdatel'stvo, 1976), the section beginning on 167.

14. Actions of the 99th Rifle Corps are described in Rumiantsev, *Razgrom vraga*, 207—16; and Khudalov, *U kromki*, 174—77.

15. Rumiantsev, *Razgrom vraga*, 212.

16. Rumiantsev, *Razgrom vraga*, 215. The 284th Separate Motorized Special-Purpose Battalion (*otdelnyi motorizovannyi batalon osobogo naznacheniia*) was equipped with ninety-four American-made Ford amphibious jeeps. See Mikuskii and Absaliamov, *Nastupatel'nye boi*, chart on 13 (284 *ombon*); and Kh. A. Khudalov, "Na glavnom napravlenii" [On the main axis], in *Cherez fiordy* [Through the fjords], compiled by V. G. Korshunov (Moscow: Voenizdat, 1969), 82, hereafter cited as Khudalov, "Na glavnom napravlenii"; the book is hereafter cited as *Cherez fiordy*.

17. Rumiantsev, *Razgrom vraga*, 215—16. During a field research trip in October 1987, the author visited this bridge site on the Norwegian side. Soviet metal engineer stakes are still visible in the water at the exit point. On the Soviet side, the road break in the tree line can be seen.

18. Rumiantsev, *Razgrom vraga*, 202.

19. Ibid. During phase two of the offensive, the 126th Light Rifle Corps had little contact until it approached Lake Klistervatn. Rumiantsev gives the 126th a sentence on page 209 and a paragraph on page 214. See also General Ferdinand Jodl, "Kursbericht ueber die Kampfhandlungen im Petsamo und Varangerraum" [A short report regarding the combat actions in Petsamo and Varanger area], 5 November 1944, microfilm series T-312, roll 1069, item 75034/1, NARA, hereafter cited as Jodl, "Kursbericht."

20. Mikulskii and Absaliamov, *Nastupatel'nye boi*, table 10 on 90.

21. Ibid., 87.

22. Ibid., 96.

23. Rumiantsev, *Razgrom vraga*, 209; and Mikulskii and Absaliamov, *Nastupatel'nye boi*, 99—100.

24. Pestanov, *Soldaty*, beginning on 111.

25. Mikulskii and Absaliamov, *Nastupatel'nye boi*, 102—3.

26. Ibid., 146.

27. Ibid., 104—5.

28. The three Soviet accounts of this action are contradictory. Absaliamov asserts in his 1959 account that the withdrawing Germans pushed aside the 127th Light Rifle Corps units blocking the road, and his accompanying map also indicates this. Mikulskii and Absaliamov, *Nastupatel'nye boi*, 119. Rumiantsev, on the other hand, writing in 1963 and citing an archival source, contends that the 127th LRC unit was not astride Arctic Ocean Highway at all but had occupied a sector of the road between Nikel and the airfield. Rumiantsev, *Razgrom vraga*, 217. Pestanov, who was with the 70th Naval Rifle Brigade, vaguely describes small-unit actions southwest of Nikel, indicating that the "3d Battalion reached the road, but met strong enemy fire, and went to ground." Pestanov, *Soldaty*, 119. German war diary entries support the Absaliamov account. See Germany, 20th Army, KTB 5, entries for 20 and 21 October 1944, microfilm series T-312, roll 1061, NARA. Narrative and map notations are also contained in Germany, 2d Mt Div, KTB 1, "Gefechtsberecht ueber das Gefecht am 20. und 21.10.1944 sudlich der Kolosjokibrucke" [Action report for the action on 20—21 October 1944 south of Kolosjoki bridge], 15 December 1944, frames 1044—54, microfilm series T-315, NARA. For a detailed description of the German counterattack conducted on the morning of 21 October, see MS P-060m, 131—48. This account was written several years after the war.

29. Rumiantsev, *Razgrom vraga*, 212; and Mikulskii and Absaliamov, *Nastupatel'nye boi*, 106.

30. Rumiantsev, *Razgrom vraga*, 214.

31. MS P-060m, 134.

32. Ibid., 150.

Chapter 4

1. Rumiantsev, *Razgrom vraga*, 219; and V. I. Shcherbakov, "Nastuplenie" [The offensive], 60, in *Cherez fiordy*.

2. Rumiantsev, *Razgrom vraga*, 222. This unusually heavy ammunition expenditure is explained in part by the fact that Kirkenes was the supply base for the region, and anything not consumed or destroyed would fall into Soviet hands. The Germans, realizing this, probably chose to fire it at targets rather than destroy it.

3. Major General Khudalov writes in *U kromki*, 185, that Lieutenant General Shcherbakov gave him this order by radio at 1600, 24 October. His corps commander, Lieutenant General Mikulskii, appeared at the division command post fifteen to twenty minutes later with additional guidance for the regiment.

4. Ibid., 190.

5. The entry of KV heavy tanks into Kirkenes is described by V. Arshinevskii, former commander of the tank regiment, in "Tiazhelye tanki v zapoliar'e" [Heavy tanks in the polar region], in *Eto bylo na krainem severe*, 225—30.

6. Khudalov, *U kromki*, 187; and Ella Mathisen, interview with author, Munkelv, Norway, 17 October 1987.

7. Khudalov, *U kromki*, 187.

8. Unnamed Norwegian civilian, interview with author, Neiden, Norway, 17 October 1987.

9. Meretskov, *Na sluzhbe*, 381—82.

10. Rumiantsev, *Razgrom vraga*, 226.

11. Mikulskii and Absaliamov, *Nastupatel'nye boi*, 125.

12. Ibid., 127.

13. Ibid., 120; Terekhov, *Boevye deistviia tankov*, 130; and Rumiantsev, *Razgrom vraga*, 223.

14. Pestanov, *Soldaty*, 121.

15. Rumiantsev, *Razgrom vraga*, 233; and Mikulskii and Absaliamov, *Nastupatel'nye boi*, 129.

16. The battle fought here is described in detail by the former chief of operations, 163d Infantry Division, in MS P-060m, 112—17, and by Major General Absaliamov in Mikulskii and Absaliamov, *Nastupatel'nye boi*, 130—34. These two accounts coincide in all significant details of the combat but differ on the unit designation of the German defenders.

17. Mikulskii and Absaliamov, *Nastupatel'nye boi*, 134.

18. Rumiantsev, *Razgrom vraga*, 236. Pestanov, *Soldaty*, beginning on 123, indicates that the 127th Light Rifle Corps crossed into Norway in approximately twenty boats manned by Norwegian civilians on an unspecified date. In the following several pages, he mentions the corps encountering two prisoner-of-war camps, one for Soviet military personnel and the other for civilians, but no combat actions. The corps recrossed the Norwegian-Finnish border and advanced as far as Nautsi.

19. Ole Sotkajervi, interview with author, Stenbakk, Norway, 18 October 1987. According to this source, "hundreds and hundreds" of Russian soldiers crossed the Pasvik River at Stenbakk early on the morning of 25 October 1944 on log rafts. The Germans in the area had fled southward three to four hours before the Soviets arrived. The local Finnish farmers gave these soldiers, who were described as "starving teen-age boys," fresh meat from recently slaughtered cattle.

20. Ibid. Local inhabitants interviewed recalled the flooding downstream that resulted from the destruction of the dam.

21. Mikulskii and Absaliamov, *Nastupatel'nye boi*, 140.

22. See MS P-060m, 117—21, for a description of this action from the German perspective. See also Mikulskii and Absaliamov, *Nastupatel'nye boi*, 141—42.

23. Meretskov, *Na sluzhbe*, 382. During the Great Patriotic War, artillery salutes were fired in Moscow in honor of Soviet forces that had achieved a significant victory at the front. The first such salute was fired on 5 August 1943 in recognition of the liberation of the cities of Orel and Belgorod. By war's end, 354 ceremonial salutes had been fired. See *SVE*, 7:219.

Chapter 5

1. I. A. Kozlov and V. S. Shlomin, *Krasnoznamennyi severnyi flot* [Red Banner Northern Fleet] (Moscow: Voenizdat, 1983), 70, hereafter cited as Kozlov and Shlomin, *Krasnoznamennyi*. The development and growth of Soviet naval power in the Barents Sea area accompanied the rapid economic development of the entire Kola Peninsula infrastructure during the 1930s. Murmansk, for example, grew from a population of 10,000 in 1930 to 119,000 by 1939.

2. Golovko's memoir, *Vmeste*, which recently was published in English by Progress Publishers, begins with his fleet command appointment in 1940. For a brief biographical sketch, see *SVE*, 2:592.

3. In June 1941, when Germany attacked the U.S.S.R., the ages of the Soviet fleet commanders were Golovko (Northern)—34, Tributz (Baltic)—41, Oktiabrskii (Black Sea)—42, and Iumashev (Pacific)—46.

4. Kozlov and Shlomin, *Krasnoznamennyi*, 84.

5. Ibid., 88.

6. Ibid., 154—55.

7. In 1944, through lend-lease, the Northern Fleet received three minesweepers, fifteen large subchasers, thirty-one small subchasers, and forty-four patrol torpedo boats. B. A. Vainer, *Severnyi flot v Velikoi Otechestvennoi voine* [The Northern Fleet in the Great Patriotic War] (Moscow: Voenizdat, 1964), 206, cited in V. Konavalov, "Iz opyta popolneniia sostava severnogo flota v gody velikoi otechestvennoi voiny" [From the experience of the replenishment of the complement of the Northern Fleet during the Great Patriotic War], *VIZh*, August 1978:109. The patrol torpedo boats were of the British Vosper design, built in Annapolis, Maryland, and Bristol, Rhode Island. See Robert J. Bulkley, *At Close Quarters: PT Boats in the U.S. Navy* (Washington, DC: U.S. Government Printing Office, 1962), 484.

8. Alekseev, "Severnyi," 63.

9. Kozlov and Shlomin, *Krasnoznamennyi*, 183.

10. Ibid., 156.

11. Admiral of the Fleet G. Egorov, "Sovershenstvovanie upravleniia silami VMF v pervom periode voiny" [The improvement of command and control of forces of the Navy in the first period of the war], *VIZh*, May 1979:26. The term used in Russian is *operativnoe podchinenie* (operational subordination).

12. Discussed in G. Egorov, "Sovershenstvovanie upravleniia silami VMF vo vtoroi i tret'em periodakh voiny" [The improvement of command and control of forces of the Navy in the second and third periods of the war], *VIZh*, January 1980:21.

13. Ibid., 22. See also L. I. Olshtynskii, *Vzaimodeistvie armii i flota* [Cooperation of army and fleet] (Moscow: Voenizdat, 1983), chap. 6, hereafter cited as Olshtynskii, *Vzaimodeistvie*.

14. Meretskov, *Na sluzhbe*, 350.

15. Admiral N. G. Kuznetsov, *Kursom k pobede* [The course to victory] (Moscow: Voenizdat, 1976), 422, hereafter cited as Kuznetsov, *Kursom*.

16. Some of the evidence is linguistic; for example, the frequent use of the Russian word *vzaimodeistvie* (mutual action, cooperation, coordination) and the total absence of the term *podchinenie* (subordination) in passages pertaining to the command relationship. Other evidence is more direct. See, for example, Meretskov's Front order of 29 September (appendix A). In it, he orders (*prikazyvaiu*) the 14th Army units but not the naval infantry. See also Olshtynskii, *Vzaimodestvie*, 195.

17. Admiral V. N. Platonov, "Pravoflangovye" [The men on the right flank], a chapter in *Cherez fiordy*, 103, hereafter cited as Platonov, "Pravoflangovyi."

18. Kuznetsov, *Kursom*, 422.

19. Golovko, *Vmeste*, 224.

20. Vice Admiral A. V. Kuzmin, *V pribrezhnykh vodakh* [In coastal waters] (Moscow: Voenizdat, 1967), 179—80, hereafter cited as Kuzmin, *V pribrezhnykh vodakh*. Kuzmin was commander of Golovko's patrol torpedo brigade and was invited to this meeting.

21. This meeting is described in Golovko, *Vmeste*, 227; and Meretskov, *Na sluzhbe*, 374.

22. Ibid.

23. Golovko uses the Russian term *tsirkuliarnoe ukazanie* (circular directive). See *Vmeste*, 227. Kuznetsov, however, carefully describes the dispatch (*depesha*) and the wording of it in light of the command relationship between Golovko and Meretskov. See *Kursom*, 423.

24. Captain First Rank (Reserve) A. Alekseev and Captain Second Rank Engineer (Reserve) M. Kariagin, "Navigatsionno-gidrograficheskoe obespechenie Petsamo-Kirkenesskoi nastupatel'noi operatsii" [Navigational-hydrographic support of the Petsamo-Kirkenes offensive operation], *Morskoi Sbornik* [Naval proceedings], No. 5—1980:22—27; and Captain First Rank (Reserve) A. P. Aristov, "Navigatsionno-gidrograficheskoe obespechenie boevykh deistvii sil flota v Arkticheskom basseine" [Navigational-hydrographic support of combat operations of forces of the fleet in the arctic basin], *VIZh*, April 1987:44—51.

25. Golovko, *Vmeste*, 231.

26. Colonel I. I. Kartavtsev, "Morskaia pekhota v boiakh za osvobozhdenie sovetskogo Zapoliar'ia" [Naval infantry in battles for the liberation of the Soviet polar region], *VIZh*, March 1985:83, hereafter cited as Kartavtsev, "Morskaia pekhota."

27. Germany, 20th Army, KTB 5, entry for 2330, 9 October 1944, microfilm series T-312, roll 1061, NARA.

28. The gathering up of this force is described in Kabanov, *Pole boiia*, 308.

29. The Liinakhamari landings are described in detail in the booklet by K. F. Fokeev, *Desant v Liinakhamari* [Assault on Liinakhamari] (Moscow: Voenizdat, 1968), hereafter cited as Fokeev, *Desant*; in Kuzmin, *V pribrezhnykh vodakh*, 197—213; and in a recent article by L. Verkhogliad, "Brosok na Petsamo" [The rush at Petsamo], *Voennyi vestnik* [Military herald], November, 1988:13—15.

30. Rumiantsev, *Razgrom vraga*, 230, indicates that this hydroelectric station had an output of 30,000 kilowatts and that it was captured intact on 24 October. In an interview with the author at the site on 16 October 1987, the station operator indicated that the single turbine had a maximum output of 3,000 kilowatts. Alekseev, "Severnyi," 66, citing an archival source, indicates that this power station was captured on 22 October. Ziemke, in DA Pam 20—271, 308, makes reference to a hydroelectric station at Tarnet. This station, which is no longer functional, by external appearances is three to four times larger than the Kobbholm Fjord station, but it is not referred to in any Soviet sources.

31. Platonov, "Pravoflangovyi," 101, 107.

32. "... podgotovlennaia nami vysadka v Varde i Vadse podderzhki v Moskve ne nashla" (... the landing prepared by us in Vardo and Vadso did not find support in Moscow). Ibid., 197.

33. The single source for information on this landing is V. N. Leonov. He referred to it briefly in his memoir *Litsom k litsu* [Face to face] (Moscow: Voenizdat, 1957), 128—31, hereafter cited as Leonov, *Litsom*, and provided a few more details in his chapter "Vperedsmotriashchie" [The lookouts], in *Cherez fiordy*, 174—78, hereafter cited as Leonov, "Vperedsmotriashchie."

34. Inozemtsev, "Sovetskaia aviatsiia," 102.

35. Ibid., 103.

36. Rumiantsev, *Razgrom vraga*, 195; and Kartavtsev, "Morskaia pekhota," 85.

37. Inozemtsev, "Sovetskaia aviatsiia," 109.

38. Egorov, "Severnyi," 24; Golovko, *Vmeste*, 229; Captain First Rank V. Shlomin, "Boevye deistviia Severnogo Flota v 1944 gody" [Combat operations of the Northern Fleet in 1944], *Morskoi Sbornik* [Naval proceedings], No. 9—1974:11; and A. V. Basov, *Flot v Velikoi Otechestvennoi voine 1941—1945: opyt operativno-strategicheskogo primeneniia* [The fleet in the Great Patriotic War, 1941—1945: The experience of operational-strategic utilization] (Moscow: Nauka, 1980), 175.

Chapter 6

1. Meretskov briefly mentions these detachments, calling them "not simple scouts, but detachments of sappers." See *Na sluzhbe*, 376. Their designation as special-purpose detachments (*otriadov spetsialnogo naznacheniia*) comes from Major General D. S. Krutskikh in "Udary po tylam" [Strikes in the rear area], in *Eto bylo na krainem severe*, 203, hereafter cited as Krutskikh, "Udary po tylam." Lieutenant Colonel Krutskikh, an engineer officer on the Karelian Front engineer staff in 1944, was responsible for training the detachments. G. Emelianov calls them "detachments of sappers-demolitions men" in "V glubokom tylu vraga" [In the deep enemy rear area], *VIZh*, October 1974:55—59, hereafter cited as Emelianov, "V glubokom tylu." Colonel General A. F. Khrenov, who in 1944 was Karelian Front chief of engineer troops and Krutskikh's superior, uses "sappers of reconnaissance-diversionary detachments" in his memoir, *Mosty k pobede*, 318.

2. Krutskikh, "Udari po tylam," 203. The 6th Guards Battalion of Demolitian Specialists was a far from ordinary engineer unit. According to a recently published history of Soviet engineer troops, each Front had such a battalion by October 1942. See S. Kh. Aganov, ed., *Inzhenernye voiska Sovetskoi Armii 1918—1945* [Engineer troops of the Soviet Army, 1918—1945] (Moscow: Voenizdat, 1985), 459—63. According to this source, all guards demolition specialists battalions were specially trained and equipped for reconnaissance and diversionary actions in German rear areas.

3. Khrenov, *Mosty k pobede*, 319.

4. Emelianov, "V glubokom tylu," 55.

5. Khrenov, *Mosty k pobede*, 317.

6. Ibid., 320.

7. The detailed descriptions that follow come from Krutskikh, "Udary po tylam," 204—5; Emelianov, "V glubokom tylu," 56—59; and Khrenov, *Mosty k pobede*, 319—37. (Beginning on 320, Khrenov quotes from written recollections of Guards Major A. F. Popov, who commanded the 6th Separate Guards Battalion of Demolition Specialists in the operation.)

8. Germany, 2d Mt Div, KTB 1, "Gebirgsjagerregiment 137, Gefechtsbericht ueber die Kampfhandlungen am 7.u.8.10.44 im Abschnitt Isar" [Mountain rifle regiment 137, action report on the defensive battle on 7 and 8 October 1944 in the Isar sector], microfilm series T-315, roll 109, frame 1089, NARA.

9. Germany, 20th Army, KTB 5, Anlage 4, Morning report, to the entry of 8 October 1944, microfilm series T-312, roll 1063, NARA.

10. Germany, 20th Army, KTB 5, Anlage 1, Daily report, to the entry of 10 October 1944, microfilm series T-312, roll 1063, NARA.

11. Krutskikh, "Udary po tylam," 206.

12. Jodl, "Kursbericht," entry for 13 October.

13. Emelianov, "V glubokom tylu," 59.

14. Khrenov, *Mosty k pobede*, 324.

15. Meretskov, *Na sluzhbe*, 376.

16. Golovko, *Vmeste*, 227; and Kuznetsov, *Kursom*, 423.

17. Barchenko-Emelianov finished a brief memoir shortly before his death in January 1984, *Frontovye budnyi Rybach'ego* [Days at the front on the Rybachii Peninsula] (Murmansk: Knizhnoe Izdatel'stvo, 1984), hereafter cited as Barchenko-Emelianov, *Frontovye*.

18. The best Soviet accounts of the early history and combat actions of this detachment are by M. A. Babikov, *Letom sorok pervogo* [The summer of forty-one] (Moscow: "Sovetskaia Rossiia," 1980) and *Otriad osobogo naznacheniia* [Special-purpose detachment] (Moscow: "Sovetskaia Rossiia," 1986). An analysis of these accounts in English appears in William H. Burgess III, ed., *Inside Spetsnaz: Soviet Special Operations* (Novato, CA: Presidio Press, 1989)

19. Leonov's memoir does not give specific dates for these events; they are estimates based on textual analysis. See Leonov, *Litsom*.

20. Four eyewitness accounts have been used to reconstruct the events of the raid: Barchenko-Emelianov, *Frontovye*, 138—54; Leonov, *Litsom*, 106—26; Leonov, "Vperedsmotriashchie"; and A. N. Sintsov, "Shturm Krestovogo" [The storming of Krestovyi], in *Eto bylo na krainem severe*, 215—21, hereafter cited as Sintsov, "Shturm." Sintsov was an officer in Barchenko-Emelianov's detachment. Another detailed but secondary source is Fokeev, *Desant*, 20—34.

21. Leonov, "Vperedsmotriashchie," 172; and Sintsov, "Shturm," 218.

22. Leonov, "Vperedsmotriashchie," 173; and Sintsov, "Shturm," 219.

23. Germany, 20th Army, KTB 5, Anlage 2, Daily report, to the entry of 12 October 1944, microfilm series T-312, roll 1063, frame 9265168, NARA. See also Leonov, "Vperedsmotriashchie," 174; Sintsov, "Shturm," 220; and Barchenko-Emelianov, *Frontovye*, 146.

24. Golovko, *Vmeste*, 235. Also see Inozemtsev, "Sovetskaia aviatsiia," 107; and P. I. Khokhlov, *Nad tremia moriami* [Over three seas] (Leningrad: Lenizdat, 1988), 223.

25. Barchenko-Emelianov, *Frontovye*, 147, provides the most details on this point. Leonov, "Vperedsmotriashchie," 174, gives the time of the counterattack as dawn on 13 October.

26. Golovko, *Vmeste*, 236; Platonov, "Pravoflangovye," 106; and Egorov, "Severnyi," 23. German war diary entries corroborate the fact that, at night on 12 October, an enemy force under cover of fog and low visibility made a surprise landing in the harbor at Liinakhamari and occupied the port and town. See Germany, 20th Army, KTB 5, Anlage 4, Morning report, to the entry of 13 October 1944, microfilm series T-312, roll 1063, frame 9265184, NARA.

27. See, for example, Golovko, *Vmeste*, 234—37.

Chapter 7

1. Meretskov, *Na sluzhbe*, 366.

2. It is difficult to know what *STAVKA* really knew about German intentions, since all that is available are secondary accounts, such as Shtemenko, *Soviet General Staff*, 2:392—97.

3. Rumiantsev, *Razgrom vraga*, 256.

4. K. Meretskov, "Razgrom vraga v Zapoliar'e" [The defeat of the enemy in the polar region], a book review published in *VIZh*, September 1963:86—88.

5. The article that prompted the discussion was Major General V. V. Gurkin and Lieutenant General (Reserve) M. I. Golovnin, "K voprosy o strategicheskikh operatsiiakh Velikoi Otechestvennoi voiny 1941—1945gg" [To the question about strategic operations of the Great Patriotic War, 1941—1945], *VIZh*, October 1985:10—23. This article contained a list of fifty-two operations, with an invitation by the editors to the readers to discuss the criteria for naming operations to the list. Follow-up discussion articles were published in April, May, and July 1986, but substantive issues on Petsamo-Kirkenes were not discussed again until the concluding and summarizing article, "Itogi diskussii o strategicheskikh operatsiiakh Velikoi Otechestvennoi voiny 1941—1945gg" [Results of the discussions about strategic operations of the Great Patriotic War, 1941—1945], *VIZh*, October 1987:8—24.

6. Ibid., 12.

7. Rumiantsev, *Razgrom vraga*, 257.

8. Ibid., 257—58. See also Mikulskii and Absaliamov, *Nastupatel'nye boi*, 72.

9. Mikulskii and Absaliamov, *Nastupatel'nye boi*, 70.

10. This command change was discovered by careful examination of tabular data in *Eto bylo na Karel'skom fronte*, 187; and Babin, *Karel'skii front*, 316.

11. Major General Alekseev's replacement was Major General F. F. Korotkov, who went on to command the 132d Rifle Corps and became the Soviet military commandant of the Danish island Bornholm. See A. Basov, "Desant na ostrov Bornkhol'm" [Assault on Bornholm Island], *VIZh*, May 1966:27—39, hereafter cited as Basov, "Desant."

12. Rumiantsev, *Razgrom vraga*, 274. See also Lieutenant General V. Lobov, "Boevye deistviia v Zapoliar'e" [Combat operations in the polar region], *Voennyi vestnik* [Military herald], No. 7—1984:18.

13. Rumiantsev, *Razgrom vraga*, 259.

14. Ibid. See also Khudalov, *U kromki*, 188. He suggests that helicopters and parachute troops will be used to perform a mission like that assigned to the 126th Light Rifle Corps in the third phase of the operation.

15. Mikulskii and Absaliamov, *Nastupatel'nye boi*, 50, 70.

16. Ibid., 74.

17. Ibid., 70, 151.

18. Khrenov, *Mosty k pobede*, 316.

19. Mikulskii and Absaliamov, *Nastupatel'nye boi*, 71.

20. Ibid., 35.

21. Ibid., 70.

22. Ibid., 150.

23. Rumiantsev, *Razgrom vraga*, 267—68.

24. Ibid., 268.

25. Inozemtsev, "Sovetskaia aviatsiia," 109; Mikulskii and Absaliamov, *Nastupatel'nye boi*, 151; and Rumiantsev, *Razgrom vraga*, 212.

26. Mikulskii and Absaliamov, *Nastupatel'nye boi*, 74; and Rumiantsev, *Razgrom vraga*, 270.

27. Rumiantsev, *Razgrom vraga*, 212.

28. Mikulskii and Absaliamov, *Nastupatel'nye boi*, 151.

29. Rumiantsev, *Razgrom vraga*, 264—65.

30. Mikulskii and Absaliamov, *Nastupatel'nye boi*, 82.

31. Maliugin, "Tyl," 101.

32. Rumiantsev, *Razgrom vraga*, 275—76. One wonders what happened to the other 30 percent.

33. Ibid., 260.

34. German losses include the total for XIX Mountain Corps and the 163d Infantry Division (Battle Group Ruebel) of the XXXVI Corps. See Germany, 20th Army, KTB 5, microfilm series T-312, roll 1063, frame 9265810, for the XIX Mountain Corps, and roll 1065, frame 9268200, for the 163d Infantry Division. The Soviet casualty figure of 15,773 appears in the official Semiriaga, ed., *Istoriia*, 9:152. The casualty rate for both sides was thus approximately 16 percent.

Epilogue

1. I. Shinkarev, comp., "Sovetskaia pomoshch' norvezhskomy narody (1944—1945gg)" [Soviet assistance to the Norwegian people (1944—1945)], *VIZh*, October 1979:32.

2. Khrenov, *Mosty k pobede*, 336—39, 342—44.

3. A. A. Grechko, *Cherez Karpaty* [Through the Carpathians] (Moscow: Voenizdat, 1972), 472.

4. Pestanov, *Soldaty*, 158.

5. Albert Z. Conner and Robert G. Poirier, *Red Army Order of Battle in the Great Patriotic War* (Novato, CA: Presidio Press, 1985), 43, 212, 254, 266—67, 287.

6. The commander of this corps was Major General F. F. Korotkov, who commanded the 14th Rifle Division, 131st Rifle Corps, from 1 September 1943 to 18 October 1944. He took command of 131st Rifle Corps on the eve of the assault on Kirkenes on 24 October and held it until 4 November 1944 when he took command of 132d Rifle Corps. For a Soviet description of the Bornholm landing, see Basov, "Desant," 27—39.

7. The best description of Leonov's activities in the Pacific theater are contained in M. A. Babikov, *Na vostochnom beregy* [On the eastern shore] (Moscow: Izdatel'stvo "Sovetskaia Rossiia," 1969).

8. *Voennyi entsiklopedicheskii slovar'* [Military encyclopedic dictionary] (Moscow: Voenizdat, 1986) 386.

9. Khrenov, *Mosty k pobede*, 291 n.

10. Peredelskii, "Primenenie artillerii," 17.

11. *Voennyi entsiklopedicheskii slovar'*, 690.
12. *SVE*, 5:247.
13. *SVE*, 2:592.
14. *SVE*, 8:552.
15. Tomas Ries and Johnny Skorve, *Investigating Kola: A Study in Military Bases Using Satellite Photography* (London: Brassey's Defence Publishers, 1986) 49, 52.

Bibliography

Documents

Brockelmann, Klaus, and Hans Roschmann. "Small Unit Tactics, Combats in Taiga and Tundra." Foreign Military Studies no. MS P-060m. Historical Division, U.S. Army, Europe, 1952.

Erfurth, Waldemar. "The Last Finnish War (1941—1944)." Foreign Military Studies no. MS C-073. Historical Division, U.S. Army, Europe, 1952.

Germany. Heer. 2. Gebirgs-division. Kriegstagebuch nr. 1 [War diary no. 1]. Microfilm series T-315, roll 109, National Archives and Records Administration, Washington, DC.

Germany. Heer. 20. Heer. Kriegstagebuch nr. 5 [War diary no. 5]. Microfilm series T-312, rolls 1061—69, National Archives and Records Administration, Washington, DC.

Germany. Heer. 20. Heer. "Zustandbericht" [Status reports]. Microfilm series T-312, rolls 1064 and 1065, folder 65635/14, National Archives and Records Administration, Washington, DC.

Jodl, Ferdinand, General. "Kursbericht ueber die Kampfhandlungen im Petsamo und Varangerraum" [A short report regarding the combat actions in Petsamo and Varanger area]. Dated 5 November 1944. Microfilm series T-312, roll 1069, item 75034/1, National Archives and Records Administration, Washington, DC.

U.S. Department of the Army. Field Manual 90—11. *Cold Weather Operations*. Preliminary Draft. Fort Leavenworth, KS: Doctrinal Literature Management Office, U.S. Army Command and General Staff College, 20 November 1988.

————. Field Manual 100-5. *Operations*. Washington, DC, May 1986.

————. Pamphlet no. 20—269. *Small Unit Actions During the German Campaign in Russia*. Washington, DC: U.S. Government Printing Office, July 1953.

————. Pamphlet no. 20—271. *The German Northern Theater of Operations, 1940—1945*. By Earl F. Ziemke. Washington, DC: U.S. Government Printing Office, 1959.

U.S. War Department. "Lend-Lease Shipments, World War II." Washington, DC, 31 December 1946.

Vneshnaiia politika Sovetskogo Soiuza v period Velikoi Otechestvennoi voiny [Foreign policy of the Soviet Union in the period of the Great Patriotic War]. Vol. 2. Moscow: Politizdat, 1946.

Maps

Joint Operations Graphic 1:250,000, Series 1501

Sheet No. 35, 36-8   (Kirkenes)
          35, 36-9   (Severomorsk)
          35, 36-11   (Verkhne Tulomskiy)
          35, 36-12   (Murmansk)

Map symbols: STANAG 2019, Edition no. 2, 5 February 1976.

Interviews

During a field trip to the Kirkenes area on 14—22 October 1987, the author conducted several interviews, some with the aid of an interpreter, with Norwegian civilians who witnessed the events of October 1944.

     Robert Dahl, Ospeli
     Jure Kasereff, Grense Jakobselv
     Kare Kristensen, Elvenes
     Ella Mathisen, Munkelv
     Ole Sotkajervi, Stenbakk
     Aase Stavem, Tarnet
     Knut Tharaldsen, Jarfjordbotn

Several interviewees declined to identify themselves.

Books

Achkasov, V. I., and N. B. Pavlovich. *Sovetskoe voenno-morskoe iskusstvo v Velikoi Otechestvennoi voine* [Soviet naval art in the Great Patriotic War]. Moscow: Voenizdat, 1973.

Aganov, S. Kh., ed. *Inzhenernye voiska Sovetskoi Armii 1918—1945* [Engineer forces of the Soviet Army, 1918—1945]. Moscow: Voenizdat, 1985.

Andreev, V. P., D. S. Borisov, and A. F. Evtushenko, comps. *Inzhenernye voiska Sovetskoi Armii v vazhneishikh operatsiiakh Velikoi Otechestvennoi voiny* [Engineer troops of the Soviet Army in the most important operations of the Great Patriotic War]. Moscow: Voenizdat, 1958.

Babikov, M. A. *Letom sorok pervogo* [The summer of forty-one]. Moscow: "Sovetskaia Rossiia," 1980.

─────── . *Na vostochnom beregy* [On the eastern shore]. Moscow: Izdatel'stvo "Sovetskaia Rossiia," 1969.

─────── . *Otriad osobogo naznacheniia* [Special-purpose detachment]. Moscow: "Sovetskaia Rossiia," 1986.

Babin, A. I. *Karel'skii front v Velikoi Otechestvennoi voine 1941—1945gg* [Karelian Front in the Great Patriotic War, 1941—1945]. Moscow: Izdatel'stvo "Nauka," 1984.

─────── . *Na volkhovskom fronte 1941—1944gg* [On the Volkhov Front, 1941—1944]. Moscow: "Nauka," 1982.

Barchenko-Emelianov, I. P. *Frontovye budnyi Rybach'ego* [Days at the front on the Rubachii Peninsula]. Murmansk: Knizhnoe Izdatel'stvo, 1984.

Basov, A. V. *Flot v Velikoi Otechestvennoi voine 1941—1945: opyt operativno-strategicheskogo primeneniia* [The fleet in the Great Patriotic War, 1941—45: The experience of operational-strategic utilization]. Moscow: "Nauka," 1980.

Bulkley, Robert J. *At Close Quarters: PT Boats in the U.S. Navy.* Washington, DC: U.S. Government Printing Office, 1962.

Burgess, William H., III, ed. *Inside Spetsnaz: Soviet Special Operations.* Novato, CA: Presidio Press, 1989.

Chew, Allen F. *Fighting the Russians in Winter: Three Case Studies.* Leavenworth Papers no. 5. Fort Leavenworth, KS: Combat Studies Institute, U.S. Army Command and General Staff College, December 1981.

Chirkova, Z. K., ed. *Eto bylo na Krainem Severe* [It was in the far north]. Murmansk: Knizhnoe Izdatel'stvo, 1965. Collection of memoirs.

Clausewitz, Carl von. *On War.* Edited and translated by Michael Howard and Peter Paret. Princeton, NJ: Princeton University Press, 1976.

Conner, Albert Z., and Robert G. Poirier. *Red Army Order of Battle in the Great Patriotic War.* Novato, CA: Presidio Press, 1985.

Dudarev, S. N., and B. V. Shipov. *Artilleriia v osobykh usloviakh* [Artillery in special conditions]. Moscow: Voenizdat, 1970.

Eto bylo na Karel'skom fronte [It was on the Karelian Front]. Petrozavodsk: Izdatel'stvo "Karelia," 1985. Collection of photographs.

Fokeev, K. F. *Desant v Liinakhamari* [Assault on Liinakhamari]. Moscow: Voenizdat, 1968.

Gamst, Thorbein. *Finnmark under Hakekorset* [Finnmark under the swastika]. Arendal, Norway: Agdin Forlag, 1984.

Garfield, Brian. *The Thousand Mile War: World War II in Alaska and the Aleutians.* Garden City, NY: Doubleday and Co., 1969.

Goldhurst, Richard. *The Midnight War: The American Intervention in Russia, 1918—1920.* New York: McGraw-Hill Book Co., 1978.

Golikov, S. *Vydaiushchiesia pobedy Sovetskoi Armii v Velikoi Otechestvennoi voine* [The greatest victories of the Soviet Army in the Great Patriotic War]. Moscow: Gosudarstvennoe izdatel'stvo politicheskoi literatury, 1954.

Golovko, A. G. *Vmeste s flotom* [Together with the fleet]. Moscow: Voenizdat, 1979. English translation *With the Fleet*. Moscow: Progress Publishers, 1988.

Grechko, A. A. *Cherez Karpaty* [Through the Carpathians]. Moscow: Voenizdat, 1972.

Holter, Hermann. *Armee in der Arktis* [Army in the Arctic]. Bad Nauheim: Verlag Hanse-Henning Podzun, 1953.

Inozemtsev, I. G. *Krylatye zashchitniki severa* [Winged defenders of the north]. Moscow: Voenizdat, 1975.

Kabanov, S. I. *Pole boiia-bereg* [The battlefield is the shore]. Moscow: Voenizdat, 1977.

Kamalov, Kh. Kh. *Morskaia pekhota v boiakh za rodinu* [Naval infantry in battles for the motherland]. Moscow: Voenizdat, 1966.

Khokhlov, P. I. *Nad tremia moriami* [Above three seas]. Leningrad: Lenizdat, 1988.

Khrenov, Arkadii F. *Mosty k pobede* [Bridges to victory]. Moscow: Voenizdat, 1982.

Khudalov, Kh. A. *U kromki kontinenta* [At the edge of the continent]. Moscow: Voenizdat, 1974.

Kirian, M. M., ed. *Fronty nastupali: po opytu Velikoi Otechestvennoi voiny* [Fronts attacked: According to the experience of the Great Patriotic War]. Moscow: "Nauka," 1987.

Korshunov, V. G., comp. *Cherez fiordy* [Through the fjords]. Moscow: Voenizdat, 1969.

Kozlov, I. A., and V. S. Shlomin. *Krasnoznamennyi severnyi flot* [Red Banner Northern Fleet]. Moscow: Voenizdat, 1983.

Krashobaev, A. I., and V. P. Zagrebin, comps. *V boiakh za sovetskoe Zapoliar'e* [In battles for the Soviet polar region]. Murmansk: Knizhnoe Izdatel'stvo, 1982.

Krautler, M., and Karl Springenschmid. *Es war ein Edelweiss* [It was an edelweiss]. Graz and Stuttgart, Germany: Leopold Stocker Verlag, 1962.

Kupriianov, G. N. *Vo imia velikoi pobedy* [In the name of the great victory]. Petrozavodsk: "Karelia," 1985.

Kuzmin, A. V. *V pribrezhnykh vodakh* [In coastal waters]. Moscow: Voenizdat, 1967.

Kuznetsov, N. G. *Kursom k pobede* [The course to victory]. Moscow: Voenizdat, 1976.

Leonov, V. *Litsom k litsu* [Face to face]. Moscow: Voenizdat, 1957. Memoirs of a naval reconnaissance scout in the literary notes of S. Glukhovskii.

Meretskov, K. A. *Na sluzhbe narodu* [In the service of the people]. Moscow: Voenizdat, 1983.

Mikulskii, S., and M. Absaliamov. *Nastupatel'nye boi 99-go i 31-go strelkovykh korpusov v Zapoliar'e (Oktiabr 1944g)* [Offensive battles of the 99th and 31st Rifle Corps in the polar region (October 1944)]. Moscow: Voenizdat, 1959.

Olshtynskii, L. I. *Vzaimodeistviia armii i flota* [Cooperation of army and fleet]. Moscow: Voenizdat, 1983.

Panov, N. N., ed. *Severomortsy: Severnyi Flot v Velikoi Otechestvennoi voine 1941—1945*, [Men of the Northern Fleet: The Northern Fleet in the Great Patriotic War, 1941—1945]. Moscow: Voenizdat, 1956.

Pestanov, S. A. *Soldaty morskoi pekhoty* [Soldiers of the naval infantry]. Petrozavodsk: "Karelia," 1976.

Polozov, S. I., and V. P. Zagrebin, comps. *V boiakh—morskaia pekhota* [Naval infantry in battles]. Murmansk: Knizhnoe Izdatel'stvo, 1984.

Pospelov, P. N., ed. *Great Patriotic War of the Soviet Union, 1941—1945*. Moscow: Progress Publishers, 1974.

Radzievskii, A. I., ed. *Taktika v boevykh primerakh: divisiia* [Tactics in combat examples: division]. Moscow: Voenizdat, 1976.

―――――. *Taktika v boevykh primerakh: polk* [Tactics in combat examples: Regiment]. Moscow: Voenizdat, 1974.

Rendulic, Lothar. *Gekampft, Gesicht, Geschlagen* [Engaged, victorious, defeated]. Heidelberg: Verlag Weisermuhl, 1952.

Ries, Tomas, and Johnny Skorve. *Investigating Kola: A Study of Military Bases Using Satellite Photography*. London: Brassey's Defence Publishers, 1986.

[Rudenko, S. I., et al.]. *Sovetskie voenno-vozdushnye sily v Velikoi Otechestvennoi voine 1941—1945gg* [Soviet air forces in the Great Patriotic War, 1941—1945]. Moscow: Voenizdat, 1968.

Rumiantsev, Nikolai M. *Razgrom vraga v Zapoliare (1941—1944gg): Voenno istoricheskii ocherk* [The defeat of the enemy in the polar region (1941—1944): A military-historical outline]. Moscow: Voenizdat, 1963.

Semiriaga, M. I., ed. *Istoriia vtoroi mirovoi voiny 1939—1945* [History of the Second World War, 1939—1945]. Vol. 9. Moscow: Voenizdat, 1978.

Shamshurov, V. K. *Inzhenernoe obespechenie boia v osobykh usloviiakh* [Engineer support of combat in special conditions]. Moscow: Voenizdat, 1985.

Shtemenko, Sergei M. *The Soviet General Staff at War, 1941—1945*. Vol. 2. Moscow: Progress Publishers, 1986.

[Stepanov, M. A., et al.]. *Deistviia voenno-morskogo flota v Velikoi Otechestvennoi voine* [Operations of the fleet in the Great Patriotic War]. Moscow: Voenizdat, 1956.

Terekhov, Petr V. *Boevye deistviia tankov na severo-zapade v 1944 g* [Combat operations of tanks in the northwest in 1944]. Moscow: Voenizdat, 1965.

Vecher, M. N., and E. V. Medvedev. *Ot tiumeni do kirkenesa: O boevom puti 368-i Pechengskoi Krasnoznamennoi strelkovoi divisii* [From Tiumen to Kirkenes: The combat path of the 368th Pechenga Red Banner Rifle Division]. Sverdlovsk: Srednie-Uralskoe knizhnoe izdatel'stvo, 1976.

Voennyi entsiklopedicheskii slovar' [Military encyclopedic dictionary]. Moscow: Voenizdat, 1986.

Vnotchenko, L. N. *Pobeda na dal'nem vostoke* [Victory in the far east]. Moscow: Voenizdat, 1971.

Webster's Ninth New Collegiate Dictionary. Springfield, MA: Merriam-Webster, c1983.

Ziemke, Earl F. *Stalingrad to Berlin: The German Defeat in the East.* Army Historical Series. Washington, DC: Office of the Chief of Military History, United States Army, 1968.

Articles

Alekseev, A., Captain First Rank (Reserve), and Captain Second Rank Engineer (Reserve) M. Kariagin. "Navigatsionno-gidrograficheskoe obespechenie Petsamo-Kirkenesskoi nastupatel'noi operatsii [Navigational- hydrographic support of the Petsamo-Kirkenes offensive operation]. *Morskoi Sbornik* [Naval proceedings], No. 5—1980:22—27.

Alekseev, V., Admiral. "Severnyi flot v osvobozhdenii sovetskogo Zapoliaria i severnoi Norvegii" [The Northern Fleet in the liberation of the Soviet polar region and northern Norway]. *Morskoi Sbornik* [Naval proceedings], No. 10—1974:61—69.

Altukhov, P. K. "Upravlenie voiskami" [Troop control]. *Sovetskaia voennaia entsiklopediia* [Soviet military encyclopedia]. Moscow: Voenizdat, 1980. 8:203—4.

Ammon, Georgi. "Tactical Amphibious Assaults." *Soviet Military Review*, No. 3—1986:55—56.

Andresian, G. A., Lieutenant General. "Osobennosti boevogo primeneniia aviatsii v Zapoliare" [Peculiarities of the combat employment of aviation in the polar region]. *Voennyi Vestnik* [Military herald], No. 12—1980:34—38.

Aristov, A. P., Captain First Rank (Reserve). "Navigatsionno-gidrograficheskoe obespechenie boevykh deistvii sil flota v Arkticheskom basseine" [Navigational-hydrographic support of combat operations of the forces of the fleet in the Arctic basin]. *Voenno istoricheskii zhurnal* [Military history journal], April 1987:44-51.

Arshinevskii, V. "Tiazhelye tanki v Zapoliar'e" [Heavy tanks in the polar region]. In *Eto bylo na krainem severe* [It was on the Far North], 225—30. Petrozavodsk: Izdatel'stvo "Karelia," 1985.

Averianov, A. I. "Posledovatel'noe sosredotochenie ognia" [Subsequent concentration of fire]. *Sovetskaia voennaia entsiklopedia* [Soviet military encyclopedia]. Moscow: Voenizdat, 1977. 6:467.

Basov, A. "Desant na ostrov Bornkhol'm" [Assault on Bornholm Island]. *Voenno istoricheskii zhurnal* [Military history journal], May 1966:27—39.

Bodarevskii, Iu. S., Vice Admiral. "Vysadka morskikh desantov v nastupatel'nykh operatsiiakh Velikoi Otechestvennoi voiny" [Naval amphibious landings in offensive operations of the Great Patriotic War]. *Voenno istoricheskii zhurnal* [Military history journal], April 1986:39—47.

Buchner, Alex. "Attack in the Tundra." *Military Review* 36 (April 1956):98—109.

Bull-Hansen, Fredrik, General. "Norway, NATO's Strategic Pivot?" *RUSI, Journal of the Royal United Services Institute of Defence* 132 (September 1987):13—18.

Coffman, Edward M. "The Intervention in Russia, 1918—1921." *Military Review* 68 (September 1988):60—71.

DeLeon, Peter. "Emerging Security Considerations for NATO's Northern Flank." *RUSI, Journal of the Royal United Services Institute of Defence Studies* 130 (June 1985):34—39.

"Dorozhnye voiska" [Highway troops]. *Sovetskaia voennaia entsiklopediia* [Soviet military encyclopedia]. Moscow: Voenizdat, 1977. 3:251—55.

Egan, Dennis M., and David W. Orr. "Sea Control in the Arctic: A Soviet Perspective." *Naval War College Review* 61 (Winter 1988):51—80.

Egorov, G., Admiral of the Fleet. "Severnyi flot v Petsamo-Kirkenesskoi operatsii" [Northern Fleet in the Petsamo-Kirkenes Operation]. *Voenno istoricheskii zhurnal* [Military history journal], October 1974:19—26.

_____. "Sovershenstvovanie upravleniia silami VMF v pervom periode voiny" [The perfecting of command and control of forces of the Navy in the first period of the war]. *Voenno istoricheskii zhurnal* [Military history journal], May 1979:24—31.

_____. "Sovershenstvovanie upravleniia silami VMF vo vtoroi i tret'em periodakh voiny" [The perfecting of command and control of forces of the Navy in the second and third periods of the war]. *Voenno istoricheskii zhurnal* [Military history journal], January 1980:20—26.

Emelianov, G. "V glubokom tylu vraga" [In the enemy's deep rear area]. *Voenno istoricheskii zhurnal* [Military history journal], October 1974:55—59.

Glantz, David M., Colonel. "Documents: Concerning the Soviet Use of War Experience." *Journal of Soviet Military Studies* 1 (April 1988):133—44.

Grushevoi, K., Colonel General. "The Liberation of Northern Norway." *Soviet Military Review*, No. 10—1969:47—49.

Gurkin, V. V., Major General, and Lieutenant General (Reserve) M. I. Golovnin. "K voprosy o strategicheskikh operatsiiakh Velikoi Otechestvennoi voiny 1941-1945gg" [To the question about strategic operations of the Great Patriotic War, 1941—1945]. *Voenno istoricheskii zhurnal* [Military history journal], October 1985:10—23.

Howlett, Geoffrey, Sir. "Concepts and Future Capabilities in NATO's Northern Region." *RUSI, Journal of the Royal United Services Institute of Defence Studies* 133 (Autumn 1988):13—18.

Iaroshenko, I. V., Colonel, and L. I. Smirnova, comps. "Osvobozhdenie sovetskogo Zapoliar'ia" [The liberation of the Soviet polar region]. *Voenno istoricheskii zhurnal* [Military history journal], June 1985:33—36.

Inozemtsev, I. G., Lieutenant Colonel. "Osobennosti boevogo primeneniia aviatsii v Zapoliare" [Features of combat utilization of aviation in the polar region]. *Voenno istoricheskii zhurnal* [Military history journal], November 1976:20—28.

――――. "Sovetskaia aviatsiia v Petsamo-Kirkenesskoi operatsii (Oktiabr 1944g)" [Soviet aviation in the Petsamo-Kirkenes Operation (October 1944)]. *Istoriia SSSR* [History of the U.S.S.R.], February 1975:101—10.

――――. "Udari po aerodromam protivnika na severnom i severo-zapadnom napravleniiakh (1941—1944g)" [Strikes against enemy airfields on the northern and northwestern axes]. *Voenno istoricheskii zhurnal* [Military history journal], December 1974:17—24.

"Itogi diskussii o strategicheskikh operatsiiakh Velikoi Otechestvennoi voiny 1941—1945gg" [Results of the discussion about strategic operations of the Great Patriotic War, 1941—1945]. *Voenno istoricheskii zhurnal* [Military history journal], October 1987:8—24.

Kartavtsev, I. I., Colonel. "Morskaia pekhota v boiakh za osvobozhdenie sovetskogo Zapoliar'ia" [Naval infantry in battles for liberation of the Soviet polar region]. *Voenno istoricheskii zhurnal* [Military history journal], March 1985:81—86.

Khrenov, A., Colonel-General. "Petsamo-Kirkenesskaia operatsiia" [Petsamo-Kirkenes Operation]. *Voenno istoricheskii zhurnal* [Military history journal], October 1984:10—16.

Khudalov, Kh. A., Lieutenant General (Reserve). "Na glavnom napravlenii" [On the main axis]. In *Cherez fiordy* [Through the fjords], compiled by V. G. Korshunov, 66—92. Moscow: Voenizdat, 1969.

――――. "Na norvezhskoi zemle" [On Norwegian soil]. *Voenno istoricheskii zhurnal* [Military history journal], October 1979:36—39.

――――. "Petsamo-Kirkenesskaia operatsiia" [The Petsamo-Kirkenes Operation]. *Voenno istoricheskii zhurnal* [Military history journal], October 1969:113—19.

Kiselev, A. A. "Krushenie planov fashistskoi Germanii v Zapoliare" [Collapse of the plans of fascist Germany in the polar region]. *Voprosy istorii* [Questions of history], No. 11—1984:25—38.

Komarov, N., Lieutenant Colonel. "Voiska PVO strany v Petsamo-Kirkenesskoi operatsii" [Troops of national air defense in the Petsamo-Kirkenes Operation]. *Voenno istoricheskii zhurnal* [Military history journal], October 1974:28—33.

Konavalov, V. "Iz Opyta popolneniia sostava severnogo flota v godi velikoi otechestvennoi voiny" [From the experience of the replenishment of the complement of the Northern Fleet during the Great Patriotic War]. *Voenno istoricheskii zhurnal* [Military history journal], August 1978:107—10.

Kozlov, I., Captain First Rank. "Vzaimodeistvie raznorodnykh sil Severnogo Flota na kommunikatsiiakh protivnika" [Mutual cooperation of various types of forces of the northern fleet on enemy lines of communication]. *Voenno istoricheskii zhurnal* [Military history journal], July 1975:22—28.

Krutskikh, D. S., Major General. "Udary po tylam" [Strikes in the rear area]. In *Eto bylo na krainem severe* [It was in the far north], edited by Z. K. Chirkova, 203—7. Murmansk: Knizhnoe Izdatel'stvo, 1965.

Kunitskii, P. T., Major General. "Dostizhenie vnezapnosti po opytu Velikoi Otechestvennoi voiny" [The achievement of surprise according to the experience of the Great Patriotic War]. *Voenno istoricheskii zhurnal* [Military history journal], October 1985:24—30.

Kurov, N., Major. "Victory Beyond the Polar Circle." *Soviet Military Review*, No. 11—1974:52—54.

Kuzmichev, Iu., Major. "S marsha v boi" [From the march into battle]. *Voenno istoricheskii zhurnal* [Military history journal], November 1974:48—55.

Kuznetsov, G., Colonel General. "Boevye deistviia aviatsii Severnogo Flota na morskikh soobshcheniiakh protivnika" [Combat operations of aviation of the Northern Fleet on enemy sea lines of communication]. *Voenno istoricheskii zhurnal* [Military history journal], March 1976:39—46.

Legkaia pekhota" [Light infantry]. *Sovetskaia voennaia entsiklopediia* [Soviet military encyclopedia]. Moscow: Voenizdat, 1977. 4:587—88.

Leonov, V. N. "Vperedsmotriashchie" [The lookouts]. In *Cherez fiordy* [Through the fjords], compiled by V. G. Korshunov, 157—78. Moscow: Voenizdat, 1969.

Leontev, S., Captain. "Otvazhnyi razvedchik Zapoliar'ia" [Courageous scout of the polar region]. *Voenno istoricheskii zhurnal* [Military history journal], January 1975:47—50.

Lobov, V., Lieutenant General. "Boevye deistviia v Zapoliar'e" [Combat operations in the polar region]. *Voennyi Vestnik* [Military herald], No. 7—1984:18—22.

Maikov, E. I., Colonel. "Inzhenernoe obespechenie boevykh deistvii voisk v Zapoliar'e (Petsamo-Kirkenesskaia operatsiia)" [Engineer support of the combat operations of the troops in the polar region (Petsamo-Kirkenes Operation)]. In *Inzhenernye voiska Sovetskoi Armii v vazhneishikh operatsiiakh Velikoi Otechestvennoi voiny* [Engineer troops of the Soviet Army in the most important operations of the Great Patriotic War], compiled by V. P. Andreev, D. S. Borisov, and A. F. Evtushenko, 176—83. Moscow: Voenizdat, 1958.

Maliugin, N., Colonel. "Tyl 14-i armii v Petsamo-Kirkenesskoi operatsii" [The rear services of the 14th Army in the Petsamo-Kirkenes Operation]. *Voenno istoricheskii zhurnal* [Military history journal], February 1973:97—102.

Meretskov, K. "Razgrom vraga v Zapoliar'e" [The defeat of the enemy in the polar region]. A book review in *Voenno istoricheskii zhurnal* [Military history journal], September 1963:86—88.

Orlov, A., Colonel, and Colonel P. Varakin. "Osvoboditel'naia missia Sovetskoi Armii v Severnoi Norvegii" [Liberating mission of the Soviet Army in northern Norway]. *Voenno istoricheskii zhurnal* [Military history journal], October 1974:12—18.

Ovsiannikov, V. V., Colonel, and Lieutenant Colonel V. V. Shmidt. "Tylovoe obespechenie 14-i armii v Petsamo-Kirkenesskoi operatsii" [Rear support of the 14th Army in the Petsamo-Kirkenes Operation]. *Voenno istoricheskii zhurnal* [Military history journal], October 1985:82—87.

Pavozkov, A. "Reid korpusa polkovnika solov'eva" [The raid of Colonel Solovev's corps]. In *Eto bylo na Krainem Severe* [It was in the far north], 208—214. Murmansk: Knizhnoe Izdatel'stvo, 1965.

Peredelskii, Georgii, Marshal of Artillery. "Boevoe primenenie artillerii v Petsamo-Kirkenesskoi operatsii" [Combat utilization of artillery in the Petsamo-Kirkenes Operation]. *Voenno istoricheskii zhurnal* [Military history journal], October 1984:17—21.

"The Petsamo Region." *Geographical Review* 34 (July 1944):409.

Platonov, V. N., Admiral. "Pravoflangovye" [The men on the right flank]. In *Cherez fiordy* [Through the fjords], compiled by V. G. Korshunov, 93—110. Moscow: Voenizdat, 1969.

Portugalskii, R., and N. Fomin. "Nekotorye voprosy sovershenstvovaniia struktury organov upravleniia fronta i armii" [Some questions about the improvement of the structure of the command and control organs of the Front and army]. *Voenno-istoricheskii zhurnal* [Military history journal], August 1978:33—41.

―――――. "O nekotorykh osobennostiakh organizatsii Petsamo-Kirkenesskoi operatsii" [Concerning several peculiarities of the Petsamo-Kirkenes Operation]. *Voenno istoricheskii zhurnal* [Military history journal], October 1964:45—51.

Rassokhin, V. V., Major General (Reserve). "Ikh podvig v pamiati narodnoi" [Their feat is in the national memory]. In *V boiakh-morskaia pekhota* [Naval infantry in battles], compiled by S. I. Polozov and V. P. Zagrebin. Murmansk: Knizhnoe Izdatel'stvo, 1984.

Rumiantsev, N. "Primenenie olen'ego transporta v 14-i armii karel'skogo fronta" [Utilization of reindeer transport in the 14th Army of the Karelian Front]. *Voenno istoricheskii zhurnal* [Military history journal], November 1972:86—90.

Sadovskii, V., Captain Third Rank. "Komandir 'Chernykh d'iavolov'" [Commander of the "black devils"]. *Sovetskii Voin* [Soviet warrior] No. 3—1985:36—37.

Selivanov, V. "Rabota organov upravleniia v boevykh deistviakh na primorskikh napravleniiakh" [The work of command and control organs in combat actions on coastal axes]. *Morskoi Sbornik* [Naval proceedings], No. 1—1989:22—28.

Sergeenko, B. "Rol' vnezapnosti v morskom desante" [The role of surprise in a naval amphibious landing]. *Morskoi Sbornik* [Naval proceedings], No. 11—1988:18—23.

Semenov, V., Major General. "Iz opyta organizatsii i vedeniia operatsii na Severo-Zapadnom napravlenii" [From the experience of the organization and conduct of operations on the Northwest axis]. *Voenno istoricheskii zhurnal* [Military history journal], September 1967:40—50.

Shcherbakov, V. I. "Nastuplenie" [The offensive]. In *Cherez fiordy* [Through the fiords], compiled by V. G. Korshunov, 52—65. Moscow: Voenizdat, 1969.

Shinkarev, I., comp. "Sovetskaia pomoshch' norvezhskomy narody (1944—1945gg)" [Soviet assistance to the Norwegian people (1944—1945)]. *Voenno istoricheskii zhurnal* [Military history journal], October 1979:31—33.

Shlomin, V., Captain First Rank. "Boevye deistviia Severnogo Flota v 1944 gody" [Combat operations of the Northern Fleet in 1944]. *Morskoi Sbornik* [Naval proceedings], No. 9—1974:8—13.

_____. "Dvadtsat' piat' morskikh strelkovykh" [Twenty-five naval rifle]. *Voenno istoricheskii zhurnal* [Military history journal], July 1970:96—99.

Shtemenko, S., General of the Army. "Na severnom flange sovetsko-germanskogo fronta letom i oseniu 1944 goda" [On the northern flank of the Soviet-German front in the summer and autumn of 1944]. *Voenno istoricheskii zhurnal* [Military history journal], July 1972:63—75.

Sidorov, A., Lieutenant Colonel. "Pobeda v Zapoliare" [Victory in the polar region]. *Voenno istoricheskii zhurnal* [Military history journal], October 1979:28—31.

Sintsov, A. N. "Shturm Krestovogo" [The storming of Krestovyi]. In *Eto bylo na Krainem severe* [It was in the far north], edited by Z. K. Chirkova, 225—30. Murmansk: Knizhnoe Izdatel'stvo, 1965.

Sunde, Hjalmar I., Major. "Kampene p Ishavsfronten" [Campaign on the arctic front]. *Norsk Militaert Tidsskrift* [Norwegian military journal], No. 12—1977:545—58.

Timokhovich, I., Major General, and Captain First Rank L. Olshtynskii. "Vzaimodeistvie VVS s aviatsiei VMF po opytu tretego perioda voiny" [Close cooperation of the air forces with aviation of the navy according to the experience of the third period of the war]. *Voenno istoricheskii zhurnal* [Military history journal], March 1978:27—34.

"Ukreplennyi raion." *Sovetskaia voennaia entsiklopediia* [Soviet military encyclopedia]. Moscow: Voenizdat, 1950. 8:185.

Utenkov, F. N. "Petsamo-Kirkenesskaia operatsiia" [Petsamo-Kirkenes Operation]. *Sovetskaia voennaia entsiklopediia* [Soviet military encyclopedia]. Moscow: Voenizdat, 1978. 6:321—22.

Verkhogliad, L. "Brosok na Petsamo" [The rush at Petsamo]. *Voennyi vestnik* [Military herald], November 1988:13—16.

Volkotrubenko, I., Colonel General (Reserve). "Obespechenie voisk boepripasami v operatsii po razgromu vraga v Zapoliare" [The supplying of ammunition to the forces in the operation for the defeat of the enemy in the polar region]. *Voenno istoricheskii zhurnal* [Military history journal], October 1984:81—82.

"Zasluzhili v boiakh za rodinu" [They served in battles for the motherland], *Morskoi Sbornik* [Naval proceedings], No. 7—1980:1—63.

Zavizion, Iu. "Nastupleniie v zapoliar'e" [Offensive in the polar region]. *Voennyi vestnik* [Military herald], February 1984:31—34.

LEAVENWORTH PAPERS

1. *The Evolution of U.S. Army Tactical Doctrine, 1946—76*, by Major Robert A. Doughty
2. *Nomonhan: Japanese-Soviet Tactical Combat, 1939*, by Dr. Edward J. Drea
3. *"Not War But Like War"; The American Intervention in Lebanon*, by Dr. Roger J. Spiller
4. *The Dynamics of Doctrine: The Changes in German Tactical Doctrine During the First World War*, by Cpatain Timothy T. Lupfer
5. *Fighting the Russians in Winter: Three Case Studies*, by Dr. Allen F. Chew
6. *Soviet Night Operations in World War II*, by Major Claude R. Sasso
7. *August Storm: The Soviet 1945 Strategic Offensive in Manchuria*, by Lieutenant Colonel David M. Glantz
8. *August Storm: Soviet Tactical and Operational Combat in Manchuria, 1945*, by Lieutenant Colonel David M. Glantz
9. *Defending the Driniumor: Covering Force Operations in New Guinea, 1944*, by Dr. Edward J. Drea
10. *Chemical Warfare in World War I: The American Experience, 1917—1918*, by Major Charles E. Heller, USAR
11. *Rangers: Selected Combat Operations in World War II*, by Dr. Michael J. King
12. *Seek, Strike, and Destroy: U.S. Army Tank Destroyer Doctrine in World War II*, by Dr. Christopher R. Gabel
13. *Counterattack on the Naktong, 1950*, by Dr. William Glenn Robertson
14. *Dragon Operations: Hostage Rescues in the Congo, 1964—1965*, by Major Thomas P. Odom
15. *Power Pack: U.S. Intervention in the Dominican Republic, 1965—1966*, by Dr. Lawrence A. Yates
16. *Deciding What Has to Be Done: General William E. DePuy and the 1976 Edition of FM 100—5,* Operations
17. *The Petsamo-Kirkenes Operation: Soviet Breakthrough and Pursuit in the Arctic, October 1944*, by Major James F. Gebhardt

RESEARCH SURVEYS

1. *Amicicide: The Problem of Friendly Fire in Modern War*, by Lieutenant Colonel Charles R. Shrader
2. *Toward Combined Arms Warfare: A Survey of 20th-Century Tactics, Doctrine, and Organization*, by Captain Jonathan M. House
3. *Rapid Deployment Logistics: Lebanon, 1958*, by Lieutenant Colonel Gary H. Wade
4. *The Soviet Airborne Experience*, by Lieutenant Colonel David M. Glantz
5. *Standing Fast: German Defensive Doctrine on the Russian Front During World War II*, by Major Timothy A. Wray
6. *A Historical Perspective on Light Infantry*, by Major Scott R. McMichael
7. *Key to the Sinai: The Battles for Abu Ageila in the 1956 and 1967 Arab-Israeli Wars*, by Dr. George W. Gawrych

✿U.S.G.P.O. 1990 754-001/02114

www.ingramcontent.com/pod-product-compliance
Lightning Source LLC
Chambersburg PA
CBHW080503110426
42742CB00017B/2985